DATE DUE

Demco

THE
SUNKEN
GOLD

THE
SUNKEN
GOLD

A Story of World War I
Espionage and the Greatest
Treasure Salvage in History

JOSEPH A. WILLIAMS

CHICAGO
REVIEW
PRESS

Published by Chicago Review Press Incorporated
814 North Franklin Street
Chicago, Illinois 60610

ISBN 978-1-61373-758-3

Library of Congress Cataloging-in-Publication Data
Names: Williams, Joseph A., 1973- author.
Title: The sunken gold: a story of World War I espionage and the
   greatest treasure salvage in history/Joseph A. Williams.
Description: Chicago, Illinois: Chicago Review Press Incorporated,
   [2017] | Includes bibliographical references and index.
Identifiers: LCCN 2016057951 (print) | LCCN 2017004741 (ebook) |
   ISBN 9781613737583 (cloth: alkaline paper) | ISBN 9781613737590
   (pdf) | ISBN 9781613737606 (kindle) | ISBN 9781613737613 (epub)
Subjects: LCSH: Laurentic (Steamship: 1909-1917) | World War,
   1914-1918—Naval operations, British. | Shipwrecks—Ireland—Swilly,
   Lough, Region—History—20th century. | Mines (Military
   explosives)—Ireland—Swilly, Lough, Region—History—20th century. |
   Damant, Guybon Chesney Castell, 1881-1963. | Treasure
   trove—Ireland—Swilly, Lough, Region—History—20th century. |
   Salvage—Ireland—Swilly, Lough, Region—History—20th century. |
   Espionage, British—History—20th century. | Submarines
   (Ships)—Germany—History—20th century.
Classification: LCC D582.L38 W55 2017 (print) | LCC D582.L38
   (ebook) | DDC 940.4/57—dc23
   LC record available at https://lccn.loc.gov/2016057951

Typesetting: Nord Compo
Map design: Chris Erichsen

The author has made every effort to secure permissions for the images
in this book. If there is an oversight, please contact the publisher.

Printed in the United States of America
5 4 3 2 1

For my daughter, Zoë Margot

CONTENTS

PREFACE

THE *LAURENTIC* MADE ITS FIRST impression on me while I was conducting research for my previous book, *Seventeen Fathoms Deep*. I found reference after reference to this salvage operation, especially to its central character, Captain G. C. C. Damant. I was amazed to find that there had been no books fully devoted to him or the topic, although there had been a chapter or two written about it. This naturally led me to assume that either it wasn't worthwhile writing about the *Laurentic* at length or it was a forgotten gem of a story.

It turned out to be the latter.

The bulk of my research came from thousands of pages of documents in the British National Archives—mainly official reports, records, and correspondence from the Admiralty records. This formed the underlying foundation of my narrative. However, since these records were official, by their nature they were largely devoid of human, personal touches. What I really wanted was to experience the *Laurentic* from the perspective of Captain Damant.

I explained my situation to Ruth Bloom, an able researcher with whom I had been working. She then tracked down Captain Damant's relatives. A letter was then sent to the captain's youngest and last surviving child, Mary Harrison. Mary, albeit getting on in years, was still very sharp, but she could not help me because of personal issues. My letter was put aside.

Leaving it at that, I continued my research and writing until some months later I received a letter in the mail from the United Kingdom. It was a cousin of Mary's, Charles Darwent, who was visiting her and discovered my letter. Being a scholar, he knew firsthand about the problems of research and offered to help.

About a month later I found myself driving to the Country Corner Diner in Bethany, Connecticut. Charles, who was writing a biography of the artist Josef Albers, happened to be in the United States doing research at the Josef and Anni Albers Foundation in Bethany. I was passing through since I was doing some lectures in New England on *Seventeen Fathoms Deep*. I arrived and sent a text message. I slid into a booth and waited, nursing an ice water.

Charles arrived and introduced himself to me. He was surprised by my appearance. He commented, "Mary asked me what I thought you'd look like, and I said, 'I don't know—probably an old guy with a beard.'"

As it turns out, Charles and I were about the same age, and perhaps because of my friendly, beardless face we easily slipped into talk concerning his family. I found it quite remarkable that cousins to what must have been the tenth degree still had close relationships. Charles explained to me, "Lots of East Anglian interbreeding. I'm surprised we don't all have two heads."

Over Reubens and French fries, Charles handed over photographs and a précis that detailed the career of Captain Damant and was the basis for an unpublished memoir Damant had written but that had gone missing.

The précis was enough for me to start, although it created even more tantalizing questions. After a few days, I wrote to Charles thanking him and urging him to track down the manuscript if it was practicable in any way. He graciously put the call out to all the Damant relatives across the world on my behalf.

Sure enough, Derek Damant, the sixth bishop of George in South Africa (now retired), wrote to Charles and attached a transcribed copy of the forgotten autobiography. The thousand thank-yous I extended to the family were not enough, for here was a document that provided dimensions of character to truly augment the story. What is more, hitherto unknown details concerning the covert work he and his divers performed on U-boats during the First World War further enriched this deep-sea-diving tale. After integrating this source into my working manuscript, I found that it increased the size of the initial manuscript by about 20 percent.

As my work progressed I found more resources still. A case in point is Mr. Ray Cossum, the current wreck owner of the *Laurentic*. I was only able to contact him via post, and we began a correspondence that culminated in a transatlantic phone call. The call, while awkward at times owing to our accent differences, nevertheless impressed upon me the ever-infectious enthusiasm that people have for the story of the *Laurentic* disaster and salvage, which by the time of the publication of this book will be one hundred years passed.

I was amazed by all the help I received on this project. I had a suspicion that I was going to be dismissed out of hand as an interloping Yankee. The opposite was true. Every person I met who knew the outline of the *Laurentic* and the life and work of Captain Damant affirmed that the story needed to be told in full. I took some solace in this and the fact that Arthur J. Marder wrote the definitive work on this period of British naval history as an American while living in Hawaii and California. While my book has neither the scope nor size of Marder's multivolume *From the Dreadnought to Scapa Flow*, I hope that the reader finds Captain Damant and the *Laurentic*'s tale of courage, outstanding tenacity, and patriotism educational, entertaining, and ultimately inspirational.

PART I

I

The *Titanic* in Miniature

THE CITY OF LIVERPOOL was the strategic entry and exit port of Great Britain's western approaches during the First World War. Foodstuffs, munitions, equipment, and weapons all passed through Liverpool first. Likewise, ships debarked from the city to voyage all around the globe to Britain's far-flung colonies and dependencies. HMS *Laurentic* was one of these vessels and on January 24, 1917, was being loaded for its dangerous voyage to Halifax, Canada.

The *Laurentic* was a former transatlantic liner, built in 1908 by the famous White Star Line. The White Star Line was known for the outstanding design of its vessels and gave the world some of the most memorable ships of the age, especially its gigantic *Olympic*-class liners: the eponymous *Olympic*, the *Britannic*, and the *Titanic*. The *Laurentic* was smaller than the great liners, being roughly a third the size of the *Titanic*. This did not diminish its grace. The ship's black hull gleamed, and its single red funnel poured out a column of smoke and steam that thickened against the winter cold. Pennants fluttered on its fore and aft masts, with the most prominent of all being the British Union Jack.

HMS *Laurentic.* © *Derry City and Strabane District Council, Ray Cossum Papers*

Observers had lauded the *Laurentic*'s splendid stateliness, revealed in the ship's long, handsome lines, and while the vessel did not have the fame of the great liners, it reflected their luxury. Its public rooms were high-ceilinged and ornate. The first-class lounge on the upper promenade was fashioned in the rococo manner of the court of Louis XV of France, where oaken panels matched a fine parquet floor. The first-class dining saloon, paneled in the intricate style of the court of Charles II, extended the entire width of the vessel, contained a veranda for a bandstand, and could seat up to 212 passengers. The first-class reading room was fashioned with neoclassical columns that rose high into the ceiling. The smoking room was bright with sunlight beneath a ceiling partially made of glass. Even the second- and third-class accommodations were designed with aesthetics in mind—stately and ornate.

The *Laurentic* was also built with some of the latest technologies. An electric elevator connected the decks. First-class staterooms were equipped with portable electric lamps, which passengers used to read while resting on Pullman beds. Even individual cabins were rigged with manual thermostats. The ship was equipped with the latest Marconi wireless devices, assuring passengers that if the *Laurentic* met danger, it could signal for help. For those who could not afford the price of the large liners, the *Laurentic* was an affordable option that offered most of the same innovations and opulence. The *Laurentic*, in effect, recalled the *Titanic* in miniature.

Photographs of the interior of the *Megantic*. The *Megantic* was the sister ship of the *Laurentic* and had virtually identical interiors. *Courtesy of Rich Turnwald*

The *Laurentic* was also fast. Its designers had experimented by giving it triple propellers, also known as screws, instead of the standard two. The ship proved its speed in 1911 by setting a record for a round-trip voyage to Canada from Britain in thirteen days. The *Laurentic* became one of the most popular ships in the White Star Line's Dominion service line between Liverpool and Montreal or Quebec City. The company, seeing the effectiveness of the ship's design, incorporated elements of it into its *Olympic*-class ships. The *Titanic*, for example, was given the same triple-screw design.

It was because of this speed that the Royal Navy saw fit to impress the *Laurentic* into military service at the outbreak of war in August 1914. The *Laurentic* was refitted into an armed merchant cruiser. Casks of stowed wine were replaced by artillery shells, and within the ship's labyrinthine passages where passengers once ambled, men in blue woolen uniforms marched out to the decks where they manned eight six-inch guns.

The *Laurentic* was under the command of forty-two-year-old Captain Reginald Arthur Norton. He had served on at least two dozen different ships since entering the Royal Navy as a cadet in 1887. Comments found in his official record include "zealous," "very attentive to duty," and "reliable."

Norton, perhaps more than anybody aboard the *Laurentic*, could appreciate the unique dangers presented by the naval war against Germany. At the outset of the conflict, Norton had been assigned as executive officer aboard the battle cruiser HMS *Hogue*. The *Hogue* was attached to two other vessels, the *Aboukir* and *Cressy*, as part of a squadron to support the Royal Navy, which was trying to hem the German fleet into its ports on continental Europe. The ships were old, out of date, and manned by inexperienced reservists. Several senior officers in the Royal Navy feared that the ships were at extreme risk of destruction by the enemy. Within the fleet, these ships became known as the Live Bait Squadron.

On September 22, 1914, at 6:00 AM, the squadron was on patrol near the Dutch coast in an area known as the "broad fourteens," since the depth remained roughly consistent throughout the region at fourteen fathoms—eighty-four feet deep.* At the same time, the *U-9*, an *Unterseeboot* (better known in English as a German U-boat or submarine) of the Imperial German Navy, came upon the ships. The *U-9*'s commander, Kapitänleutnant Otto Weddigen, positioned his submarine and stalked the ships with his periscope.

At 6:20 AM the *U-9* fired its first torpedo at the *Aboukir*, which struck home. The captain of the *Aboukir* assumed his ship had crashed into a mine. Being the senior officer of the flotilla, he ordered the other ships to render assistance. Two of the *Hogue*'s lifeboats were launched. Soon after, the *U-9* launched two torpedoes at the *Hogue*, which exploded into the ship's starboard side near the center. All hands now realized that a German submarine was single-handedly destroying the Live Bait Squadron.

This German propaganda postcard depicts the sinking of the Live Bait Squadron. *Courtesy of Library of Congress Prints and Photographs Division, George Grantham Bain Collection, LOT 11274-1*

---

* A fathom equals six feet in depth.

Norton's commanding officer, unable to raise the engineering room on the voice tube, ordered him to go down to assess the damage. After Norton spent precious minutes disciplining crew to prevent panic, he descended into the ship. As he hurried, he met a crew member coming from the other direction. The seaman informed Norton that the engine room was fully flooded. The watertight doors below the decks had all been (carelessly) left open, thus making the ship sink quicker than it should have.

Norton turned back to the bridge. But suddenly the *Hogue* listed, tilting to starboard. The ship was rolling over in what mariners call "turning turtle." In these last moments, desperate sailors jumped from the ship. Norton grasped a ringbolt and hung in the air for some time before crashing onto the deck. Then a great wave washed him into the sea. Norton tried to regain the ship by climbing onto the *Hogue*'s side, but he was again washed off as the ship fully turned over and sank. Norton clung to pieces of wreckage until he was rescued.

The *U-9* sank all three ships, killed 1,459 men, and managed to spread terror of U-boat attacks among the Allies. The scale of the disaster was unprecedented. If so much destruction can be caused by one U-boat manned by twenty-five crew and four officers, what would happen if the Germans launched a full-scale submarine war? Otto Weddigen was feted in Germany and decorated with the Pour le Mérite and the first- and second-class Iron Cross, prestigious medals. He even published an article, "The First Submarine Blow Is Struck."[*]

As for Reginald Norton, he was eager to return to sea. Perhaps he felt his own personal honor was stained by the disaster, or maybe he believed it was his patriotic duty to avenge the *Hogue*. When he made his report to the Admiralty, he wrote, "I have the honour to submit that I may be appointed to another ship as soon as I get a kit."

Norton's new "kit" was the *Laurentic*, to which he was assigned in December 1916. Norton was acting captain, since as a commander he was not senior enough to formally take the command of such a large vessel. Since there was a shortage of senior officers in the Royal Navy,

---

[*] British anxiety was alleviated somewhat after Weddigen was killed on March 15, 1915, when his U-boat was rammed by HMS *Dreadnought*.

Commander Reginald Norton, acting captain of the *Laurentic. London Daily Mirror, January 29, 1917*

the appointment was not unusual. Norton proved capable, leading the *Laurentic* on hunts for German raiders and making the run to Halifax, Nova Scotia, twice. Norton had learned lessons from the *Hogue* and had become as cautious as the war would allow. He ensured that the *Laurentic* was fully equipped with life jackets and that the watertight doors below decks were shut at all times.

Norton had 475 officers, crew, and passengers in his charge. All were either Royal Navy or Royal Navy Reserve (RNR) personnel. But there was a strange quality to the upcoming voyage. Secret consignments consisting of small plain wooden boxes, each twelve inches long, twelve inches wide, and six inches deep, weighing in at approximately 140 pounds, had been brought by train from London in the early hours of January 20.

The boxes were carefully counted, stacked, and stowed inside the second-class passenger baggage room instead of the cargo holds. Meanwhile, sentries prowled the decks, and crew searched the magazine and ammunition holds for bombs. Plainclothes detectives maintained a watch on the gangplank, checking all persons who sought entry for a pass.

As to what lay in those boxes, only Norton and perhaps a couple of the other senior officers aboard the *Laurentic* knew.

2

The Damants of Cowes

WHEN MR. HENRY CASTELL DAMANT married Mary Wilson on September 30, 1879, the future seemed bright. Harry, as Mr. Damant was known, was the son of a prominent solicitor on the Isle of Wight who had followed his father in practicing law, setting up shop in the town of Newport. Mary was a lady of Irish Protestant heritage and an amateur author and thespian who drew admiration for her charitable theatrical performances. Harry set up a residence at Bedford House in Northwood, a village just south of the town of Cowes, before moving in 1887 to a new house named Forest View, which had magnificent views of the sea. It was a comfortable life, with Harry Damant earning somewhere between £300 and £500 annually, which allowed them the luxury of keeping two servants who were paid up to £18 a year.

The Damants had dwelled on the Isle of Wight for two generations. Harry had seven siblings who, by the time of his marriage, had spread to all corners of the island. But not all the Damant siblings chose to stay there. Harry's eldest brother, Guybon,[*] was a political officer in India. Harry had last seen his brother at Guybon's wedding a year prior. Just three weeks after Harry's own wedding, he received unfortunate news. On October 14 Guybon had led a contingent of

---

* The name Guybon, pronounced "Gibbon," comes from another family who had in prior generations married into the Damant line.

British soldiers to confiscate weapons from a tribe of headhunters in the Nagaland, where he was killed. It was said that his widow saw Guybon's head thrown down a well, and there were rumors that he was cannibalized. Officially, Guybon was shot.

In June 1880 Mary gave birth to a son they named George Sancroft. But three months later the child died of an unknown cause. They buried their son in the West Cowes Cemetery, marking the grave with a small Celtic cross.* Mary and Harry conceived again, and on July 25, 1881, she gave birth to a boy whom they named Guybon. The infant's full name, Guybon Chesney Castell Damant, took into account other pedigreed Norfolk and Suffolk families that had intermarried with the Damant line. Usually, he went by Guy. He was joined in quick succession by three brothers: James Charles Wilson, Henry Kirkpatrick, and John Alister.

Guybon Chesney Castell Damant as a toddler.
Courtesy of Mary Harrison

---

* The grave is no longer there; it was removed because of bombings during the Second World War.

The Damants left Forest View and Harry built a new home, named Lammas, after the family's ancient estate on mainland Great Britain. Harry made sure to build the house just outside the boundary of East Cowes, to avoid the higher tax rate. As such, the home lacked certain services. Lammas had water shortages, and on one occasion after a well had been sunk, paraffin leaked into the well, contaminating it. Guy always suspected that his father built Lammas "on the cheap" and was relieved when East Cowes's boundaries were shifted in the 1890s to include their home. Not that this improvement in municipal services alleviated the somewhat backward, bucolic nature of the Isle of Wight in the 1890s. Tollgates, for example, remained long in force on the island after they were done away with on mainland Great Britain. The roads were plagued with thick mud in the winter and threw about such a dust in the summer that it was more common to wear boots than shoes out of doors.

But this backwater had its own special attractions. Guy delighted in exploring the fauna found in the rock pools with his friends. The best times were at low tide, when Guy overturned rocks exposing butter-fish, crabs, and small eel and would imagine that beneath the stones was the lost treasure of some ancient Celtic prince. Then there were the long, meandering walks he took with his mother to visit his older brother's grave. Although Mary Damant was strict and industrious, she was loving and regaled Guy with stories. Sitting straight-backed in an armless chair, she read to her boys either stories such as *The Middy and the Moors* or the works of Charles Dickens. Dickens became Guy's favorite author.

Guy often visited his relatives on the isle, and there were many— from his grandparents to his uncle Arthur, an eccentric doctor with no patients. He also mingled with royalty. For several generations the Isle of Wight had played host to the British gentry, and this was especially the case after Queen Victoria established a residency at the Osborne House in 1851 in East Cowes. Every summer, especially during the famous Cowes Week, the island attracted visits from the rich, the royal, and the famous who came to see the yacht races and regattas that graced the Solent, the bright strait that separates the Isle from mainland Great Britain. There were parties, banquets, celebrations, and spectacles. In 1897 Harry was clerk to the council

Mary Wilson Damant. *Courtesy of Mary Harrison*

that helped arrange for the celebration of Queen Victoria's Diamond
Jubilee. Harry, a keen yachtsman himself, was also a founder of the
Island Sailing Club, the first to service its residents.

Guy was delighted to witness the yacht races during Cowes Week
and on one of those grand occasions actually saw Queen Victoria.
It was exciting, but Guy personally never aspired for that kind of
recognition. He had grown into a handsome young man, albeit of
unremarkable height, with a friendly face, copper-colored hair, and
slightly protruding ears. His most distinct trait was his keen and mis-
chievous gray eyes. He was laconic, unassuming, and not the least
interested in developing new friendships.

Guy's curiosity was stoked when he visited shipwrecks on the south of the Isle of Wight with his father, who acted as an agent of the famous shipping insurance firm Lloyd's of London and made arrangements for salvaging ships. There for the first time Guy saw divers salvaging what they could from the *Irex*, a ship carrying a cargo of huge water main pipes. He also saw sailing ships passing through the Solent or seeking shelter from contrary winds. It was hard to avoid the sea on the Isle of Wight.

Guy's early education was conducted at home by his mother and governess. When it came time to attend a proper school, his father made the choice for him. It seems that Harry Damant would allow his sons either to practice the law like himself or enter military service. There was no debate about it. Harry decided to send Guy into the Royal Navy.

But a boy from a prominent family could not just enlist in the navy. To be respected and maintain status, Guy needed to become an officer. Harry, therefore, approached his friend, Reverend Arthur Watson, who was the headmaster of a school called the Grange, which had a reputation for getting boys cadetships. As a favor to Harry, Guy was allowed to be a day student rather than boarder with the other thirty or so students. It was near to home, albeit by a meandering route, so it was a natural choice. He was enrolled at age eight and a half.

To become a cadet Guy needed to obtain a nomination, typically from a flag-ranked officer, produce testimonials of his good character, and be free of any physical defects. His father obtained the necessary nomination from Lord Colville. The other part was a competitive test, for which the Grange prepared him. He only had a year and a half window to take the test since cadets could only enter the Royal Navy between the ages of thirteen and fourteen and a half. Guy studied mathematics, composition, scripture, French, Greek, Latin, geography, and English history. He needed to be able to draw both freehand and geometrically. Boys were typically lined up from the head of the class to the bottom of the class. Watson would ask a question. If a boy got a question wrong the teacher moved on down the row until a boy got it right. Then that boy would move ahead of all the boys who got it wrong, thus going to the head of the class. Guy's class standing depended on where he was in the line. Sometimes, as punishment, boys were demoted to the bottom of the class and had to work their way back up. Guy also needed to keep himself fit. This was done by playing goalie on the Grange's football team.

There was more to school besides academics and sports. In typical fashion of the day, and especially to prepare the young men under his charge for naval service, corporal discipline was maintained by Watson's cane either on the hands or astern. The headmaster gave Guy his first beatings. As a measure of how devoted the old schoolmaster was to discipline, although he was at times bedridden with gout he managed to conduct beatings from his bed—albeit the blows were weaker since he could not fully flick his cane from the lying position. Guy's initial reports from school were bad—"Careless and Dirty"—and he apparently had trouble in spelling.

Guy found solace through the tutelage and companionship of his mother, who assisted him in his studies. When not at school she would take him on occasional trips to London and spend holidays and Sundays sailing on his father's yacht. Slowly, Damant focused and improved his academics.

Guy sat for his multiday examination in Westminster beginning on December 3, 1895. His score was 1,394 out of a total possible score of 3,200. While the score, approximately 44 percent, may seem low by modern testing standards, he was still ranked fourteenth out of the seventy-one who were admitted to cadetships. Hundreds of others failed. He received word of his appointment while visiting his grandparents. Guy was fitted out with his uniform and, feeling somewhat self-important, left the Isle of Wight in 1896.

3

The U-Boat War

AFTER ALL THE CARGO WAS loaded aboard the *Laurentic* on January 24, 1917, the ship was ready to debark from Liverpool. The only thing that Captain Reginald Norton lacked was sailing orders. The British Admiralty had made it common practice to issue final directions only on the date of departure as a precaution against German intelligence. There were two routes that Norton could take: a route south of Ireland that was designated by the code E-F-G or a northern route encoded by the letters R-S-T.

At 11:30 AM the Admiralty sent a telegram: R-S-T. The *Laurentic* was to sail out of Liverpool and proceed west across the Irish Sea until the ship drew near Ireland. Then Norton was to sail north, hugging the coast until the ship reached the open Atlantic and thence Halifax, Nova Scotia.

By 3:00 PM Norton's crew cast loose the ship's moorings. Tugs eased the ship off the Canada Dock and helped it slip into the mouth of the dark River Mersey. With a sound of its horn, the *Laurentic* passed into the Irish Sea, where a cold storm crept in from the west. Two destroyers, HMS *Dee* and HMS *Dove*, greeted the ship as escorts.

Shortly after leaving Liverpool, a message came in on the wireless telegraph from the Admiralty. Apparently, there were four seamen who had boarded the ship that had contracted a kind of spotted fever. Norton was to divert the ship to Lough Swilly in the north of

Ireland to discharge the men. It was not a great course change, and Norton expected to lose little time.

The destroyers stayed with the *Laurentic* while it was still daylight. But as the sky darkened, the escort dropped away. The *Laurentic* extinguished its exterior lights, lest they provide a target for U-boats. Norton and his crew were now on their own until they reached Lough Swilly in the morning. He gave orders to sail at maximum speed hoping for a clear passage.

* * *

Great Britain's Royal Navy was the most powerful in the world, but in the years running up to the war Germany had built its own powerful High Seas Fleet to challenge it. This had been the era of large steel battleships modeled after HMS *Dreadnought*, that grew more powerful with each new construction. As Germany built its ships, Britain, fearful of losing its hegemony of the seas, accelerated its own construction program in an unprecedented naval arms race.

When war broke out in 1914, there was an expectation that these two massive fleets would clash in the greatest naval battle in world history. However, the German navy became "a fleet in being" since the Royal Navy's Grand Fleet, led by the cautious Admiral Sir John Jellicoe, did not wish to risk forces in a titanic battle. Instead, the British took up a strategy of containment and maintained a blockade against the German ports at a distance.

The only sign of any break to the stalemate came at the end of May 1916 off Jutland, the peninsula that forms the mainland portion of Denmark. Vice Admiral David Beatty found his squadron drawn into battle with the German High Seas Fleet commanded by Admiral Reinhard Scheer. The German admiral had adopted a strategy of trying to destroy portions of the British navy. After chase and engagement, Beatty, seeing the more numerous German ships, turned his squadron about and retreated to the main force of ships commanded by Jellicoe. Known to the Germans as *Skagerrakschlacht*,* the Battle

---

* So named after Skagerrak, the name of the strait between Norway and Jutland.

of Jutland was the largest, albeit inconclusive, sea battle in the First World War. The Germans managed to destroy more ships and kill more personnel than the British, but the British still maintained their blockade, and the Germans were forced to remain in port.

German naval strategists realized the implications of *Skager-rakschlacht*. There was no way to destroy the British Grand Fleet and break its blockade. If Germany could not counter the British, its citizens and soldiers would slowly starve. They also could not simply build more ships to try to wear down the British in a naval war of attrition since they would not be able to keep pace. Germany, therefore, looked to another weapon: the submarine.

By early 1915 combatants realized that the Great War was to be a war of attrition. They turned to innovations to break the stalemate. On land, the Central Powers employed poison gas against the trenches while the Allies first tested the use of tanks. At sea, Germany's strategy was to lay a counter blockade against Britain by destroying as much shipping as it could with U-boats. At the outset of the war, Britain dominated all other nations in gross registered tonnage in its merchant fleet at over 11.5 million tons. Its nearest rival was Germany at a little over 3 million tons. Britain was dependent on these ships to transport troops, munitions, food, and all other sorts of goods. Germany declared the British Isles a war zone and focused its attention on sinking British merchant ships using U-boats that were primarily based at the captured Belgian ports of Zeebrugge and Ostend, which were much closer to British waters than the German harbors.

Traditionally and legally, naval combatants were expected to follow so-called prize or cruiser rules that set the bounds of appropriate behavior for navies at war. If a warship was blockading a country or port, the ship could make a merchant vessel that was potentially carrying contraband heave to. Then, after boarding the ship, the seizing navy could confiscate the vessel as a prize if there was contraband aboard. In these types of encounters, captured passengers were usually taken aboard the attacking ship and, if not genially treated, were at least not killed. For example, the *Laurentic*, armed as a patrol ship in East Asia, performed this kind of search and seizure duty. On February 18, 1916, the ship stopped the American-flagged *China*, and seized thirty-eight nationals of the Central Powers who were believed to be plotting against British holdings in Asia. The US government, after learning about the matter, objected, stating that it was "an unwarranted invasion of the sovereignty of American vessels on the high seas." The British government eventually released the prisoners.

Submarines by their nature could only inelegantly employ cruiser rules against enemy merchant ships. A submarine's strength lay in its ability to conceal itself and conduct surprise attacks. Submarines could not off-load civilians from a ship that was to be scuttled since U-boats were far too small to carry additional passengers. In the rare cases when a U-boat attempted to follow such a code, the submarine captain would inform the soon-to-be-destroyed ship that it was about to be sunk and that those aboard should flee to the lifeboats. Five minutes of time given to evacuate was not unusual. After this was done, the U-boat would blast at the ship's hull using its deck guns—torpedoes were far too expensive.

This strategy, however, was untenable since U-boats were much more vulnerable at the surface and liable to be sunk by swift destroyers. What is more, at the start of the war Britain armed its merchant fleet. While Winston Churchill was first lord of the Admiralty he declared that this was for defensive purposes only, but to a German submarine commander it made the idea of surfacing to halt an enemy merchant ship ludicrous since they themselves stood a great chance of being sunk. Furthermore, Churchill introduced "Q-ships." These were heavily armed merchant vessels that disguised their weapons through the use of screens and other mechanisms. Their job was to lure submarines close to them and, once they surfaced, sink them. To German naval sensibilities this was foul play and, strictly speaking, against cruiser rules. To Germany, in order to have any parity in the war at sea they had to wield a submarine as it was built to be used—unrestricted.

As a result, victims of U-boat depredations complained that the attacks violated the rules of war as stipulated by the Hague Convention and the 1909 Declaration of London, which required that merchant ships be stopped, searched, and personnel allowed to disembark from the vessel to a place of safety. In practice, international law did not fully comprehend the reality of what submarine warfare *had* to be like in order for it to be effective. There could be no stopping. There could be no capture. The submarine's genius was ambush. Germany therefore turned to unrestricted submarine warfare in 1915 in which enemy merchant ships could be sunk without notice. Germany warned that they could not guarantee the safety of neutral ships in the declared war zone area since they may be mistaken for the enemy.

The consequence of this strategy was to alienate neutral countries, especially the United States, which often had citizens traveling aboard Allied merchant ships. This strain reached crisis proportions after the sinking of the RMS *Lusitania* on May 7, 1915, which had aboard 128 American passengers. Germany insisted that the *Lusitania* was a valid target since it was classed as an auxiliary cruiser and had munitions aboard. Nevertheless, international outrage over unrestricted submarine warfare mounted, and as more incidents occurred Germany agreed to limit its use of submarines. Admiral Scheer, the German commander at Jutland, noted how the U-boat matter became more of a political than military issue. He wrote:

> The course of events hitherto had shown that America interfered on England's behalf as soon as the U-boat campaign began to have perceptible results. For ever so long America had systematically prevented us from using our most effective weapon. Our attitude gave our people the false impression that, despite America's objections, we were still going to use our U-boat weapon with all our might. The people did not know that we, pledged to the nation by our big talking, were only pretending to carry on the U-boat campaign, and America laughed because she knew that it lay with her to determine how far we might go. She would not let us win by it.

Jutland forced a change. With little hope for a German naval victory using its High Seas Fleet or an outright victory by the army on the continent; and with Britain's military blockade strangling Germany, advocates of unrestricted submarine warfare grew more outspoken. Admiral Scheer commented, "There is no possibility of bringing the war to a satisfactory end without ruthless U-boat warfare."

The head of the German naval general staff, Admiral Henning von Holtzendorff calculated in December 1916 that if the U-boats were unfettered and could sink at least 630,000 tons of shipping per month, "England will be forced to sue for peace within five months as the result of launching an unrestricted U-boat war."

Germany naturally realized that this strategy would inevitably draw the Americans into the war, but it was a calculated risk. They considered that even if the United States declared war on Germany, it would be months before the Americans could effectively mobilize and get troops to Europe. By that time the war would be over. The Germans adopted this policy on January 9, 1917, and it was to be fully implemented on February 1.

While the full escalation of the U-boat campaign would occur just after the *Laurentic*'s departure from Liverpool, the effects of Germany's new intensified submarine warfare strategy were already being felt. In June 1916, 73 vessels were victims of U-boat attacks, which resulted in 108,851 tons of cargo lost. In December that number had grown to 223 vessels with 355,139 tons of cargo lost. Captain Norton was fully aware of the growing U-boat peril, although he was unaware of the impending unrestricted war. When considering also his experience in the Live Bait Squadron his own fear must have been palpable, which makes his commitment of duty to his ship even more impressive as he led his ship north through the Irish Sea.

4

"I Have No Good Word to Say for It"

IN 1896 GUYBON DAMANT ENTERED as a cadet aboard the *Britannia*, a special floating school used to train future navy officers. Cadet training in the late nineteenth century consisted of eighteen months of intense drilling, studying, and hazing. The hazing was probably the toughest to handle. The upperclassmen shook down the underclassmen for money or items of value. Corporal punishment was commonplace. Damant would later write of the *Britannia*, "I have no good word to say for it."

As a cadet, Damant took part in Queen Victoria's Diamond Jubilee, where he saw miles of stands with thousands of cheering people, including many crowned heads of state, such as the Austrian archduke Franz Ferdinand. Damant weathered his time as a cadet well, with his official record describing him as "zealous & attentive. Promises well."

After graduating from the *Britannia*, Damant served on a variety of ships as a midshipman, starting with the battleship HMS *Camperdown*, upon which he cruised the Mediterranean. It was a time of practical training during which he learned to take sights of sun and stars to mark the ship's position from the ship's chaplain, who had no practical experience in the matter except that he passed a course in spherical trigonometry. Some of the more memorable moments were of the warm, clear waters of the Aegean Sea, where the crew would swim, some daring to swim completely under the *Camperdown*. On one occasion, Damant was on deck with the officer of the watch and a signalman who were observing two to three hundred men in

Guybon Damant in cadet uniform circa 1896. *Courtesy of Mary Harrison*

the water. They got in and out via a boom, a long projecting spar that nearly touched the water, as well as other routes such as ladders and ropes. As the men were swimming, the signalman noticed a shark's fin in the water. But the officer of the watch stopped the man from shouting the alarm and gave the word to the bugler to recall the men in normal order. The men, dripping and somewhat resentful of only having a few minutes in the water, trickled aboard. The officer then looked to Damant and said, "There my boy, what do you think would have happened if I had started any emergency nonsense?"

"Don't know, sir," Damant replied.

"Well there would have been fifty or a hundred men on that boom at once and the topping lift would have carried away," the officer said.

Damant had his own growing pains in learning how to handle men. When in Souda Bay, Crete, the *Camperdown* sent boats on trips of ten miles to the shore to fetch provisions of beef. Damant managed one crew of the boats, and he made them row the entire ten miles without a break. The men pulled at the oars without complaint, but word soon got back to the senior midshipmen, who promptly beat Damant for not knowing his duty. Damant would later write, "Administration has always been my bugbear but I could heave the lead remarkably well for my size."

After the *Camperdown*, Damant served on the battleship HMS *Prince George* on the Channel Fleet and cruised about the British Isles. It was during this time that he took up boxing. Damant later admitted that he had inflated ideas about his own prowess since his first boxing partners "knew nothing whatever about it and were less pugnacious." Still, in 1901, while preparing in London to sit for his sublieutenant exams, he saw an advertisement that read, "The Knockout Blow and How to Avoid It." Responding to the ad, he took lessons from a "Professor" Andrew Newton, who had been an amateur lightweight champion some years prior. The Professor, who operated a smelly ring in a little house, was also hired by a bookmaker as a bodyguard. In one case, the bookmaker ran into another rival bookmaker whose bodyguard was an amateur heavyweight—the bookmakers decided to settle their differences by having their protectors fight. Despite the longer odds, since Newton was a lightweight, the Professor had to make a living and went at it, all the while a ring of boys who knew him shouted, "Come on, Andrew! The knock out blow and how to avoid it!" Newton managed to hang in until the police came. Probably the best boxing trick Damant learned from Newton was to always wear kid gloves when going into any place where trouble might erupt. Damant wrote, "This saves one from gashing one's knuckles against the other man's teeth and are more likely to bust his face open than bare fists. 'Fighting in kid gloves' is not all it seems." Damant was so enthusiastic about boxing that he showed up with a black eye to his grandfather's funeral.

It was also during this time that Damant read H. G. Wells's "The Moth," a dark satire written in 1895 about the intense rivalry between two entomologists. In the story, one of the entomologists published a paper concerning the mesoblast of the death's-head hawkmoth. "What the mesoblast of the Death's Head Moth may be does not matter a rap in this story," wrote Wells in good humor. But Damant wondered, "What could this be?" He was inspired, went to a pawnshop, and bought a microscope and secondhand histology textbooks, which he intended to use while he was away on his long duty to the China station.

The outward voyage, which he took on the cruiser HMS *Amphitrite*, had its own set of adventures, but Damant, aside from his normal duties, became the captain of the officer's football team while at the same time intensely read his books to sate his growing interest in natural biology. The voyage itself provided ample opportunities to a budding physiologist. He delighted in observing flying fish and sea snakes. Upon arriving in Singapore, he was especially excited. Damant had read that the mangrove marshes outside Singapore had giant earthworms. Obtaining leave, he explored them. Damant did not find the worms but instead caught a fever. When the ship arrived at Hong Kong he was taken to the naval hospital in a stretcher. Damant wrote, "Though not feeling particularly ill, I grew feeble and exhaled a most peculiar smell. The medical people could not put a name to my illness, and, after a few weeks, with no improvement were on the point of invaliding me home when I began to mend."

The *Amphitrite* had left, so Damant joined the armed cruiser HMS *Blenheim*, a happy ship where he made several good friends. He then visited China and Japan, where he was promoted to lieutenant (an automatic appointment based on time served) and was placed on the armored cruiser HMS *Argonaut*. The *Argonaut* was commanded by Captain George H. Cherry, who was infamous for being the most severe commanding officer in the service. Damant later wrote that Cherry was said "to have court martialled each of his officers twice over and never to have less than ten percent of the men doing ninety days in the shore gaol." As an example, the bell-bottoms of a sailor's trousers were by regulation supposed to be exactly thirty-one and a half inches in circumference. During inspections, Cherry would come with the master of arms, who had a tape measure, and meted out severe punishments for those who violated even this minutest detail of code. Cherry ordered the master at arms to turn up trouser legs to make sure that socks were properly inscribed with the owner's name. Damant noted that there was a long waiting list for the ship cells.

"Private subscriptions awarded a silver 'Cherry Medal' to every officer who survived a year in the ship," he wrote. He had one memorable encounter with Cherry:

> One morning at sea with the fleet I was on watch at daybreak when the flagship made an unexpected signal for a violent alteration of course which, as she was a battleship with quite different turning circle to than us, involved some rather delicate steering. By good luck I manage to put over the helm, ease it and steady, at exactly the right moment but nearly jumped to hear a croak in my ear of "That was done correctly." The old villain had stolen up from below in slippers and pajamas hoping for trouble. It was said to be the only time he had approved of anything anyone did.

In his spare time, Damant continued to box, dissect dogfish and frogs, and practice with his microscope. Upon arriving in Singapore in early 1904, the *Argonaut* was paid off and headed home, but Damant's time on the station was not over. Much to his delight, he was assigned back to his friends on the *Blenheim*, upon which he made his homeward cruise. He returned to Britain for a long leave in 1904.

On the whole, Damant disliked the navy, but it did provide him an opportunity to see the world and at least look at some of the exotic flora and fauna he had come to admire. The Royal Navy had him slated to start the long course in gunnery instruction at HMS *Excellent* in March 1905. As a specialist gunner lieutenant, Damant would receive extra pay and enhanced promotional opportunities. With several months before the new assignment, the navy offered him an interim appointment. However, Damant had his fill of the navy for the moment and was much happier with his friends and brothers, and the various girls he met. So he returned to the family home of Lammas and remained there on half pay. While he waited for his new assignment, he worked at his father's law office copying names and other data into deeds and other legal papers. To stimulate his scientific enthusiasm, he attended a meeting of the British Science Association, where he met and was further inspired by scientists. He then regretfully turned to his coursework at the *Excellent*.

HMS *Excellent* was what was called a stone frigate, or a shore establishment as part of the navy's training regimen. While in former days there actually had been a hulk in the water named the *Excellent,* by Damant's time the whole business had been moved ashore mostly onto Whale Island near Portsmouth. Damant described Whale Island as a "mass of mud" that was reclaimed from the sea by prison labor. The heart of the island was a vast gravel-covered parade ground, which was used for exercise, next to a proving range where big guns were fired at armor plate backed by six feet of English oak to check the quality of the shells.

Damant's coursework consisted of the study of ballistics and field drills on the island's large parade ground. He was to master calculus and learn how to lead battalion drill. As part of the process, he took part in mock battles put on for King Edward VII. The commanding officer's motorcar stood in for an armored vehicle. There were also elaborate dinners, sports, and paperwork. Damant skived off on the latter and snuck away to the Empire Music Hall in Portsmouth. Whale Island was in close proximity to the Isle of Wight, and he was able to visit Lammas on a regular basis either by ferry or occasionally by his new yacht, *Scart,* over the short distance. Despite these perks, Damant felt displaced and uninspired in the anti-intellectual boredom of military training. He desired something more.

5

The Lake of Shadows

THE *LAURENTIC* SPED THROUGH a night that brought a cold southeast gale of over twenty-six knots. Snow fell in either a blizzard or a flurry. Captain Reginald Norton and his crew sought solace in the ship's electric-lit interior, relaxed in the unexpected security of bad weather, since it was unlikely that a U-boat would attack the *Laurentic* during a storm.

There was no sign of a break in the weather even as dawn rose cold, windy, and gray. But with the growing light, all hands could see that the ship had reached the mouth of Lough Swilly, Ireland. Even during a winter storm, the coastal fjord would be hard not to appreciate—especially for Captain Norton who had never been there before. The deepwater channel penetrated twenty-five miles into the Irish interior, a haven that could hold multiple fleets. At its farthest reaches into the countryside, the Swilly seemed not so much a coastal estuary as a true loch—a deep, dark, and beautiful sea lake surrounded by wintry pasture and highlands. The original Irish *Loch Súilí* is sometimes translated as "Lake of Eyes," but the more common rendering is "Lake of Shadows."

The great inlet was strategically important for the Royal Navy. In October 1914, shortly after the disaster that sunk the Live Bait Squadron, Admiral Sir John Jellicoe had temporarily relocated a portion of the British Grand Fleet from its main base at Scapa Flow, in the Orkney Islands, to Lough Swilly, which was less vulnerable to submarine attacks. The Royal Navy built a great boom manned by trawlers to fence the waterway so that none but friendly ships could pass.

By the time of the *Laurentic*'s voyage, the Grand Fleet was no longer there, having been relocated back to the Royal Navy's main base at Scapa Flow, which by that time was better protected. However, at Lough Swilly the boom remained in place with its string of heavy nets running across the inlet from Macamish Point east to Ned's Point, just north of the small town of Buncrana.

To a British sailor fighting in the First World War, the boom was a physical manifestation of the war's frontline at sea. Behind the safety of the boom, men could breathe easy but forget for a while to be constantly vigilant for a periscope's feather or the foamy track of a darting torpedo. As a precaution the channels leading toward Buncrana were swept for mines at least once a week.

After the *Laurentic* passed inside the boom, it sailed for two miles before setting down its anchors in sight of Buncrana, where Norton was to discharge the men with spotted fever. An officer from the shore base came aboard with a message from Admiral Frank Finnis, the senior naval officer in Buncrana. Retired, the sixty-five-year-old former flag officer had been given a temporary commission of captain by the Royal Navy Reserve. At the beginning of the war he was given command of a yacht converted to a patrol ship named the *Sagitta*. However, after a collision with a trawler and then a second mishap on the rocks near Whitby, which not only sank the *Sagitta* but also resulted in Finnis losing all his belongings including two sets of false teeth, he was reassigned. False teeth were hard to replace at that time, and subsisting on a diet of porridge and soup, he was placed in charge of Naval Area 18, which encompassed Lough Swilly and extended into the adjoining waters for some miles. Finnis had received an encoded message from the *Laurentic* that stated that Norton was sailing under Admiralty orders, and the ship would anchor outside Buncrana during the day of January 25. They would leave at dusk.

Finnis's officer asked if Norton needed anything before the Atlantic crossing, but he declined. The *Laurentic*'s stores were full, its cargo secure, and its hands ready—that is, except for three crew members imprisoned in cells. Whether it was attempted desertion, disobedience, or some other infraction, the prisoners' crimes are lost to the historical record. However, it is known that they were firemen, those who maintained the coal-burning fires that ran the *Laurentic*'s engines. They were being held for the voyage across the Atlantic, and it is likely that they were only guilty of minor infractions.

With time to spare after the discharge of the sick men, some of the officers took boats into Buncrana, where they went to the Lough Swilly Hotel to enjoy a meal. They were in good spirits, but then a message came in with new orders. The *Laurentic* was now to depart before dusk. The officers, who expected more than a couple of hours ashore, were shocked—angry even. There was to be no shore leave until Canada.

At 4:00 PM, with darkness coming on, preparations to depart commenced. Norton ordered action stations. Alarms echoed through the ship. The crew ran across the decks to man the guns, look out for the enemy, seal doors, or to shovel coal to feed the *Laurentic*'s fires to build steam. At 5:00 PM, the ship drew up its anchors. Norton ordered the ship to edge away from Buncrana and make for the boom. Twenty minutes later, the trawlers opened the barrier to allow the *Laurentic* to proceed north, steam being steadily whipped from the ship's funnel by a cold gale.

Norton reasonably thought that if there was a German submarine in the area, it might try to get out of the storm by seeking the relative protection of Lough Swilly. He ordered full speed ahead. The engines roared and the *Laurentic*'s speed built to seventeen and a half knots. Norton decided that the best thing to do was zigzag—a common tactic to avoid U-boats. The *Laurentic* swung a point to starboard. After five minutes, the ship made two points to port, aligning its course to magnetic north.

The *Laurentic* was now coming to the mouth of Lough Swilly. Two miles to the west lay Fanad Head, a rocky promontory that rose

into high cliffs. In the dark, it was a gray mass with a single beacon
of light emanating from its lighthouse. Beyond were the open waters
of the North Atlantic. There would be no more land until Halifax.

6

Through the Looking Glass

ONE DAY IN 1905, LIEUTENANT GUYBON DAMANT and the other young officers were taken down to the docks of Whale Island where they were met by a thirty-six-year-old warrant officer named Andrew Yule Catto. A slightly built Scotsman, Catto was known through the service as *the* expert on diving. He was reputably capable of feats underwater that put larger divers to shame. Described as having a "singularly attractive personality, modest, clean minded, with ill-feelings toward none, yet with that brave and fearless—a true sailor of the best type," Andrew Catto was to give the officers a one-week crash course on diving.[*]

Divers were used to clean inlets, scrape barnacles from ships' bottoms, or look for lost items that were thrown overboard. Officers in general did not think much of diving, and there were few, if any, commissioned officers in the Royal Navy that regularly dived. The young lieutenants might have groaned at the thought of learning this unglamorous subject. Damant wrote, "It was an unpopular item. Besides the physical discomfort of partial suffocation it involved handling wet, muddy chain and gear, work more suited to a labourer than to the smart brainy young officers whom it disgusted. Moreover it is only a minority of either officers or men who can face isolated submergence

---

[*] Catto's younger brother, Thomas, would become a successful businessman and later the governor of the Bank of England.

without funk, however courageous they may be in ordinary matters." But by some quirk of the service gunnery officers were in charge of diving on ships. Officers needed to know what to expect while commanding and ensuring the safety of the divers while they were on the bottom.

The course was an overview of diving and lasted fourteen days. Damant saw the cumbersome equipment that encased a man's body in canvas topped by a heavy diving helmet, also called a bonnet, which was screwed onto a corselet worn by the diver. He learned of the dangers of sea pressure and how divers worked on the bottom through the delivery of compressed air into the suit that was weighted to keep a man stable in the water. All told, there were about 175 pounds of gear that a diver wore. Aside from the helmet and weights, divers who went deeper than twelve fathoms—seventy-two feet—wore what was referred to as the "shackle" or the "crinoline," named after a traditional woman's petticoat that was stiffened outward. This wickerwork was attached around the diver's stomach and waist on the unproven theory that it was to hold pressure off the diver's vital organs in order to allow him to breathe more freely.

Damant also learned about the lifeline, also called a breast-rope, which tethered a diver to a tending boat as well as the air pipe[*] that delivered the all-important compressed air that allowed the diver to work. Then there was communication. Divers could use a telephone transmitter in the diver's helmet that was wired through the lifeline, or lacking that, employ a series of tugs on the line to request more air, less air, or to report an emergency. There were all sorts of signals.

Catto would have taught Damant about the troubles divers had underwater. Men worked slower on the bottom, and it was considered impractical to send divers deeper than one hundred feet since their breathing became labored and their motions slowed. He would have learned how a man's diving dress could either "blow up" due to outlet valves getting clogged, or men getting squeezed by water pressure during a fall or sudden increase in depth. The squeeze was particularly dangerous on account of the nature of the suit. The 1924 *Diving Manual* stated,

---

[*] Called an air hose in the US Navy.

Suppose a diver at work on a stage cleaning the ship's bottom slips off the stage and falls 5 fathoms.... At this depth the absolute pressure is twice as much as it is close to the surface, so by the descent the volume of the air in his dress is halved. He has an additional pressure of nearly 15 lbs suddenly applied to every square inch of his body, or about 2,000 lbs to every square foot. As the helmet is rigid, his body will be crushed into it with overwhelming force.... If, however, the diver is at 165 feet ... and falls 5 fathoms, pressure has only increased in the proportion of seven to six, and the volume of air has only diminished by less than one-seventh of its volume, so that the effect will be proportionately less. From this it follows that the deeper a diver is the less serious is a fall.

Then there was fouling, when a man's lifeline and air pipe become snagged against some obstruction. This was all too easy when working at depth since a diver's lines had to be paid out farther than the straight-line distance between the diver and the surface in order to account for current and tide. This created belly-like loops of slack in the lines that always threatened to catch on something.

But the most insidious danger of all the hazards Damant learned was diver's palsy. Examples of this affliction were well known to those whose profession brought them underwater or into extended contact with compressed air. One case occurred in 1900 when a thirty-three-year-old diver with a lean, strong physique was working in 24½ fathoms of water, about 147 feet. The diver took his time getting to the bottom—forty minutes—and worked there for another forty minutes before it became too dark to continue. He surfaced slowly over the course of twenty minutes and climbed aboard the little diving boat that was the typical kind of platform used for the work. His tenders opened the faceplate of his helmet, and the diver said he felt fine. He was cheerful and made a joke. The men who tended him thought they never saw anybody come up in better condition.

About eight or nine minutes later the diver suddenly complained of pains in his stomach. He pleaded with the tenders to take off his diving dress and get him back aboard the main ship. Then he uttered, "Send for the doctor," before collapsing onto the boat's deck, limp and unconscious. When they got him to the ship, he was comatose. The medical report read that "his skin was cyanosed and his breathing was stertorous, laboured, and difficult. His lips were blowing and covered with froth." He died before they got him to the sick bay. Only fifteen minutes had passed since he came to the surface.

The next morning, an autopsy was performed. The surgeons found that "on incising the scalp, a quantity of very dark coloured, almost black, fluid blood flowed from the cut vessels, principally the temporals." But what was most striking was the presence of bubbles throughout the body. "The heart was normal in size, but the veins on its surface under the serous membrane were markedly beaded by air. On lifting it up, it felt like a bladder half full of water, and, on making pressure to raise it, was heard to gurgle loudly, and a quantity of black frothy blood flowed from the sinuses at the base of the skull." Most of the major organs had this intrusion of air and froth that blocked circulation.

The cause of diver's palsy, also called caisson disease, decompression sickness, or the bends (due to the position the afflicted often took), was well known by the time Damant was at HMS *Excellent*. Divers imbibed nitrogen from the compressed air into their tissues. While working on the bottom, everything was normal since under the compression the nitrogen remained in solution. But when a diver returned to normal air pressure, the nitrogen would, as gases do, come out of solution and enter the tissues, joints, spinal column, and organs. The best and most ubiquitous example of how to describe the bends is to compare it to a bottle of soda water. Soda water in a bottle is kept under pressurized air. When you look at the bottle when it is sealed there are few, if any bubbles. However, when the bottle is opened the pressure equalizes to the air pressure outside the bottle. The carbon dioxide gases inside the bottle suddenly come out of solution and form bubbles. Symptoms of the bends could be mild, from headaches, joint pain, and double vision, to severe, such as brain damage, paralysis, and death. The condition was classified as caisson disease when physiologists in the 1870s studied workers who labored on the Brooklyn Bridge in caissons that were filled with compressed air.

While the symptoms and causes of the affliction were understood, the remedy for it was at best unreliable. In shallow dives, up to roughly forty feet, divers were not afflicted by the bends, meaning that the body could withstand breathing in a moderate level of compressed air. However, if a diver went deeper, higher pressurized air needed to be delivered to him since the air had to overcome the greater water pressure of the deep.[*] The best scientific advice was to come up slowly, at about the rate of one atmosphere of pressure per twenty minutes. But even so, the bends still occurred. Fortunately, divers could be sent back down if they showed symptoms, or they could be placed into a recompression chamber, which was a sealed iron cylinder in which pressurized air was delivered, forcing nitrogen bubbles back into solution. Then, through trial and error, the pressure could be relieved. Finding a reliable way to prevent diver's palsy was a mystery that needed to be solved.

As part of the course, Catto guided Damant and the other officers in making dives. It was not to be a true deepwater dive where there was a danger of contracting the bends but simply to appreciate what it was like to be a diver and how the equipment operated. When it came time for Damant's first dive he recalled, "I felt like Alice through the looking glass. The new underwater world fascinated me, and, unlike my shipmates, I felt perfectly at home in it. Technique was easily acquired, and I would have stayed down all day if I could." After his own thrilling experience, Damant was amused to see how Catto would interact with the half-scared, half-indignant lieutenants he was teaching—ostensibly Catto's superior officers.

It was a life-changing experience for Damant. He would later state, "I found going under water to be a delightful experience and infinitely preferred Catto's fatherly instruction to the study of ballistics and field gun drill. I loved it. Diving amused me." Catto, in fact, would become one of Damant's lifelong friends.

The two weeks of instruction passed too quickly for Damant, and afterward he volunteered to go with Catto's seaman divers to scrub

---

[*] If you took a straw and blew it into a glass of water, you would find no difficulty in doing so. However, if you took the straw and extended it to the bottom of a ten-foot pool, there is no person who could blow air out of the straw.

and chisel barnacles off ships' bottoms or clear hawsers from propellers. He loved diving in and of itself but could not imagine how as an officer these newfound skills could be of service. Damant wrote, "Officers did not dive and the trained seamen divers never had anything to do more important than to search, usually unsuccessfully, for lost anchors and the like."

7

Spark

IN THE *LAURENTIC*'S WIRELESS TELEGRAPHY OFFICE, twenty-two-year-old Arthur Bower had just finished transmitting a message to the station at Malin Head, the most northerly point of Ireland, and was waiting for an acknowledgment. However, he found that the wireless's alternator had malfunctioned. The warrant officer puzzled over this for a moment, but was confident that he could fix the problem.

While a teenager, Bower had been trained by the Marconi Company in London to operate the complex equipment that was the state-of-the-art in wireless communications in the early twentieth century. The wireless telegraph was commonly referred to as a Marconi, after its inventor, Guglielmo Marconi. The device worked through the use of an alternator that generated an electrical current, which created a blue arc of electricity called a spark between two electrodes. The spark was then transformed into Morse code radio signals. A wireless operator aboard a ship needed to be completely fluent in international Morse code to translate the signals.

The wireless telegraph revolutionized naval communications. Before Marconi's invention, ships could only communicate by direct signal, be it by flashing light, cannon shot, or signal flag. Now, fleets could be dispatched to intercept the enemy from a faraway signal, or a ship could summon help if it was in trouble. Even non-naval ships benefited from the wireless technology.

The *Laurentic* itself became tied to the history of the wireless telegraph in 1910. Dr. Hawley Harvey Crippen, who had murdered his wife, fled from England to Canada with his lover (dressed as a boy) aboard the liner *Montrose*. The captain of the *Montrose*, suspecting that Crippen was aboard, sent a message by wireless telegraph to authorities ashore. Chief Inspector Walter Dew of Scotland Yard boarded the *Laurentic*. Even with the *Montrose*'s three-day lead, the swift *Laurentic*, which could make eighteen knots to the *Montrose*'s twelve, beat the *Montrose* to Canada, where Dew arrested Crippen at the dock. It was the first time that wireless telegraphy was used to apprehend a criminal.

The *Titanic* had its own Marconi device in 1912 to call for assistance before it sank. By the time of the First World War, these devices were ubiquitous, and there was a great demand for experts who could work them. So Bower at the start of the war was assigned to the *Laurentic* as its wireless telegraph officer. He had remained in charge there ever since.

The cabin itself was divided in two, with all the Marconi equipment behind a partial enclosure. Bower, alone in the section by the equipment, was surrounded by boxes filled with ciphers, codebooks, and messages. The most important materials were kept in a locked box that contained such confidential items as the *Wireless Telegraphy Code—1915*, the call signs of all of His Majesty's ships as well as commercial vessels, operating signals, and the wireless telegraph manual. Some of these had been removed for Bower's use and were to be returned after he was done working with them. Generally, however, the only organization to the cluttered office was seemingly in Bower's head. He refused to dispose of old messages, using them instead to train a ship's boy named O'Callaghan in wireless telegraphy. He also had under him three other men who helped him at his work—but none of them were on duty, leaving Bower alone with his boxes, books, and broken alternator.

Bower's thoughts of the alternator were suddenly disturbed by an explosion that lit a terrible white froth of water on the forward port side of the *Laurentic*'s hull abeam of the forward mast. The ship trembled and the windows shattered, allowing bitter air to whip through the cabin. A cascade of boxes avalanched onto the deck, along with the wall clock, several codebooks, and almost anything else that was not fastened down.

Bower knew he had to get a signal out. There was a page in the wireless signal instruction book that he had tacked to the wall, which gave directions for what to do in an emergency. In the case of a ship striking a mine or torpedo—and Bower could not imagine the explosion being anything else—he must send out a signal indicating the ship had been struck and upon which side.

Bower turned to his equipment. He tested his receiver, found it working, and adjusted it for sensitivity. He needed to find out specifics from Captain Norton as to what signal to send. He rose from his chair and started to gather the codebooks together—if the *Laurentic* sank, the books needed to be destroyed, even as his staff began coming in from the other part of the cabin to assist him.

Just then, about twenty seconds after the first explosion, a second more violent blast hurled Bower off his feet.

He scrambled in darkness. The electricity had cut out.

8

Suffer

ON JANUARY 23, 1906, Lieutenant Guybon Damant headed down to
the piers to board a ship in order to practice firing its six-inch guns.
On the way, he saw Andrew Catto and the other divers dressed spit-
and-polish. Catto informed Damant that "professors from Oxford" led
by a Dr. John Scott Haldane were coming to try to figure out how
divers may dive deeper than ever before.

It would have been surprising if Damant had not known who
John Scott Haldane was. Haldane was distinctive not only for his
Scottish burr and his bushy mustache but also for his creative intellect and guts. The forty-five-year-old professor was a world-renowned
physiologist who had achieved celebrity for his work on combating
noxious gases in mines. In 1893 he hypothesized that respiration was
regulated by carbon dioxide. He and a colleague sealed themselves
in an airtight box dubbed the "coffin" and stayed inside for eight
hours recording their reactions as carbon dioxide built up. In 1895
Haldane investigated sewer gas which had caused several workers to
die. This turned out to be noxious hydrogen sulfide. His recommendations were to aerate sewers and make sure workers were tethered
by ropes to the surface.

Haldane's family motto was "Suffer."

Haldane's brother, Richard Burdon Haldane, happened to be
the British secretary of war. When the Admiralty made it known that

it wanted to conduct experiments on diving, Richard helped swing the research director position to his brother. Despite the blatant nepotism, Haldane was still the most qualified person in the British Empire to conduct experiments in diving since he understood the nature of gases and how these behaved under pressure better than anyone.

The Admiralty first engaged Haldane to work on the problem of ventilation aboard the Royal Navy's new submarines. Haldane's suggestions were readily adopted. The Admiralty then tasked Haldane to look into deep diving. The Admiralty had long known that divers who went deeper than fifteen fathoms (ninety feet) often had labored breathing, which slowed down the diver and the amount of work he could do on the bottom.

Haldane was now at HMS *Excellent* to direct a series of tests using the experimental diving tank. As a supplement to this, Catto and his divers were taking part in tests at Spithead along the Solent diving to depths of 19 fathoms (114 feet). While underwater, divers collected samples of air from their helmets for analysis. Simultaneously, Haldane examined the diving equipment used to deliver air for efficiency and leaks. The pumps were hand-cranked affairs that took squads of men to operate. Haldane found air was leaking out of the pumps, which grew worse as a diver went deeper. At two hundred feet, Haldane found a 57 percent leakage rate and exposure to too much carbon dioxide. Divers were simply not getting enough breathable air. New, efficient pumps needed to be designed. While that was underway, Haldane had carbon dioxide–absorbing canisters installed into the divers' helmets. Haldane returned to Oxford to teach after the initial round of tests was completed.

Damant then had an epiphany. Here was an opportunity to combine his newfound enthusiasm for diving with his love of science. After considering the matter, he wrote a carefully constructed letter to Haldane, expressing his keen interest in the subject. Damant explained that he was an *officer* who could combine Haldane's theories with Catto's practice. He appealed to Haldane to allow him to join the research.

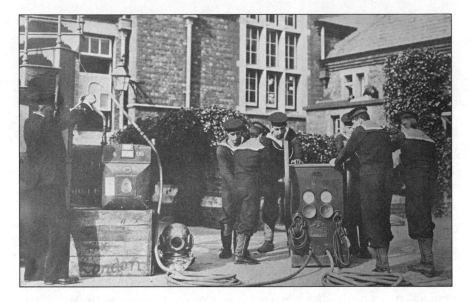

Sailors demonstrate the use of hand-cranked pumps. *Report of a Committee Appointed by the Lords Commissioners of the Admiralty to Consider and Report upon the Conditions of Deep-Water Diving, 1907*

To Damant's astonishment, he received a reply. Haldane cautiously expressed interest and wrote, "Experiments are still needed. Would you go down in twenty five to thirty fathoms? There is less risk for a young man and that could be minimised ... if you care to talk the matter over I shall be very glad to see you here [Oxford University] and, should you be here for a night, I hope you will stay with us. I enclose a paper on the subject."

The paper was Haldane and John Gillies Priestley's 1905 article "The Regulation of the Lung-Ventilation." Damant found the paper dense but managed to master enough of it to feel like he could have some semblance of a conversation with the famous physiologist. When Damant returned to Lammas to tell the news of his impending visit to Oxford, his parents encouraged him and did not object to the possibility of diving in up to thirty fathoms of water. His brother Henry suggested that he wear a false beard and glasses to impress Haldane.

It was with a good measure of anxiety that Damant visited Oxford in 1906 and called upon the Haldane household. He found that Haldane was busy at work but was immediately invited to a tea party, which was generally considered a female affair—Damant felt awkward. But soon after, he met the great scientist himself in his study, which was littered with journals, papers, letters, and diagrams. Haldane was gracious and they talked deep into the night as he sized up the young lieutenant. He invited Damant to visit his laboratory the next day. After further observing Damant's eagerness and intelligence, Haldane said he would try to get him appointed to the experiments as long as he passed the gunnery course at Whale Island.

It was with this final impetus that Damant passed the course work (near the bottom of his class) and was (to the surprise of those who did not know about the diving experiments) appointed a junior staff member of the *Excellent* on March 20, 1906. Since Damant was an officer, he was placed in charge of the diving side of the experiments over Catto.

But Damant had only taken the short course designed for officers who were not expected to dive regularly. In order to expand his limited experience, Damant took the full seaman diver's course and received the personal tutelage of Catto. Both Damant and Catto carried on multiple tests in Whale Island's experimental tank then off Spithead where Damant dived to a maximum depth of nineteen and a half fathoms—a

Guybon Chesney Castell Damant as a staff officer at HMS *Excellent* circa 1910. *Courtesy of Mary Harrison*

personal record for him. He then visited Siebe Gorman, the preeminent British diving equipment company that was desperately working on the pump leakage problem that Haldane had discovered. There Damant was fitted for his own diving dress.

Meanwhile, diving practice continued. Damant dove in Portsmouth Harbor taking on miscellaneous diving jobs that would have been considered beneath his status as an officer—such as cleaning ship bottoms and clearing inlets and fouled propellers—just to gain practical experience. Rather than feeling demeaned, Damant fully enjoyed it, taking delight in seeing undersea creatures like lobsters in their native habitat. He was also amazed at the sheer amount of debris that could be found under the sea. He hunted for long-forgotten cannon, bottles, and anchors. Some of the anchors he recovered he sent to his yachting friends at Cowes.

Damant also kept on the lookout for potential new species of plants and animals. On one occasion, as he wandered through the inky darkness of the muddy harbor he felt some sort of marine growth, about the size of a football, swaying from a slimy stem. The stem was curiously attached to a chunk of iron. Since this unknown colony—of something—was straining on the stem, he cut it and telephoned to the surface to stand by to collect the new specimen and wash it with clean seawater. Damant dreamed of zoological fame as he hurried up after the object, which rose balloon-like to the surface. As he climbed up the diving boat's ladder he said, "Have you got it? Let me see it!"

The reply, "Well, sir, it was only a stinking dead cat and Mr Catto said don't take that carrion into the boat, but you can still smell it sir if we stop the pump a minute."

Damant was also put to use testing new diving equipment. In one instance he was tasked to test a Fleuss apparatus, a type of rebreather developed by Henry Fleuss in the late nineteenth century. The equipment, which theoretically allowed a diver to rebreathe his own air and also provided a supply of pressurized oxygen, was invented as an effort to make divers independent of any connection to the surface. The apparatus proved to be fairly successful in rescue situations such as in mines and tunnels, but not appreciably so under the sea. In

1906, working with the Siebe Gorman Company, Fleuss had made some modifications to the equipment and asked Damant to test it.

Damant entered the diving tank at the *Excellent*. But the dress had so many complicated valves that he neglected to turn one of the taps. Damant passed out in the tank. He recalled:

> I suddenly woke up to find myself lying on dry ground with a fat doctor performing artificial respiration. Wet through and deathly cold it seemed imperative to get warm by violent exercise, so flinging him and his pale satellites aside, I jumped up and ran like a maniac across the astonished parade ground with a pursuing tail of divers and sick bay attendants! They could not begin to catch me till the sudden idea of a hot bath caused a reversal of course.

To help round out his knowledge of working with compressed air, Damant took courses at Portsmouth Technical College for a physiology certificate. He ranked first. His only leisure at this time was racing his small yacht, the *Corella*, on the weekends. It was after this grueling crash course in the science and practice of diving that Damant was considered ready to leave the *Excellent* and join the main research.

The Admiralty, however, was resistant to the idea of Damant taking leave from the *Excellent* to take part in the studies. Haldane interceded by having a word with his brother, who then contacted the first sea lord, Admiral John Fisher, who allowed Damant to go. Damant was directed to the Lister Institute of Preventive Medicine where he was to work with a pathologist and naturalist named Arthur Edwin Boycott. Damant took immediately to the twenty-nine-year-old Boycott, who became one of his closest friends.

The Lister Institute, founded in 1891 as a counterpart to the Pasteur Institute in Paris, was one of the preeminent facilities in the world for the study of disease and microbiology. Standing in a brick building on an embankment of the Thames in London, Damant was seduced by the large white-tiled laboratories and the little rooms designed for individual researchers and equipped with the best microscopes, incubators, and sterilizers. There were hot rooms, darkrooms, workshops, a library, and an animal house on the roof. It was "like

The experimental air compression chamber at the Lister Institute.

heaven on earth," Damant wrote. The institute had recently become a school of the University of London and was the beneficiary of a large steel compression chamber from a Dr. Ludwig Mond, who had been contacted by Haldane for this purpose.

A few initial experiments had been conducted on mice, rats, guinea pigs, and one old hen by putting them into the compression chamber. But smaller-bodied creatures tended to exchange gases quicker and disperse the nitrogen from compressed air rapidly. They needed larger-bodied animals so that an approximation to human respiratory function could be measured. Dogs, pigs, and monkeys were considered. But dogs had a respiratory exchange ratio quite different from humans, pigs were hard to come by, and monkeys were simply too small and difficult to obtain.

The researchers wrote of the matter, "Goats, while they are not perhaps such delicate indicators of as monkeys or dogs, and though they are somewhat stupid and definitely insensitive to pain, are capable of entering into emotional relationships with their surroundings, animate and inanimate, of a kind sufficiently nice to enable those who are familiar with them to detect slight abnormalities with a fair degree of certainty." A herd of eighty-five goats was obtained for the research and kept at the Lister Institute.

They needed to determine a goat's respiratory rate first. To do so they put them in the compression chamber, sealed it, then measured carbon dioxide content as it built up. Based on the tests they calculated the goats had a respiratory exchange ratio 1.7 times that of a grown man.

Next, over the course of several months, the researchers put groups of up to eight goats inside the chamber. The air pressure was then raised to a specific amount, and the goats were left inside from a few minutes to a few hours in order for compressed nitrogen to be absorbed into their bodies. The goats were visible during the proceedings through windows into the chamber. Then, the experimenters would decompress the chamber at different rates. The change in pressure would fog the windows, which obscured observations until the air pressure was normalized and the goats were released to roam the yard.

In the yard, the researchers carefully observed the goats for signs of the bends. Since the goats could not tell Damant and Boycott how they felt, the researchers had to become quite familiar with their behavior. The researchers remarked, "During the breeding season it is advisable to keep the males and females separate, and by removing any sources of interest, to allow the animals to fall into a state of meditative boredom."

If they saw goats refusing food, they knew something was wrong. They found the most common symptom of the bends was when a goat seemingly developed an injury in one of its four legs. It was likely that bubbles had formed in the knees. Some goats were stricken by temporary paralysis. Others showed pain through bleating and constant restlessness. Others were permanently paralyzed. Then goats died. Some of these were first afflicted with dyspnea, or shortness of breath and labored respiration, which would gradually worsen before the goat expired. Animals that were suffering were dispatched and the researchers limited experiments that they knew would outright kill the goats, not just to be humane but to keep a number alive for future tests.

As for Damant, since he was working ashore, he was living on reduced pay. He generally lived hard for a blue blood at a bed-and-

The researchers at the Lister Institute found that one of the most common symptoms of decompression sickness in goats occurred in the knees, where bubbles of nitrogen would lodge in the animals' joints. This picture illustrates how a goat lifted his foreleg to indicate it was suffering from the bends in that leg. Journal of Hygiene 8, no. 3 (1908), courtesy of Cambridge University Press

breakfast in London. After working through the day he would bid farewell to Boycott, who returned to the suburbs while Damant would get a cheap meal at Harris the Sausage King or another such place. But he was happy. His life had found focus as he had come serendipitously to an occupation that ignited his love of science, which was compounded by the important purpose of enhancing safety under the sea. He was duly proud when the professor of physiology at the University of London recommended him to the home secretary to hold a vivisection license, which allowed him to dissect animals for research purposes. It was through these dissections that the researchers could clearly see bubbles of nitrogen that had formed in the bodies of their test subjects.

Haldane only appeared once or twice a week at Lister during the experiments, but was at the same time gathering much anecdotal data from divers and other written accounts. Haldane learned that the common way to bring divers to surface, based on the best advice of scientists, was to draw up the diver at a rate of one atmosphere of pressure of water for every twenty minutes. Everything he read and everybody he spoke to confirmed that this kind of gradual, steady decompression did not work. "It is needlessly slow at the beginning and usually dangerously quick at the end." If divers were to come up gradually, Haldane concluded the safe way would be to draw up a diver at one and a half hours per atmosphere.

Haldane also learned that divers never contracted the bends if they were in shallow water in which the compressed air being delivered to them did not exceed a little over two atmospheres absolute.* Haldane hypothesized that the body could withstand a drop in pressure by one half no matter what depth the person was at. So a diver who is at a pressure of one hundred pounds per square inch (psi) could immediately rise to where the pressure was fifty psi, wait for a while as the nitrogen dispersed, and then be raised up to where the pressure was twenty-five psi and so on. This method was faster than slowly inching up a diver since he covered more ground by doing halves. Haldane dubbed this "staged decompression."

The goats that were stage decompressed consistently did not exhibit symptoms of caisson disease. Now it was time to experiment on human subjects. It was potentially lethal work. Haldane "did not want publicity-seeking 'human guinea-pigs' but experienced divers with brains, courage, and patience."

Lieutenant Damant was ready.

---

* There are two ways of describing ambient pressure. *Absolute pressure* includes the one atmosphere of pressure exerted by the atmosphere at sea level. Thus, at sea level the absolute pressure is one atmosphere and at a depth of ten meters (thirty-three feet) the absolute pressure is two atmospheres. *Gauge pressure* ignores the pressure at sea level, thus at sea level the gauge pressure is zero and at a depth of ten meters the gauge pressure is one atmosphere. For the purposes of this book, unless otherwise specified, pressure will be expressed in absolute terms.

9

SOS

AFTER THE FIRST EXPLOSION, which had hit the *Laurentic* near holds numbers two and three, the equipment was still functional. But the second explosion occurred on the port side by the engine room, just next to the three dynamos that provided electricity to the ship.

On the bridge, Captain Norton pulled the telegraph lever, which gave instructions to the engine room to stop. There was no response. He pulled the lever again indicating FULL ASTERN. Nothing. He tried using the voice tube to call to the engineering room. The lack of response confirmed his worst fear: that the second explosion had destroyed the engine room and killed any man within it.

The *Laurentic* took a heavy list to port. The ship lost its heading completely and swung about so that its broadside faced the southeastern gale. As it came to a dead stop, Norton commanded, "Abandon ship!"

. . .

Telegraphist Arthur Bower never heard Norton's command. His voice tube was inoperable. However, the warrant officer had a good notion that the *Laurentic* was in serious jeopardy. With the electrical power out, Bower could not use the wireless to signal for assistance. Fortunately, he had an emergency backup: a Marconi one and a half kilowatt battery-operated wireless telegraph. He set up the equipment while fumbling for a life jacket.

After a few minutes, Bower had the device ready. But when he hit the key to send a signal, there was no blue spark between the electrodes. In the dark, he traced his hands over the equipment. The fuses felt fine. The circuits seemed in proper order. Then his hands felt the accumulators—essentially open batteries filled with chloride—and he discovered that they had been overturned by the explosions. He was standing in a pool of battery acid.

Bower started repairing the equipment—or at least jury-rigging it, a slow process in the dark. Meanwhile, his staff rushed into the wireless cabin. Bower ordered his men to take old messages from the boxes and burn the paper to produce light. Each time they attempted to set a message on fire the match would blow out due to the gale sailing through the broken windows.

In this flitting light Bower saw that O'Callaghan, the boy he had been training in telegraphy, did not have a life jacket. Bower removed his own jacket and gave it to the boy. At the same time, he also assigned his men to take a chest of materials up to the bridge. This chest contained the most important codebooks, call signs, operating signals, and memoranda.

Just then, a voice called from the entryway to the office. It was Captain Norton.

Neither man could see the other. Norton had already ordered a yeoman to launch emergency rockets and send signals to Fanad Point using an oil-powered flashing lantern. Unable to raise Bower on the telephone, he decided to go personally. The captain asked, "Have you sent for help?"

"No, sir," replied Bower, not explaining that the wireless was not working.

Bower, thinking of his directive from the wireless instruction manual, was about to ask Norton what side of the ship had been struck, but the captain cut him off, ordering him to send an SOS signal, and stormed away.

After a few minutes, Bower's men had produced enough light by burning messages to allow him finally to get the emergency Marconi operational. He tested it by hitting the telegraph key. A spark of electricity crackled between the electrodes. Tapping the key, Bower struck off an SOS signal to Malin Head, followed by "15R," the *Laurentic*'s call sign.

While Bower waited for a return signal, he considered all the information that had been placed in his trust. While most of the important materials were being sent up to the bridge, there were still plenty of ciphers, messages, and codes that remained in the office. Bower and his remaining staff began to destroy any messages that they could find so that they would not fall into enemy hands amid the flotsam of the ship.

Bower anxiously waited for a return signal from Malin Head. He adjusted his spark gap, to try to strengthen the signal. After a seeming eternity he tapped, "Have you received my S.O.S.?"

A response came. "No. What is the matter with your spark?"

Evidently, his signal was weak. Bower attempted to send another message, but the Marconi failed completely. The batteries were simply too compromised. He gave up and sent his men to the lifeboats. Alone in the office, he resumed the work of burning as many documents as he could before following his men.

10

Loch Striven

THE SUNSET OF AUGUST 20, 1906, lit the relief of a dual-funneled ship slowly steaming its way along the dark waters of the Firth of Clyde. HMS *Spanker*, a torpedo boat of the *Sharpshooter* class, stood in miniature against the sweeping hills that rose in green and gray tops out of some of the deepest coastal waters of the British Isles.

Lieutenant Guybon Damant knew that some of these waters did not reach a bottom for over a thousand feet. Even as a young and daring diver he could hardly be *that* ambitious—the hand-cranked pumps would never let a man reach that depth and live to tell the tale. Still, what was planned for him by Professor Haldane was challenging, dangerous, and groundbreaking.

Accompanying Damant was his diving instructor, Andrew Catto. Even for an old hand at diving like Catto, the experience could be nothing less than surreal. They had already tested Haldane's hypotheses by sitting inside the compression chamber at Lister where they had experimented on the unfortunate goats. The pressure was built up to 6.4 atmospheres absolute pressure, or over ninety-four psi, which is what divers would experience at a little over two hundred feet. Then, using Haldane's theories and following the example of the goats, Damant and Catto were repeatedly stage decompressed without ill effects. But now they were coming to Loch Striven where a finger of the sea extended from the Firth of Clyde into the Scottish hinterland. Here they were to practically test these theories.

Preparations for the tests were intense. The *Spanker* was furnished with all the latest in diving equipment from Siebe Gorman (which included improved pumps), and Damant recruited the strongest team of seamen and marines he could find. They would be needed to turn the stiff hand-cranked pumps in order to get the divers to the deepest depth that had ever been achieved.

Professor Haldane met the research team at Rothesay where he had brought along a bit of an entourage, which included a staff surgeon, Oswald Rees, family members, and his thirteen-year-old son, Jack, who the professor had promised would be allowed to dive.[*]

The experiments began at Loch Striven on August 21. To test the pumps an open-ended air pipe was connected at one end to an air pump and the other end attached to a lead line. The pipe was then lowered to a depth of two hundred feet. Sailors turned the pump handles hard and fast, building up pressure in the pipe and sending the air deeper down the pipe until it escaped at the open end, two hundred feet down. At this point, the pressure displayed on the pressure gauge stopped increasing and indicated one hundred psi. No leaks were found, so the pump was deemed to be working effectively.

Under Haldane's observant eye, the crew hooked up a Whitehead torpedo charging cylinder to the coffin-like steel recompression chamber. They released compressed air from the column and using gauges could see that the air pressure could be increased to forty psi in four minutes. There was leakage, but it was negligible, a mere pound per minute. If either of the divers were stricken by diver's palsy after they had been pulled to the surface, they could be placed in the chamber which would expose them to compressed air and then recompress any nitrogen bubbles that formed in their bodies.

---

[*] "Jack" or John Burdon Sanderson Haldane, would become a famous scientist in his own right. He would later become an outspoken socialist, and his political dissent forced him into self-exile in India in 1956. Damant, who even at thirteen was impressed by Jack's intellect allowed him to sleep aboard the *Spanker*. Damant would later indicate his disappointment in Jack Haldane's later "underachievements."

Being hands-on, Haldane and Rees went inside the chamber to test it and understand how it functioned. As the pressure built, Haldane experienced the pain that many neophyte divers feel when the air pressure outside is greater than the pressure within the diver's middle ear. There were cases when the difference in air pressure was so great that a diver's eardrum would rupture and bleed. In order to clear the pain, Haldane would necessarily have to swallow, yawn, or perform some of the specialized maneuvers developed by divers over the years to open the eustachian tube, a 1.4-inch-long passage between the middle ear and the upper portion of the pharynx.

The *Spanker* shifted position to shallower water. Haldane deemed that fifteen fathoms was sufficiently deep to allow a trial dive. Hands cast

Professor John Scott Haldane posing in diving dress. *Courtesy of the Historical Diving Society, UK*

a shot line overboard with a weight at the end that spun down into the
loch. The water was relatively still, and conditions were ideal for diving.

Damant would have followed typical dressing procedures when
preparing to dive. He put on a woolen Guernsey, drawers, and long
stockings, as well as layers of flannels. He had the option of putting
on a red woolen cap that he had to draw tightly over the head.
Damant was not keen on the red cap, which had the noted tendency
of obstructing the helmet's air outlet.

The next part of the diving dress required the assistance of an
attendant, who took the bulky twill suit, held it high, and allowed
Damant to slip inside. His arms and shoulders came next. As Damant
pushed his hands through the sleeves, the tender forced open the
tight rubber cuffs with his fingers to help Damant slip his hands
through. Often divers used soft soap to allow the hands to slip through
more easily. Then the tender stretched rubber rings called "greys" over
Damant's wrists and let them snap shut at the end of the sleeve of the
diving dress in order to assure a watertight seal around the wrists.[*]

Damant sat down on a stool, and the inner collar of the diving
dress, called the bib, was pulled up and gathered around his neck.
The bib was overlaid with an outer rubber collar with six holes in
it.[**] Then Damant's attendant put on his heavy diving boots, specially
weighted so that Damant would not upend in the water. These were
strapped and tied tightly to his legs. Once done, the tender took the
corselet, also known as the breastplate, and set it over his head and
shoulders. The rubber collar was pulled carefully over the edge of
the corselet, allowing six stud bolts to protrude through the holes
in the collar. This was then overlaid with brass straps that were then
tightened down by six wing nuts. This provided the watertight seal
between the helmet and the dress. Then Damant put on a jockstrap
that helped to secure the whole ensemble of equipment.

Communication came next, and a set of headphones were
strapped to Damant's head. Through this, he would be able to hear

---

[*] They were called greys because of their color. In American diving parlance, they
were called snappers.
[**] The bib's function was to catch and retain excess water that might ship in from
the exhaust valve.

people from the *Spanker* through a telephone wire that ran through the center of his lifeline, also called a breast rope, and into the diving helmet. Inside the helmet, there was an electric switch button (the call-up button) on the left side that the diver pressed with his chin. This would sound a bell in the telephone set on the surface, letting the attendant know that the diver wished to speak.

There were several varieties of Royal Navy diving helmets, which had differing numbers of bolts that attached it to the corselet. The six-bolt variety was the British Admiralty pattern. All helmets featured a glass port in the front called the faceplate and ports to the right and left. Some models even had a port above, so that a diver would be able to look up. Since the helmet only encased the diver's head and did not move in conjunction with his movements, it was important that he be able to see in all directions. The tender screwed the helmet onto Damant's corselet, but left the faceplate off since more gear still had to be hooked up.

The lifeline and air pipe were lashed to Damant's helmet. The two lines were drawn under his right and left arms respectively and then were secured in front to the bonnet. These were the two critical lines—one that would allow the men on the *Spanker* to haul him up as needed and the other to deliver compressed air into the diving dress.

Men turned the handles of the diving pump. As air flushed through his helmet, Damant could see, hear, and feel that all was properly joined.

He stood up as heavy as a knight in armor, and helped by the squire-like attendant, clunked monstrously toward the ladder on the *Spanker*'s side. Others grabbed his air pipe and lifeline, trailing it behind him as if it were the train of a gown. But before Damant was to go into the water, there was yet more—a knight needed his weapon. His diving knife was strapped to his left side in a sheath. Divers might be required to take much more equipment, such as extra lines, tools, and submersible lamps, but for these testing purposes the knife alone was enough. Weights were then attached at his chest and back to sink him.

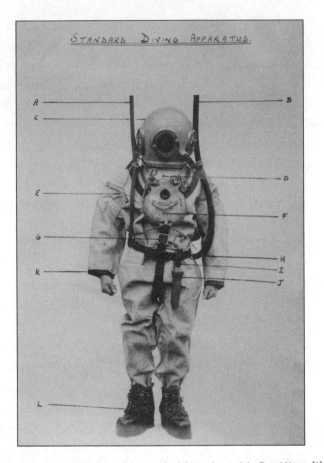

This photograph shows the distinct parts of the standard diving dress of the Royal Navy: (A) breast rope, (B) air pipe, (C) helmet fitted with telephone transmitter, (D) corselet, (E) dress of India rubber with twill covering, (F) lead weight (40 lbs), (G) jock strap, (H) leather belt, (I) knife, (J) brass knife base/sheath, (K) rubber cuffs, and (L) boots with lead soles and brass toe caps. Note that in this configuration the air pipe and lifeline are lashed to the corselet and not to the eyes of the bonnet. *Courtesy of the Historical Diving Society (UK), Royal Navy Archives*

Dressing a diver does take some time, and even at this stage, there was one last test. The tender screwed on Damant's faceplate and air wheezed into the diving suit, making it billow outward. The attendant tapped Damant's helmet to let him know that all was ready.

Damant climbed down the ladder and, pausing for a moment just when his helmet had begun to submerge, pressed his finger on

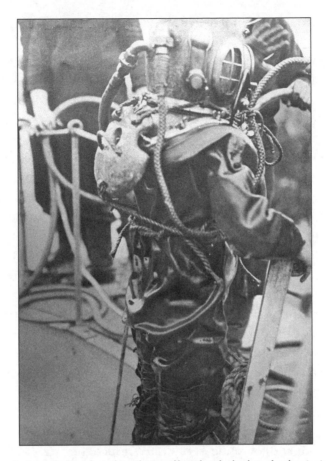

This photograph shows the diver's rig from the rear. Note that the hookups for the air pipe and breast rope are to the bonnet and that in this case the diver has chosen to lace his leggings. *Report of a Committee Appointed by the Lords Commissioners of the Admiralty to Consider and Report upon the Conditions of Deep-Water Diving*, 1907.

the exhaust valve for a few seconds and then grabbed the shot line and began to slide down. If there were any leaks in the diving dress, he would soon know. As he sank deeper and deeper he closed the exhaust valve on his helmet more and more to counter the squeeze on the suit caused by the increasing water pressure. This permitted more air to remain in the suit to compensate for the reduction in volume caused by the increasing pressure, and he felt rather buoyant in contrast to the inherent clumsiness of the diving dress on the land. To tweak his buoyancy, he occasionally used a plunger-like button

on the inside of the helmet that a diver pushed with the right side
of his head to release additional air.

Ninety feet, or fifteen fathoms, was a shallow depth for Damant
and more so for Catto—114 feet, nineteen fathoms, was Damant's
personal record, and Catto had descended to 138 feet. It took Damant
120 seconds to slide down the shot line and sink knee-deep into the
muck of the loch and Catto 75 seconds. Upon reaching the bottom
both men felt quite comfortable, although the water was very cold.
They stayed for an hour, deeply breathing in the compressed air that
was being pumped into their suits. They were to saturate themselves
with nitrogen. If the ports in their helmets fogged, they would clear
them by turning a small valve on the left side of their helmet called
the spitcock. This supplementary exhaust allowed water to enter into
the helmet, which the divers might take into their mouth and thence
spit on the faceplate to demist it.

When his time was up, Damant was pulled up to five fathoms, or
thirty feet, where it was calculated to be the shallowest place to stage
decompress. He clutched the shot line with his arms and legs. As far
as he was able, he moved his limbs about vigorously on the theory that
this would help the nitrogen disperse. Five minutes later, he was hauled
up to ten feet. The hull of the *Spanker* was so close—if this had been
done the old way he would have been pulled up almost at once. But
as tantalizing and tempting as it was to surface then and there, he had
to wait for ten minutes to allow more dissolved nitrogen to dissipate.

He came aboard the *Spanker,* and after climbing up the ladder
a tender removed the faceplate and began to relieve him of weight.
He had spent a total of eighteen and a half minutes ascending from
the bottom. There were no signs of the bends at all. It was time to
do more testing.

The next day, Catto and Damant were sent down in twenty-three
fathoms of water and stayed for twenty minutes. It was a new personal record for Damant. Again, both men were stage decompressed
without any adverse effects.

Each day brought them to new depths. On August 23 they dove
to twenty-five fathoms. On August 24, twenty-seven fathoms. On
August 25, twenty-nine fathoms. Then, on August 27 and 28, Catto

and Damant made descents to thirty fathoms of water—180 feet. To keep the air pressure going, the deckhands turned and turned the pumps at thirty-two revolutions per minute, only falling back due to exhaustion while allowing other hands to take over. For Damant, some of the work was tedious, especially when you had to wait at a stage for a prolonged period of time, dangling in midwater. But when the welcome daylight greeted him, Damant had pamphlets sent down to him that he could read. He made sure they were short since the paper disintegrated in the water.

Catto dove on the afternoon of August 28. Damant had already returned from his dive after obtaining samples of air from his helmet in order to examine the carbon dioxide content.* In Catto's case, Haldane wanted to measure how stage decompression held up when divers had to work. Catto spent a minute and a half in the descent until he reached the bottom at 180 feet. He hooked up a line to a weight and soon enough his time was up. He had been on the bottom for twelve minutes. The lines were pulled, but then Catto's voice, distorted greatly by the compressed air, came through the telephone warning them not to pull.

His lifeline had fallen foul of the hawser holding the weight. It wasn't a terrible fouling, but Catto was at a depth no diver had been fouled at before. The men working the pumps, already exhausted, could only maintain twenty-four revolutions per minute. So this meant that less air was getting pumped into his diving suit than there ought to have been. Catto became sluggish and weak from high levels of carbon dioxide. This made the work of freeing himself even harder since he was about to collapse from lack of breathable air.

It was probably just the knowledge of imminent death that kept Catto going, and in time he managed to free his line. But by the time he was clear he had been on the bottom for twenty-eight minutes and forty-five seconds. No person had ever been exposed that long to air so highly compressed. At that depth it was necessary for the air pressure in his suit to be over ninety psi.

---

* Air samples were collected by using a two-ounce bottle that was connected to a tube attached to the diver's helmet. This was then sealed with a cork stopper.

There was much care given, therefore, when they brought Catto to the surface. While there was absolute confidence in Haldane's staged decompression theories, it had never been so practically tested. Nine stops in total were made so as to ensure that Catto would be completely free of nitrogen bubbles. It took one and a half hours to get Catto to the surface, but when he got back on the deck of the *Spanker*, aside from being generally exhausted, he was fine. He did the same diving exercise the next day.

On August 31, the *Spanker* was moved to the mouth of Loch Striven, where the water was deeper. Damant reached a muddy bottom with so much sediment that he could not see. He had come to an unheard-of depth of just over 35 fathoms—210 feet—a world record. The men worked three pumps in gangs of six with five-minute reliefs. Catto soon did a similar dive at a hair shallower than Damant. In his diving log, Damant recorded the historic moment: "I dipped first in 36 fathoms. Took a sample. Quite pitch dark. Hands too cold to feel much but could not detect any solid or bottom. Nothing but mud. Catto in afternoon: same."

By September 3, Haldane wanted to experiment more with measured work on the bottom. He directed that a hawser be threaded through a system of pulleys on one of the ship's spars. These were attached to weights underwater with an end of the rope made available for the divers to test their strength. Then the free end was attached to a fifty-six-pound sinker. Both Catto and Damant went to the bottom at 142 feet and took an air sample from their helmets. Then they pulled on the pulley system four times at the rate of once per minute. The heavy ropes and blocks caused great friction and resistance. Then more air samples were taken. Then there was another set of pulling, this time seven times in over five minutes. Another air sample was taken. They were then stage decompressed. There were no ill effects.

There was much elation on the *Spanker*, so much so that Haldane decided one last test was needed in order to fulfill his promise. He and his thirteen-year-old son, Jack, made a descent on September 4 in six fathoms of water. It was the first time either had made a dive in their diving dress. All dives were resounding successes.

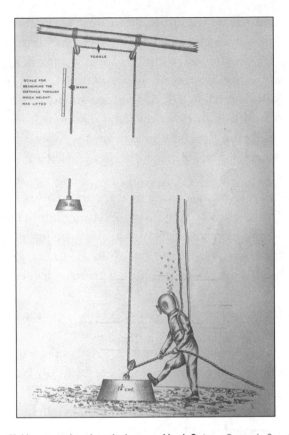

Illustration of how Haldane tested work at the bottom of Loch Striven. *Report of a Committee Appointed by the Lords Commissioners of the Admiralty to Consider and Report upon the Conditions of Deep-Water Diving, 1907.*

Still, there was some question as to whether the Admiralty would adopt Haldane's methods. Indeed, the Royal Navy at that time limited their divers to descend no more than forty feet except experimentally. Only commercial divers went deeper. The new method of staged decompression would allow for true deep diving by the navy. But Damant was worried. "It was quite possible that they would wind up the whole business and send me to sea as a gunnery officer and stopping my ambition to continue this fascinating life of diving and science, without considering what prospects it held out."

But Damant's fears were misplaced. Haldane's method of diving decompression was adopted by the Royal Navy. After slight modifications, his tables became the standard for deep-sea diving worldwide. His theories have held up even over a century later; staged decompression is still practiced by all deep-sea divers. In 2014 Egyptian diver Ahmed Gabr set a record dive at 1,090 feet. It took him twelve minutes to reach the depth. Then, using the staged decompression techniques developed by Haldane, he spent fourteen hours returning to the surface.

Damant and Catto made practical recommended changes to the traditional diving dress to make it more functional. They advocated for the suit's leggings to be laced instead of being left loose, which allowed divers who were accidentally "blown up" to remain upright. Then to Damant's great delight, he was to write a diving manual for the navy.

In the official report of the experiments they noted that the thirty-five fathoms of water reached by Damant "is the greatest depth ever definitely recorded as having been reached by divers, and considerably exceeds that at which work has hitherto been deemed to be ordinarily practicable."

After finishing the diving manual, Damant returned to HMS *Excellent* where he assisted in gunnery practice on gunboats, but his heart was now set on diving and science. Shortly thereafter, Damant was sent back to the Lister Institute to continue experiments to enhance diving speed and safety, but also to understand the true perils of deep-sea diving.

He was happy.

II

Abandon Ship!

WHILE THERE WAS NO HOPE for the *Laurentic*—Captain Reginald Norton could not even order the pumps to be used since they were housed in the destroyed engine room—his precautions to seal all the watertight doors slowed the flood and allowed him time to properly evacuate all the survivors onto lifeboats.

Norton commanded that the box of codebooks, messages, and ciphers from Bower's office be thrown overboard in a weighted chest. He also had a separate locked steel safe of orders, secret books, and documents that resided in his cabin. The safe undoubtedly contained information on the boxes in the second-class baggage room. When his assistant paymaster asked him what to do with the paperwork, Norton said, "Leave them where they are and go to your boat." The *Laurentic*'s papers would drown with the ship.

As for the boxes, there was plainly nothing Norton could do. There were too many crates, and each weighed too much to even think of salvaging. Norton probably understood the implications of what losing the cargo might mean for the war effort, but he was too concerned with the immediacy of saving his crew to give it much thought.

Meanwhile, men poured onto the deck and were shepherded to lifeboats. A good many members of the crew were ill clothed for the biting cold, especially those who had been on duty in the hot stoke-holds maintaining the fires for the engines. Light shirts, and even bare chests, were the typical uniforms in the stokeholds, where the temperature easily exceeded one hundred degrees.

All seventeen lifeboats aboard the *Laurentic* were serviceable, with a total carrying capacity of over 800 men, far greater than the 475 aboard the ship. Each boat had twelve flares, a lantern, a sea anchor, a compass, four boxes of biscuits, two boxes of tinned corned beef, a bailing bucket, an axe, and two casks of water. But since the *Laurentic* was heavily listed to its port side, it was impossible to lower the star-board boats—they would have just banged into the side of the ship when released. This left the port boats, which hung directly over the water, as the only mode of evacuation.

The sailors were forced to leap into these since, because of the list, the lifeboats hung a good distance from the ship. After the boats were loaded, the crew manned the falls, long lines that connected the lifeboats by davits, crane-like devices, to the ship, and lowered each into the water. From Norton's vantage point, he thought that some of the lifeboats were not fully loaded—it was hard to tell in the dark-ness. Since only half of the lifeboats were available it would be best for all to have the boats wait for more survivors. Shouting through a megaphone, he ordered the lifeboats that had already been lowered into the water to stay as close to the *Laurentic* as possible so that he could attempt to board more crew.

In response, the men on the lifeboats attempted to seize lifelines, ropes that were tied to the ship. Yet this proved impossible as the gale and current tore each lifeboat away. The stormy waters of Lough Swilly quickly filled with careening lifeboats, which disappeared from sight.

Then a miracle of sorts occurred: the deck of the *Laurentic* righted itself. The vessel's lower decks had become fully inundated with water, which allowed the ship to rest at an even keel. The once inoperable starboard lifeboats were now usable. Immediately, the remaining seamen swung them over the water and started to board. Almost three years of war and constant drills had inculcated the men with a grim stoicism in the face of disaster. There was no panic, just a hurried resolve. Meanwhile, Norton, as captain, knew and accepted that he must be the last man to leave the ship.

Then, quite suddenly, Norton thought of the three imprisoned men. While it was likely they had been released to go to the lifeboats, no person could confirm it. Not being able to spare another man, Norton descended from the bridge and hurried across the decks toward the cells.

He reached the forecastle, flung open the door, and peered into the dark interior. From what he could tell, the room had not sustained any damage. However, the sentry had fled his post, and two of the three prisoners were still trapped in their cells—one had apparently managed to break out. The problem was that Norton did not have a key or any means to release the trapped men.

The captain hurried back to the bridge, where he ordered his navigating officer to obtain tools to break open the prisoners' cells. As he waited, Norton watched the sea rise higher and the *Laurentic* sink lower. Fortunately, the ship was not turning turtle like the *Hogue*, but sinking evenly—as if the *Laurentic* wanted to allow time for its crew to leave.

At last, the navigating officer returned with one of the *Laurentic*'s shipwrights. The necessary tools to open the prison cells were locked in the carpenter's shop, and the key hung in one of the darkened cabins.

Norton took charge directly. He formed a party composed of himself, the navigating officer, the shipwright, and the chief steward, Charles Porter. Porter was one of the few men aboard with a working flashlight and led the way. Quickly, they marched through the ship's corridors to the cabin where the key was stored. Aside from Porter's single beam, and the occasional red radiance cast by emergency oil lanterns strung along the main corridors, all was dark.

By good fortune, the men found the key quickly. The next stop was the carpenter's shop. Porter's flashlight again lit the way. There, the men seized axes and headed back to the cells where the prisoners, undoubtedly miserable, awaited rescue.

With heavy strokes, the cell doors were chopped open, and the men were released. Norton led them all to lifeboat number five, manned by his executive officer, Hugh Rogers. Aboard were those who stayed on as long as safety allowed, including Arthur Bower, who had finished his work in the wireless office. The two prisoners boarded the lifeboat while Rogers stood by to await orders.

Captain Norton said, "I am going to lower you away now, but remain alongside for a few minutes."

Norton went with Charles Porter searching the *Laurentic* for any remaining souls. As they wandered through the empty ship, the silence was interspersed with the sounds of rushing water and groans of twisting metal. The pair headed down the main staircase and sloshed through cold water that encroached upon the first-class saloon. They could find no other living person.

Norton and Porter hurried back to the lifeboat where Hugh Rogers waited by the railing. The lifeboat itself was in the water, and the men were struggling to hold it in place by the lifelines. Norton ordered Porter and Rogers into the lifeboat by sliding down one of the ropes.

Norton was the last man left alive aboard the *Laurentic,* and he was loath to leave his command. The ship was low in the water. Norton had done all he could do—and all he was supposed to do. But still he hesitated.

His men were shouting at him, urging him to board the lifeboat. At length, Norton passed down two additional fire buckets to bail water and slid down the lifeline. It was 6:45 PM. The explosions occurred less than an hour earlier.

They cast loose. The ship quickly left Norton's sight as the wind and current carried them far away. A bitter gale blew up to fifty-five knots.

Despite Captain Norton's orders that the lifeboats stay together, the storm made this impossible. As he looked out, he saw the signal flares of other lifeboats scattered about the sea like red stars in a dark sky. All the craft were being strewn about the mouth of Lough Swilly and inexorably pulled toward the open Atlantic or careening toward rocks.

12

The Inspector

ON JULY 13, 1907, almost a year after the trials at Loch Striven, the *Spanker* was sailing along the southwest coast of England. The dramatic cliffs of Berry Head, Torbay, rose sharply four and a half miles distant, reaching two hundred feet. There, topping a gray and green cliff was a lighthouse to guide mariners about the headland. Built only a year prior, the human-made structure stood out in stark contrast in an otherwise wild and beautiful place. But Lieutenant Guybon Damant, as well as all hands aboard the *Spanker*, had their eyes turned toward the sea, looking for the grave of *Torpedo Boat 99*.

On June 19, the boat had foundered in speed trials. Another vessel, seeing what had happened, rescued the crew and set a buoy to mark the approximate spot of the accident. The wreck lay in 132 feet of water. While such a depth would usually not warrant a salvage operation, the boat had sunk where fishing vessels from the nearby town of Brixham trawled the water. Since this created an undesirable obstruction, the Admiralty decided to salvage the boat rather than suffer the complaints of fishermen. But before contemplating any salvage operation it was important to get as much information on the wreck as possible. Salvage crews needed to know how it lay and the extent of the damage. Damant, now on his second day of the work, had already confirmed that the wreck was there, and he was now going to continue to survey it.

G. C. C. Damant (in white outfit) boxing against an army opponent circa 1907. Damant lost. *Courtesy of Mary Harrison*

Since Damant's return to Lister, he had ensconced himself in a cheap flat in the Pimlico neighborhood in London. Aside from conducting research, he played football for the institute's team and boxed at night with other young staff members in the basement of the institute among the canisters of compressed oxygen. He also boxed for the Royal Navy against other services.

For entertainment, he was often accompanied by his colleague from the goat experiments, Arthur Edwin Boycott, to see prize fights or attend music halls. Boycott had become one of Damant's closest companions, and he thoroughly enjoyed their discussions at teatime on such topics as Latin chronograms, new species of slugs, or diseases spread by mouse bites. Damant was also taken by one Miss Harriette Chick, a microbiologist at Lister who prepared tea using a Bunsen burner. Damant thought her "young and so fresh looking in her spotless starched overall." But a romantic relationship never developed.*

Damant and Boycott continued to work on experiments with the surviving goats. In one case, they found a goat that seemed unwell without any of the recognizable symptoms of decompression illness a day or two after it had undergone experimentation in the air chamber. Unsure of whether this was an ordinary illness or a symptom of the bends, Damant took the goat's temperature. It was 104, but Damant had no idea what the temperature should be. There was nothing in the library, and the Royal Veterinary College had contradictory information. When Damant told Boycott of the problem, Boycott said, "Here's a chance for you Damant. We have a large herd of goats at hand. Take all their temperatures, morning and evening for a month, using standardised thermometers, if you do it properly the *Journal of Physiology* will publish your little paper and it will then be quoted in every future text book dealing with such matters."

Thus, Damant's first published piece of scientific literature was titled "The Normal Temperature of the Goat." He wrote that the findings "will be of some value in supplying the want of data for the normal rectal temperature of an animal which is now used for physiological and pathological investigations." Damant later commented, "The job was more troublesome than seemed likely because the goats resented the procedure and had to be trained to submit to it without struggling and getting hot." Damant calculated that the normal temperature of a goat was between 39.75 to 40 degrees Celsius (103.55 to 104 degrees Fahrenheit).**

He and Boycott then wrote a lengthier note in the *Journal of Physiology*, again using the herd of goats and the compressed air chamber. In "A Note on the Quantities of Marsh-Gas, Hydrogen and Carbon Dioxide Produced in the Alimentary Canal of Goats" Damant and

---

* Harriette Chick, later Dame Harriette Chick, became famous in scientific circles for helping to comprehend protein folding as well as understanding how to prevent rickets through sunlight and cod liver oil. She never married and lived to the age of 102.

** Later veterinarians have calculated the normal temperature of a goat to be between 102 and 103 degrees Fahrenheit.

Boycott measured how much gas the goats produced a couple of hours after eating hay and a small amount of oats. They also published a short note concerning the blood volume of goats and how this related to susceptibility to caisson disease as well as another paper in the *Journal of Pathology and Bacteriology,* "Some Lesions of the Spinal Cord Produced by Experimental Caisson Disease"—also using the goats as test subjects.

By the time Damant and Boycott had finished their various experiments, the herd was reduced to one survivor. This small white goat was known for her affectionate personality and seeming immunity to compressed air illnesses. Damant kept her, and brought her back to Lammas where she would accompany him along the beaches of the Isle of Wight with the family spaniel.

From time to time the Admiralty took Damant away from the research, mostly to attend to the duties that were required of gunnery officers but at other times to send him on practical missions related to diving. Thus he found himself looking for *Torpedo Boat 99.* While navy regulations limited diving for personnel to just forty feet, these rules were changing and were a mere formality in the case of Damant. But he was forced to seek civilian divers to volunteer for the deepwater work, since the rule bending would only apply to him.

The *Spanker* came to the marker buoy and set its anchors fore and aft. The buoy slightly bobbed in the calm sea—conditions were fine for diving. Damant geared up and was the first diver down. Going over the side he followed the buoy line to the wreck. Even in twenty-two fathoms of water, visibility was fine—a few feet. He could see how the wreck lay, and how the forward end projected upward about three feet. It would be possible for a pair of tugboats to sweep wires under and raise the boat.

After Damant decompressed, two other divers followed, continuing the inspection. As the day passed, the visibility got worse and the current began to run stronger. The divers' air pipes and lifelines were being pushed about but there did not seem to be a risk of a major fouling. Still, Damant sent a message to the tugboat *Industrious* for assistance. The boat came and latched a hawser to the *Spanker,* in order to stabilize it. The divers, being physically connected to the ship, relied on their diving platform to be as still as possible. A strong tide or a sudden yank on the lines could be disastrous.

At 7:10 PM, Walter Trapnell, a heavyset, mustachioed man in his late forties who worked at the Portsmouth Dockyard as a senior diver for a shipwright, went into the water for his second dive of the day. He landed on the deck of *Torpedo Boat 99* and then slipped over the side to examine the propeller shaft, sending up reports through the telephone. Satisfied with his examination, Trapnell proceeded around the wreck's side and headed toward the rudder chains. But like a gust of air, the current was pulling his lines all about, so he got on the telephone and asked that more line be paid out.

Damant by telephone told Trapnell to surface if he found the current too strong. Trapnell, who had ten years of diving experience to Damant's one, demurred, "Oh, it's not so strong as that." His voice was high pitched and nasal—one of the effects of breathing the compressed air.*

Time passed as Trapnell made observations. At times, his voice would crack through the telephone requesting more air pipe as it felt too tight. So more air pipe was given out as dusk set in.

At 7:30 PM, it was time to surface. But Trapnell noticed that something was wrong. He called to the surface. His air pipe had fallen foul of some of the wreckage and gear on the deck. Using his telephone, he communicated to Damant that he was foul, but added, "I am all right."

Damant did not sense immediate danger to Trapnell. He advised him to relax and not overexert himself. He should try to free himself—a common practice.

But soon thereafter, Trapnell called to the *Spanker* again. This time his lifeline was foul. He could not move. In the worsening visibility he could feel that his air pipe went off in one direction and his lifeline in the other. Both, from being pushed by the tide and far too extended, had fouled in two distinct locations high above him in the wreck. If he tried to head toward the source of the fouled air

---

* Another effect of compressed air was the inability of divers to whistle. This and the voice changes are due to the effects of the density of compressed air on the speech organs.

pipe, he found that his lifeline held him at bay. If he tried to go to the source of the fouled lifeline, the air pipe prevented him from moving in that direction. He was essentially shackled to the wreckage.

Trapnell signaled to be hauled up. But the men of the *Spanker* could not do it. The lines were fully fouled.

The tide grew and the seas rose. The *Spanker* started surging up and down despite the efforts of the *Industrious* to keep the ship settled. The motion threatened to sever Trapnell's lines upon the wreckage. Trapnell, for his part, was unable to do anything to free himself.

Aboard the *Spanker* was Trapnell's friend and workmate for over eight years, Sydney Leverett. He, like Trapnell, was a senior dockyard diver at Portsmouth and had been hired to work on the salvage. Leverett, getting on the telephone, spoke to Trapnell. The stricken diver was all right, but trapped. Trapnell expressed confidence that he would be free again at any moment.

Leverett then asked if he needed help.

Trapnell replied that he would be grateful for it.

Leverett said, "All right, I will come down and help you."

Damant assented to the plan. Leverett was dressed in the diving gear so that at 8:00 PM he was ready to go to the bottom. Stepping off the ladder of the *Spanker*, Leverett immediately noticed that the current was moving at about three-quarters of a knot. As he descended, the tide swept his lines out, forcing the *Spanker* to pay out more line to the diver so he could get to the needed depth. Then, with the *Spanker* heaving up and down and side to side, Damant was forced to have the diving tenders pay out another thirty feet of line to make up the difference.

Leverett followed Trapnell's lifeline. Soon enough he vaguely saw his friend standing by the boat on the seafloor like some marionette. He now had a full appreciation of the fouling. With some maneuvering, Leverett approached him. But the would-be rescuer's lines, all thirty-three fathoms, had been swept out by the current and could not reach. He could only touch Trapnell's helmet with his foot to assure him that he was working to rescue him. Leverett, explaining the situation on the telephone, was hauled to the surface. Damant needed to act quickly, but he did not have enough extra hose to give Leverett more line.

Trapnell and Leverett were each hooked up to two hand-cranked pumps. Each of these pumps had an intermediate length of hose, nowadays called a *deck whip*, that was connected to a volume tank and then to a manifold that delivered air to the divers. In order to extend the length of Leverett's hose, Damant unscrewed the deck whip from Leverett's air pump, and coupled it to the air pipe coming out of one of his pumps. This had the effect of lengthening the rescue diver's hose, but at the cost of him receiving air from a single pump only.

Leverett dove again, and at 8:45 PM he reached Trapnell. They shook hands.

The trapped diver was still doing well. Leverett immediately went to work in the dark, using an underwater hand lamp to guide him. Leverett needed to be hauled up onto the wreck's deck and free Trapnell's lines from the davits and spars. But Leverett was tired, much more tired than he should have been.

First, Leverett only had one air pump delivering air to him when he should have had two. Second, in order to deliver air through the extra-long hose to both divers, the men working the air pump had to work double time. It was an exhausting process to keep the optimal amount of air pressure up. As a result, Leverett was breathing in too much carbon dioxide, which tired him, and the sea pressure squeezed him mercilessly.

It was frustrating too, since the current was still running strong. Leverett said, "It was heartrending to find that as fast as I freed a line it got entangled again in the wreckage. I was almost … as helpless as a blind man. Things more than two or three feet away were invisible, and time and again, as I fumbled for the unseen objects that held the lines, I could have shrieked with impatience and the sense of my helplessness." It got worse as blood started to pour from his nostrils and eyes. Leverett craved fresh, free air. Close to passing out, he had to be hauled toward the surface, where the pressure was less, so he could breathe more freely.

The tide began to slacken, and Leverett dove again. As he removed length after length of Trapnell's line from the wreckage, time played tricks. Though he thought he had worked for three hours, it had in fact been forty-five minutes—still quite long. "All the time I struggled against the fearful weight of water, which seemed to be crushing the life-blood from my veins and consciousness from my brain, numbing the agonies of suspense I should otherwise have suffered."

By 9:30 PM Trapnell was free.

Despite being on the bottom for well over two hours, Trapnell was still cogent and telephoned to the *Spanker* that his lines were clear. But his hell was not quite over since the *Spanker* no longer had its recompression chamber aboard. Damant decided to stage decompress him in the most conservative way, since no man that he knew of had been fouled for so long at such a depth. In fact, Haldane's tables did not account for the length of time that Trapnell had been on the bottom. The tables only accounted for a maximum of one hour, so Damant had to make his best guesses. Trapnell for his part just hung limply by his own lifeline as he went up to the surface, stage by stage. Leverett was decompressed quicker, but for a time the two friends hung together in the water. After three hours in the water, Leverett was aboard the *Spanker*. Trapnell remained under the sea, Damant believing that he needed more decompression.

Occasionally, Trapnell would telephone to the top to let Damant know his status. By the time he got to the last stage, and was ten feet beneath the *Spanker*, he suddenly felt giddy—but that might have been from being in the water for so long. Besides, Damant believed that Trapnell "could hardly have been safely kept in the water longer." Trapnell came to the surface at 12:10 AM after a total of almost five hours underwater.

Damant spoke with Trapnell, who was bobbing at the surface for only two minutes before complaining of dizziness. He could not climb the ladder to board the *Spanker*. Men hauled him aboard. Damant noticed that Trapnell showed neither definitive symptoms of diver's palsy nor any signs of pneumonia. Trapnell complained of pains in his legs, but this disappeared. It was plain that the man needed rest. The *Spanker*, being as small as it was, did not have a sick bay. Instead, a bunk was made for him on the deck of the ship. Hot-water bottles were pressed into his aching muscles. Men massaged him. The ship weighed anchor and headed ashore.

By the next morning, Trapnell seemed much better, but Damant sent him ashore to a hospital as a precaution. During the trip inshore Trapnell suddenly become delirious and restless. When he arrived at the hospital, where his wife and daughter were waiting, he was given oxygen. Even so, he went into cardiac arrest.

Walter Trapnell died almost twenty-four hours after he was brought to the surface. The next day an autopsy was conducted. There were bubbles in the right side of his heart, in the veins of his liver and intestines, as well scattered about everywhere except in his brain. He was buried on Wednesday, July 17, 1907, in Portsmouth.

An inquiry over the incident was held. The jury ruled that the tragedy was an accident and that none aboard the *Spanker* were culpable in the death. Leverett's actions, while in vain, were praised and he was given a silver medal and a certificate by the Committee of the Royal Humane Society. However, the inquiry asserted that the *Spanker* was unsuitable as a salvage vessel.

With Haldane and Boycott, in 1908 Damant published a landmark paper on the subject of decompression sickness that broadly introduced the world to staged decompression. In it, Damant referred to the *Torpedo Boat 99* incident. He asserted that despite the diving tables, Trapnell's death came due to his age and "the mesenteric fat, which was very abundant," that held the nitrogen bubbles in his body far longer than it would in a slender man. Damant commented, "This is the only known case of prolonged exposure of a man to such a high excess of pressure as four and a half atmospheres; and although his age, heavy build, and exhausted condition combined to make the circumstances very unfavourable, the fact of his death shows that the long decompression periods recommended ... after prolonged exposure are none too long, even for a man of ordinary build. Every precaution should be taken to guard against such long exposures at high pressures."

As a follow-up, Damant and Boycott published another paper in the *Journal of Hygiene*, titled "Experiments on the Influence of Fatness on Susceptibility to Caisson Disease." After experiments on guinea pigs showed

how obese specimens died more readily in compressed air when compared to their slender counterparts, Damant and Boycott concluded,

> The practical conclusions are clear. Really fat men should never
> be allowed to work in compressed air, and plump men should be
> excluded from high pressure caissons (e.g. over +25 lbs) or in di-
> ving to more than about 10 fathoms, and at this depth their diving
> should be curtailed. If deep diving is to be undertaken, or cais-
> sons worked at pressures approximating to +45 lbs., skinny men
> should be selected. It is unfortunate that an increase of experience
> and skill in technical operations should often be associated with
> the increase in waist measurement which accompanies the onset
> of middle age. Middle aged men have a lower rate of respiratory
> exchange than young men: if fatness is not the explanation of this,
> they are at a double disadvantage, and the two factors must be mul-
> tiplied, rather than added, together.

A couple of naval periodicals printed cartoons lampooning Damant's theory.

Despite the jury's lack of confidence in the *Spanker*, Damant
returned to the wreck aboard that ship after Trapnell's funeral. The
marker buoy was lost, being severed against wreckage. Damant chose
to send himself to the bottom to try to relocate *Torpedo Boat 99.* This
he did relatively quickly, but while he was attaching a new buoy he
found that air was not coming into his suit as strongly as he would
have liked. He signaled for more air and the men at the pumps
turned the wheels to increase the air pressure.

The air filled his suit and suddenly it tore at the wrist. Water
poured in. Damant grabbed the tear as tight as possible, but still
it flooded. He telephoned to the top to haul him up. But Damant
knew full well that it was folly for him to come straight to the surface.
So he ordered a staged decompression even as water threatened to
drown him in his helmet. He was forced to hang by his lines, holding
back the water by gripping at the wrist while he waited at the stages.
Damant calculated that the supply of air to the suit would keep the
water from filling his helmet. He needed to keep his arm on the side

with the tear as low as possible to avoid further flooding. The water only managed to reach his chin, as they pulled him aboard.

An incident such as this would not usually be recorded, except that it occurred only days after Trapnell's death. As a result, the story was published in several newspapers, which made *Torpedo Boat 99* seem accursed. But Damant's survey was done, and the salvage of the vessel was handed over to the Liverpool Salvage Association, which finished raising the wreck by the end of August.

• • •

In October 1907 Damant was officially made inspector of diving for the Royal Navy. This was a new position, created by the Admiralty in response to ongoing salvage problems with navy ships. As inspector, he was put in general charge of diving instruction and to answer questions that might arise in regard to diving. He traveled to various diving schools in the British Isles, transmitting knowledge of the new staged decompression theory.

Damant became associated with some salvages over the next few years as he honed his skills. In all cases, he performed surveys of the foundered ship. Then he and his divers would enter the wreck, remove documents such as crew lists to account for the dead, and seek out secret signal books and other government materials to return to the Admiralty. The actual salvage of the vessel was then left to private salvage firms, typically the Liverpool Salvage Association. Damant was notably involved with HMS *Gladiator* in 1908 and HMS *Blackwater* in 1909. When not working at salvage, Damant continued to serve as a junior staff officer aboard the *Excellent.*

In the case of the *Gladiator*, the ship had capsized ninety degrees. Diving inside it was a surreal experience. Damant recalled, "I took a turn at getting some secret out of the desk in the Captain's cabin. The desk was floating away overhead and the cabin door was underfoot and one kept forgetting this oubliette and falling out through it into the alleyway." In the case of the *Blackwater*, where Damant attempted to salvage the entire vessel, he learned some practical lessons. During the operations a diver, Carpenter's Mate Thomas

Milne, a forty-year-old man with a fine physique, went down to clear the wreck's anchors and cables. The work required him to crawl under the forward part of the vessel, putting him at a maximum depth of ninety-eight feet. Coming up, Milne attempted to decompress following Haldane's tables, but the weather had turned rough. Damant opted to shorten the decompression period and attempt to modify the tables in order to get Milne up sooner. But the rolling and pitching of the diving boat made it difficult to keep the diver at the appropriate depth. Then, mistaking the signal given to him, Milne came to the surface too soon—he had to be sent down again.

These irregularities led to Milne contracting diver's palsy. He felt pains in his chest and became giddy. This degenerated to the point where in about an hour he could not stand and his face grew pale. His eyes made random uncontrolled movements. His pulse was irregular and weak. However, he was still cogent, even when the HMS *Edgar*, the accompanying vessel, came alongside. They transferred Milne aboard and put him in a recompression chamber.

"He became much better at once," wrote Damant. "The pulse returned, and he began to talk, spontaneously describing a sensation of warmth flowing down into his arms and legs, which was no doubt due to the rapid improvement of the circulation." In a couple of hours, brandy was passed to him as he continued his recovery. He returned to duty three days later. Damant, with the ship's surgeon, published a brief piece on the matter in the *British Medical Journal.*

Damant's superiors took notice of him and wrote on his official record that he had "acquired great skill as a diver and is a well-read physiologist." In recognition for his obvious talent and achievements in working with compressed air he was elected to the Physiological Society. Damant, seemingly modest and loathing self-promotion, claimed that this was due to the influence of his friend, Boycott, who had left Lister to become a professor of the society. Still, the Admiralty sent Damant to the International Congress on Occupational Diseases in Brussels in 1910 so he could learn how other countries were working with compressed air. On April 15, 1911, he was promoted to lieutenant commander. Damant was not quite thirty.

13

The Cold Sea

On January 25, 1917, at 6:10 pm, Admiral Finnis had received a message at his post in Buncrana from the Fanad Head station: "Observe rocket showing white stars, East by North, four miles from the station. No vessel can be seen owing to the mist." Soon, other messages came from Fanad Head as well as from vessels in Lough Swilly. Emergency red signal flares were being sighted all across the waters of the mouth of Lough Swilly. It was clear that the *Laurentic* had sunk.

Finnis commanded the trawlers *Helcia*, *Nogi*, and *St. John* to weigh anchor and head toward the site. He then ordered the trawlers *Coriettes*, *Lord Lester*, and *Scot Ferriby* and the minesweeper *Imperial Queen* to join the search. Finnis also sent a message to his minesweepers that were in nearby Lough Foyle to join the rescue. In addition, ships such as the destroyers *Sethon* and *Vale of Lennox*, which were escorting an oil tanker, picked up wireless messages of the disaster and joined in the search and rescue. There came to be a total of nineteen vessels looking for lifeboats throughout the night and into the next day.

• • •

Different lifeboats met different fates. Sublieutenant William Heathcot's boat, lifeboat seventeen, became swamped with seawater. Because of the powerful current, the thirty-four men aboard were forced to constantly pull at the oars. At the suggestion of Leading Seaman William J. Prior, they dropped a sea anchor to slow the lifeboat. Heathcot lit a red flare every half hour, but it was only at 11:30 PM that Heathcot was able to signal the *Coriettes* by using a flashlight. His lifeboat was the first to be rescued.

Lifeboat seven, under the charge of Lieutenant Richard Morgan, soon found itself separated from the others due to the heavy weather. Throughout the punishing night, his men worked the oars toward land, but found themselves perilously close to rocks. Exhausted, they abandoned the effort and let themselves drift. The seas battered the lifeboat. The saltwater soaked through and froze the men's clothes.

At midnight they broke into the provisions and ate biscuits and corned beef, washing it down with water from the emergency casks. They burned rescue flares, and at times thought they had been seen. But no ship found them that night. When morning came, seven men were dead from exposure, including Lieutenant Morgan. The living were so weak that they could hardly bail water from the lifeboat. It was only at 4:30 PM, that the trawler *Farnaby* found five survivors twenty-five miles from shore—there had originally been over thirty men aboard the lifeboat.

A similar fate awaited the men of lifeboat fourteen. None of the forty-four men aboard were wearing winter clothes. After two hours, they were awash with seawater. At length, all they could do was throw over the sea anchor and wait. Cold and exposure killed forty of them before they were picked up at 9:00 AM by the trawler *Lord Lester*.

As for Captain Norton's boat, lifeboat five, he gave orders to pull toward the Fanad Point Lighthouse, but his crew was unable to make any gain against the storm. Norton ordered his men to make an additional sea anchor with the lifeboat's mast. The anchor stabilized the boat somewhat, but there was to be no rest. Water kept slopping into the boat, which required them to constantly bail. By midnight, the water was gaining.

It was to the south that Norton saw the flashing lights of a ship, steaming out of Lough Swilly. Desperate, Norton ordered three more flares to be burned. The ship changed its course and headed directly to them. The vessel was the *Imperial Queen*, which had already picked up lifeboat seventeen. At 1:00 AM, Norton and his men were brought aboard.

Norton took command of the ship and through the night continued to work to find survivors. Finally, at 7:00 AM on January 26, the *Imperial Queen* brought Norton ashore. After conferring with Admiral Finnis, Norton was housed at the Lough Swilly Hotel in Buncrana to convalesce. There, using the hotel's stationery, he began to pen a grim report to the Admiralty.

Of the 475 men aboard the *Laurentic*, 121 survived. The vast majority of the dead perished in the lifeboats from exposure. When the matter came to a court martial in February, Norton and his officers were found blameless. The court wrote, "The evidence shows that the ship was well organised and that the general behavior of the Officers and Crew was very creditable both before leaving the ship and afterwards in the boats." In fact, Norton and several of his officers received letters of commendation.

But the *Laurentic* now rested at the bottom of Lough Swilly at a grave of approximately twenty fathoms. There, too, lay the *Laurentic's* cargo of small, heavy boxes. Norton did not tell the court of inquiry what was in those boxes, but soon enough the magnitude of the disaster reverberated in whispers throughout the British government.

14

The Fortunes of House Damant

SINCE GUY DAMANT JOINED THE SERVICE, his father Harry had continued his profitable law practice on the Isle of Wight. He had also become the official receiver for the towns of Newport and Ryde. Then in 1908 he sold Lammas to a retired merchant named Peters for £3,000—twice the market value. "It's the view, not the house I'm paying for," said Peters. The family lived in a series of homes until Harry finally bought a property called Maresfield on Cambridge Road in East Cowes, which he rechristened as a second Lammas, complete with a stately, four-story home. Meanwhile, his son James had married, and Guy had begun courting Eleanor May Brook, nicknamed Nell. Guy thought Nell, who was twelve years younger than him, was the "prettiest girl in Cowes" with her soft-pale brown hair and fine features.

All the same, Mary Damant would tell her son that the family lost its luck when they left the original Lammas. Guy never wrote much on the subject, merely stating, "We lost our unity and went different, selfish ways." This bad luck started perhaps on August 13, 1910, when Guy's father, while aboard the yacht *Coral* in the Helford River, was suddenly stricken by a heart attack. A doctor was called for from St. Keverne, five miles away, but Guy's father died before help could arrive. Harry Damant was fifty-eight years old. The will was read on October 17 and bequeathed his fortune of just over £5,490 to his widow.

Meanwhile, Guy's youngest brother, John Alister Damant, had been serving in the Royal Navy as a sublieutenant. Three days before his father's death, John was diagnosed with neurasthenia. This is a diagnosis that is not used in modern medicine but was defined by one clinician of the day as "a generalised irritable weakness of the entire nervous system, characterised (when the brain is chiefly affected) by hypersensitiveness of the sensorium, loss of mental and bodily vigour, inaptitude for work, disturbed sleep, and irritability of temper; and (when the spinal cord is chiefly affected) by general muscular weakness, restlessness, nervousness, and vague pains; and usually accompanied (in both forms) by various phenomena referable to the vaso-motor and sympathetic systems." It was also referred to as nervous exhaustion or what today would be normally called generalized anxiety disorder. In addition, John was diagnosed with organic heart disease, another medical condition that based on the medical technology of the day, indicated that he probably was suffering from heart arrhythmias brought about from anxiety and stress. This stress may have been exacerbated by the rumor that John was a closeted homosexual. He was admitted to the Royal Hospital Haslar and subjected to a three-month medical probation. He was discharged on October 1, being warned by doctors of heart trouble. John's three-month medical review did not go well. He was found unfit for service on November 10 and placed on the retired list.

Shortly thereafter, his mother Mary came for him, and they traveled to nearby Southsea where they checked into the Royal Pier Hotel, which catered to well-to-do travelers. While their plans were unknown, it can be assumed that they were to return to the Isle of Wight and try to figure out what John was going to do with his life.

The answer came shortly. On the morning of November 15, Mary Damant made repeated calls to her son's hotel room. There was no answer. At last she called upon the hotel staff, who broke open the door.

On the bed with clothes pulled over his head was John Alister Damant and a bottle of chloroform. The coroner's jury ruled the death "suicide during temporary insanity" possibly from "brain congestion due to thickening membranes, which would affect his mind." He had just turned twenty.

Guybon Damant retired from the Royal Navy in October 1911, and Andrew Catto became the new inspector of diving. After his retirement, Damant fell out of the historical record with just hints of information gleaned from local newspapers from the Isle of Wight and his descendants. He did not write much about this period, and there is no indication that he had any career ambitions during this time, aside from returning to do those things that he could not do while in the service. He lived at Lammas off his naval pension of three pounds sterling a week. He earned more in consulting fees for projects that Professor Haldane recommended him to such as developing an improved breathing apparatus used by rescuers after a disaster in a coal mine. Haldane even recommended Damant to give testimony before a parliamentary select committee, for which he was paid handsomely even though his testimony ended up not being needed. He was commissioned by C. E. Heinke & Co., a rival firm to Siebe Gorman, for consulting work. And he also conducted the scientific experiments he enjoyed so much. In fact, he was involved in the movement to found the Isle of Wight Natural History and Archaeological Society, which was eventually established in 1919. He corresponded frequently with Arthur Edwin Boycott about his experiments, which included, among other things, the speed of snails. Damant's life might be characterized to be one of leisure mixed with study—the life of a gentleman scientist.

Damant also kept busy with the Medina Sailing Club where he first served as a member of the sailing committee in 1911. In his thirteen-meter yacht *Tessa,* he won a challenge cup in 1911 with prizes of under two pounds sterling. He was then appointed secretary of the club and later vice commodore. He would eventually be an officiant of Cowes's Royal Regatta. In addition, Damant also helped start the sea scouts in Cowes becoming a "commander." According to the county commissioner for the movement, Dr. C. Gordon Brodie, the purpose of the organization was "to teach boys to think and act for themselves and to train them to be real boys and not molly coddles." Damant arranged for the purchase and moorings of a dinghy.

On July 23, 1913, he married Eleanor "Nell" May Brook. The Reverend F. C. Learoyd officiated over the ceremony at St. James's

Church in East Cowes. Nell wore a dress of white voile and an heir-loom pendant wrought with topaz and pearls given to her by Mary Damant. She also wore a pearl bangle, which Guy gave to her. She carried a bouquet of roses and smilax, and her bridesmaid was her sister. Nell's bouquet was sweet pea flowers. They received many hand-some presents and went to London for their honeymoon. At their departure, she changed to a gray cloth dress and wore a white-and-amber hat.

Nell was in many ways the opposite of Guy. She did not have the shy intellect of Guy. She was social, outgoing and, as described by her youngest daughter, Mary, had "frivolous tendencies." Not all of Guy's extended upper-class family took well to Nell, who was from a "lesser family," and some even refused to receive her. But Guy did not care for his own family's frivolities. Neither did Mary Damant, who blessed the marriage by giving to her son and daughter-in-law a portion of the Lammas estate's gardens to set up a new home. With its magnificent views of the Solent, Guy and Nell's home, Thursford, on Cambridge Road was named after the ancient estates held by the Guybon family on mainland Britain. Nell often entertained, but when Guy would see guests coming he would escape by scrambling through the serving hatch between the dining room and kitchen to find solace in the gardens by the sea.

The pair were loving and devoted, spending time at the Tessa fishing for plaice, which they caught in such abundance off Old Castle Point that they gave some away. Guy would always remember those happy days.

Then, on August 4, 1914, Great Britain declared war on Germany. All that summer Damant had heard the rumors of war, and it was no surprise to him that even before Britain entered the conflict he was called up from the retired list. Damant was not sure what to expect. He wrote, "No one had the least idea of what a war would be like but [I] imagined one great battle like Waterloo and peace signed before winter." The war was a shock to Nell, who had some trouble under-standing how somebody who was retired from the service could be called to active duty. However, Guy made arrangements for her to shut down the house at Thursford and live with his mother at Lammas.

He first served on the HMS *Royal Arthur* for patrol duty in the North Sea before he was transferred to his old home, HMS *Excellent*. Whale Island was now chiefly engaged in training reservists and new officers. Due to Damant's prior experience at Whale Island, he was promoted into the senior staff and stood in for the *Excellent*'s first lieutenant when needed. Damant rented various furnished houses and moved Nell out of Lammas and into various residencies in nearby Portsmouth where he got leave to visit two days a week. They lived a good lifestyle, since the war had the effect of reducing housing prices. Damant would write of this time:

My pay was good, my servant used to bring to the house the four pounds of meat I was entitled to draw weekly. It *was* meat, no bones. We all had bicycles and used to ride as far as Southampton in one direction and Chichester in the other on every fine afternoon and could afford the theatre once or twice a week. Nell took piano lessons and could play *Blue Bells of Scotland* and such like on the landlord's piano. The other Whale Island wives used to visit and she used to attend sewing parties for hospital comforts and so on. Altogether, a happy carefree time.

For the most part, Damant's involvement in the war was minimal. He tested experimental artillery shells, and on one occasion he and another officer were sent to the Somme to observe whether new gunnery methods used by the battling armies could be of any value to the navy. He flew in an airplane for the first time, the pilot darting over German lines. Damant lost all sense of direction. "Great black anti-aircraft shell bursts crashed all round us, some very close producing fragments which sang like hornets past our ears." Below he could see the lines of zigzagging trenches, facing one another over the dead no-man's-land. When he debarked he saw the men. "Wounded were lying in stretchers awaiting ambulances and myriads of loathsome green flies settled on quick and dead, food and bedding. I remember a regiment trailing past which had just been pulled out, after a bad time in the trenches, mud was dropping off them in great flakes and they looked too young, pale, haggard and bewildered." He wrote that compared to the brutal life on the Western Front his times with the *Excellent* were "easy ones for me."

Then, at the end of January 1917, the thirty-five-year-old lieutenant commander received new orders. He was to call upon the Admiralty, which wished to discuss an urgent matter that required his special skill set in the technically difficult and practically dangerous world of deep-sea diving.

PART II

15

The Council of the Sea Lords

LIEUTENANT COMMANDER GUYBON DAMANT did not know why he was being ordered to Whitehall, and while he was no stranger to London, it would have been difficult not to contemplate the capital of the British Empire at war in January 1917. Stretching south from iconic Trafalgar Square, Whitehall held the War Office, the Foreign and Commonwealth Office, the Treasury, and many other departments. Extending west off the southern end of Whitehall was Downing Street, where at number 10 the new British prime minister, David Lloyd George, had taken up residence a little over a month prior. Southward, the street terminated at Parliament Square, near Westminster Palace, where the British legislature met. But among all these grand buildings, Damant sought the natural center, the force that had built and maintained the greatest empire the world had ever known: the Admiralty.

Damant arrived at 26 Whitehall, where he encountered an ornate wall supported by Doric columns, which had in its center an iron gate surmounted by winged seahorses. Passing through this barrier, called the Admiralty Screen, Damant entered a wide courtyard fenced by a U-shaped brick building adorned by four more Doric columns that vaulted awkwardly to its portico. Designed by Thomas Ripley and finished in 1726, this was the Old Admiralty Building. To some, the building may have appeared grand, but to others, such as intellectual Horace Walpole, it was a spectacle, who noted it was a "most ugly edifice" for lacking classical proportions. However, according to writer Colin Brown, the building only looked this way since the "Admiralty, which wanted to use all the available space, had little time for classical sensitivities.... Ripley was ordered, despite his protests, to raise the columns carrying the portico over the windows, and to hell with the classical proportions of the pillars. Both the Admiralty and the architect became a laughing stock for the critics." The Admiralty Screen was built in part to cover up the architectural blunder from passersby on the street. The Ripley building was the oldest structure of the Admiralty complex, and was interconnected to other buildings that varied in architectural pomposity. In fact, the entire edifice had been assembled in piecemeal and coincided with the development of the British Empire in an effort to keep ahead of its rivals.

At the Admiralty, Damant saw evidence of a country at war. The number of persons working there had grown to about ten thousand—over fivefold since the start of the conflict. There were so many new workers that the Admiralty ran out of space for them, so the new hires were stationed in nearby buildings. There had also been a heavy change in personnel. Many of the civilian clerks who had served at the Admiralty before the war had gone into the armed services. In their place were *mutilés de guerre*, men who had been wounded during the war, as well as a growing number of women—something that was unprecedented. But the need for staff had grown so acute that traditional chauvinism was tossed aside. By the next year, 1918, the Admiralty employed over three thousand women. However, even with the increase in staff, the workload demanded more still. Workers served in twenty-four-hour shifts. One longtime Admiralty careerist, Sir Charles Walker, noted, "The normal day's work was a minimum of twelve hours on weekdays with a short day on Sunday, and annual leave was voluntarily restricted to a week."

All of this naval bureaucracy was governed by the Board of Admiralty. The board was composed of individuals known formally as lord commissioners of the Admiralty. The head of the group was the first lord of the Admiralty, normally just shortened to first lord. He was traditionally a civilian along with several other civil lords. The military membership of the board, those being naval flag officers, were known as the sea lords. Their head, the first sea lord, was considered the professional leader of the Royal Navy. The other three sea lords each managed broad facets of the service: personnel, material, and supply.

The board had seen heavy change in membership during the past year. The then first lord was Sir Edward Carson, an Irish Protestant who was an outspoken opponent of Irish independence. He was appointed to the board in December 1916 to replace Arthur Balfour who only briefly held the position after Winston Churchill was ousted for the disastrous Gallipoli campaign against the Ottoman Empire. On the whole, Carson took a more hands-off approach than Churchill and deferred to the sea lords, trusting professionals to make the military decisions.

The first sea lord, Admiral Sir John Jellicoe, was also new to his position, having been appointed in November 1916. But Jellicoe had extensive experience with the board as third sea lord from 1908 to 1910 and then second sea lord from 1912 until he was assigned to be the admiral of Britain's Grand Fleet in 1914. With Jellicoe came others, such as Cecil Burney as second sea lord and Lionel Halsey as fourth sea lord. These men who replaced the prior sea lords had more direct experience fighting in the war than their predecessors. With them also came many other officers, particularly from the Grand Fleet, to help administer naval affairs. While Jellicoe's reputation was so sterling that there was no objection to his tenure as first sea lord, others, particularly the staff officers, were referred to by some long-time Admiralty staff as "the mob from the north" since the Grand Fleet was stationed in the North Sea.

• • •

While the meeting's locale at the Admiralty was not recorded, owing to its importance it was possibly held in the same room where the momentous decisions that had shaped the British Empire from the Battle of Trafalgar to the explorations of Captain James Cook had taken place—the ornate Admiralty boardroom. Here, there was an imposing table, surrounded by eighteenth-century red leather chairs. The table itself had a curious semicircle cutout at its head, built during the 1870s either for the permanent secretary who carried copious papers or to accommodate First Lord George Ward Hunt's protruding belly. There was also a fireplace to drive away the late January chill, atop which was a wind dial over a circular world map. The dial was mechanically connected to a weather vane upon the roof that told the Admiralty which way the wind was blowing.

Damant was ushered into his meeting and met by admirals and other higher-ranking officers. Solemnity encompassed all.

While the full roll call for Damant's meeting at the Admiralty was never recorded, based on subsequent correspondence it is possible to reconstruct who was there, such as Captain Clement Greatorex,* the director of naval equipment and assistant to the third sea lord. There was Admiral Morgan Singer, the director of naval ordnance, and Captain Frederick Young, who had organized the navy's fledgling salvage section. Due to the special nature of the meeting, some of the sea lords were likely present, including Admiral Jellicoe who had a tendency to take a direct hand in operations and the third sea lord, Admiral Sir Frederick C. Tudor who was in charge of all matériel matters in the Royal Navy.

The admirals wanted to discuss the recent loss of the *Laurentic*. The official investigation would rule that the *Laurentic* had blundered into a pair of moored mines. During the First World War, mines came in various weights and sizes, ranging upward of 700 pounds, and each containing between 250 to 350 pounds of explosive guncotton, trinitrotoluene (TNT), or amatol. Most mines were spherical and had lead spikes, or horns, that stuck out from their sides. When a horn struck an object at a minimum of fifty pounds of pressure, a capsule containing a chemical mixture within it broke and released it into an internal battery. The battery then fired the explosives, which destroyed or damaged whatever hit it. In this case, the mines had been laid by the *U-80* commanded by Kapitänleutnant Alfred von Glasenapp.**

---

* Pronounced "Grate-rakes."

** There has always been some confusion as to whether the *Laurentic* was torpedoed or mined. This stems from some of the crew members stating the ship had been hit by a "tin fish" (the nickname of a torpedo). In addition, a comment written by

German naval mines during the World War I typically had horns that set off the explosive within them upon contact with an object. This mine has its sinker attached to the base, which would detach and anchor the mine to the seafloor on a tether. *Courtesy of the Imperial War Museum Collections, MUN 3844*

Lieutenant Commander Damant had known about the disaster, but not much more than that. He had been too busy with his duties to pay more than scant attention to it. Still, the *Laurentic* was but one of many ships sunk by U-boats—there was seemingly nothing special about it. But Admiral Morgan Singer, with his thin lips and grave eyes, informed Damant that he was to be privy to a secret known only to a few people in the British Empire: the *Laurentic* was a treasure ship.

Aboard the *Laurentic* were approximately forty-four tons of gold* composed of 3,211 individual ingots. Each bar of gold had been carefully weighed and measured. These were then packed into crates and stowed in the *Laurentic*'s second-class baggage room. The Bank of England estimated the total value of cargo to be almost £5 million,

---

the Admiralty shortly after the incident read that because no mines were found in the channel in subsequent days, and because the explosions occurred in such rapid succession and on the same side of the ship that "it appears more probable that Laurentic was torpedo[ed]." However, German documents indicate that the *U-80* indeed laid mines at that time. In fact, some later accounts indicate that the *Laurentic* was sent into the mined area by error.

* Or 1,285,286.413 troy ounces, to be exact.

or $25 million, in 1917 prices. While trying to fix a value on the cargo using later figures is difficult since the price of gold has far outpaced the rate of inflation, one estimate shows that this treasure would be worth about $1.7 billion in 2017 US dollars. But no matter what figure is used to calculate the value of the gold, the outcome is the same now and then. It was and is a hoard of monumental value.

The cost of the war for the Allies was staggering. Britain, France, and Russia had been heavily purchasing equipment and supplies from the neutral United States. To pay for it, all three countries borrowed. Britain, for example, sold war bonds and engaged foreign creditors. By the time of Damant's visit to the Admiralty, the British national debt had grown to almost 100 percent of the country's gross domestic product, something unheard of at that time. With the all-consuming war still demanding ammunition, food, and supplies, every sign showed that the financial situation was going to get worse.

The problem was more acute for Russia and France, which did not have economies as robust as Britain. The borrowing had become so intense that French and Russian credit had collapsed. As a result, both nations were dependent upon the British to pay their bills. At Calais, France, in August 1916, Britain insisted that its allies agree to send shipments of gold to Britain to back their own credit. The gold was in turn taken by the British government and designated for various destinations in order to preserve the Allies' good economic standing. Gold was not just French and Russian in origin. The British government removed gold from regular circulation, smelted it, and forged it into bars. Some bars were even American in origin, showing how frequently the ingots passed from nation to nation.

The gold aboard the *Laurentic* was bound for Halifax, Canada, but from there it was to be shipped to Ottawa where it would be tallied again before being taken by the Dominion Express Company to New York to be deposited into the vaults of J.P. Morgan and Company. According to Bank of England records, from June 1916 to February 1917 over 220 tons of gold had been sent to the neutral United States. Additional large amounts of gold specie were sent to other countries and parts of the empire in order to preserve the Allies' credit.

The entire war to this point had been quite beneficial for the United States. The amount of material being exported to Britain from the United States was gigantic. The war, in fact, brought the United States out of a recession. Between 1914 and 1916 the balance of trade deficit, the difference in the value of goods being imported and exported between Britain and the United States, had grown from £74 million to £227 million in the United States' favor. As a result, the strength of the American dollar was growing at the expense of the British pound sterling. The gold was therefore used as collateral for short-term loans, to keep the British currency strong, or to be used to directly buy equipment and supplies. This last case was what the *Laurentic*'s gold was slated for, the purchase of ammunition. The British Cabinet ordered the Admiralty to recover the gold.

The admirals informed Damant that the loss of the *Laurentic* was a tremendous blow to the national economy and the war effort. The Germans did not know yet that their mines had sunk the *Laurentic*, and they certainly did not know of the gold aboard the ship. They told Damant that they had approached the top salvage companies of the day, but they had informed them that the job was so difficult and dangerous that they required a payment of half the gold recovered in compensation.

The Admiralty then presented Damant with a question. *Could Royal Navy divers be used to recover the gold?*

Damant told the Admiralty that it was feasible to get the gold.

The Admiralty ordered him to go get it.

Damant was to have all the men and equipment that he needed if they were available. In a later interview, Damant said, "I walked on air. I knew just what I wanted and where to find old diving allies. It was quite a change for a dug-out lieutenant commander gunner to be responsible to the Admiralty only."

16

Twenty Fathoms Deep

ON A COLD FEBRUARY DAY in 1917, Lieutenant Commander Guybon Damant found himself three miles south of Buncrana near the village of Fahan. Here was a church and the ruins of a former monastery that included an ancient abandoned graveyard with grass-covered stones dating to the seventh century. In it was the famous Fahan Cross Slab, an ancient stone carved with intertwining reliefs in the shape of a cross whose design preceded the famous Irish high cross. The monastery, named St. Mura's after the first abbot of Fahan, had endured Viking attacks during the first centuries of its history until a new monastery was built in the sixteenth century. This, too, fell into ruin. In fact, the only maintained sites in St. Mura's were the church and a newer graveyard behind it.

While the exact date of Damant's visit to the cemetery is unknown, it seems fitting that he would have visited after he had received grim news. His brother Henry, who was a second-class airman in the Royal Flying Corps, had died from pneumonia on February 26 at the Tidworth Camp. It was a hard blow since Damant had already lost his youngest brother, John Alister, to suicide.

Damant headed toward a site in the confines of the newer graveyard. There was no memorial yet, though it was certain that one would be erected when the war came to an end since here sixty-four crew members of the *Laurentic* lay in a mass grave, while next to it was another burial site containing four of the ship's officers. These graves were close to the tomb of some officers of the frigate *Saldanha*, which was lost with all 238 crew in 1811 during a gale in Lough Swilly. Damant contemplated the cemetery and noted that some of the old Irish gravestones had white rounded pebbles from the seaside set on them, arranged in flowerlike rings. This was an ancient custom and Damant could not guess how long had passed since those stones had been set upon the markers. It may have been centuries. There were other such graves to contemplate all about Lough Swilly. But the lieutenant commander needed to turn all his thought to the task at hand—there was little time for grieving.

● ● ●

Damant's visit to the old cemetery at Fahan occurred after weeks of preparation for his mission. First Sea Lord Admiral Sir John Jellicoe issued orders on January 31, 1917, to salvage the wreck for "guns, mountings, rangefinders and other articles of value." In the first weeks of the *Laurentic* operation there was never any mention of the gold. To do the job, the Admiralty promised the lieutenant commander everything he needed to recover the bullion *if* the resources were available. As the German Empire was escalating its U-boat campaign against Britain, finding the assets for the salvage would be tricky, even with the mission prioritized.

Damant was detached from the *Excellent* and temporarily assigned to the Royal Navy's newly developed salvage section. As the First World War ground on and on, it became clear that defending the mercantile fleet which brought the materials to the conflict was as important as protecting the fighting navy. But the Royal Navy had never developed a great capacity for salvage. The general feeling was that such work could be subcontracted to private firms as needed since the cost of operating a special salvage wing of the navy in peacetime was not justified by the number of naval vessels that needed recovery. However, within a year of the start of the war, it became increasingly evident that the Admiralty had to take on some responsibility in recouping ships and their cargos in order to put a bandage on losses.

On October 22, 1915, the Admiralty set up the salvage section for the duration of the war under the auspices of the third sea lord. While overall charge of the department was given to a Captain Christopher Metcalfe, day-to-day operations—which included surveying government-chartered wrecks, reporting the viability of salvage on certain wrecks, and actually conducting salvage operations—were overseen by the Admiralty's special salvage adviser, Captain Frederick Young.

With a dashing goatee and eyes full of bonhomie, the sixty-one-year-old Young looked more the part of an adventurer than a workaday toiler of the sea. Damant described him as a "genial old boy who had risen from nothing and spent his large salary like water." Young was probably the most knowledgeable salvage expert in the British Empire, if not the world. He was a former Royal Navy diver who since 1906 had worked as the chief salvage officer for the Liverpool Salvage Association, the most respected marine salvage agency in the British Empire. As such, Young led the salvage of several wrecks that Damant had surveyed while he was inspector of diving, including *Torpedo Boat 99* and the *Gladiator*.

After joining the section, Young had assessed the capabilities of the Royal Navy for salvage and made considerable recommendations to change personnel, ships, and equipment. He led a crash program in salvage modeled after his own experiences with the Liverpool Salvage Association. Initially, the salvage section worked on ships that were classified as *War Risk* since the goods they carried were meant to be used for the conflict. But as the war progressed, the salvage section expanded to work on regular merchant ships and their cargoes. By 1917, as the German U-boat offensive peaked, the section was strained to the limit, handling all kinds of cases throughout British waters.

But the *Laurentic* was not a typical salvage case, even when not considering the gold. The wreck was located off the North Irish coast, where the salvage team would be, as Damant wrote, "exposed to the full run of North Atlantic weather from the Westward and Northward, while any force of wind from the Southward fetched a nasty sea down Lough Swilly."

To cope with the conditions, Damant needed a vessel that was not unduly large and was seaworthy enough to keep a good position over the wreck. The ship needed flexibility so that it could be heavily anchored by its four corners and used as a platform for the divers, and the derricks needed to haul up recouped materials and debris. It may seem strange that large ships make for poor salvage vessels, but larger ships swing proportionally greater distances in rough weather and become highly dangerous to the divers who are physically connected to them. Even the *Spanker* was rather large at 242 feet. Though the Admiralty would have provided Damant with a larger ship, he demurred, "I had had just enough experience of diving in the open sea to realise that the most important thing is to be able to hold your ship vertically over the wreck, the smaller the ship the easier she is to hold." Since the salvage section could not spare any of its primary salvage ships, he chose the mooring lighter *Volunteer*.

The *Volunteer* was a part of the Royal Fleet Auxiliary (RFA), which were those ships owned by the Admiralty but crewed by reserve personnel, men of the merchant marine who were attached to the Royal Navy at the outbreak of war. With its single, squat funnel and spidery mast, the ship, while new—it was launched in 1916—would win no beauty contest. Damant called it a "bug trap." And it would be crowded. The *Volunteer* was 135 feet long, 28 feet abeam, and displaced 750 tons of seawater—there were only two cabins aboard for the captain and his mate. Still, it was large enough to be seaworthy while at the same time not so big as to endanger the divers. It also had two powerful capstans, capacious holds, and a reinforced structure at the bow called an apron that cables ran over to enable the *Volunteer* to engage in heavy lifting. Lieutenant Robert Arthur Tanner of the Royal Navy Reserve was the *Volunteer*'s commanding officer. Tanner, who had commanded passenger ships to and from the Isle of Man before the war, was considered by Damant to be a "quiet, decent man." Tanner's mate, Sylvester Platts, was described by Damant as a "splendid seaman and rigger who had spent years in sailing ships and coasters and could weave spells with wires and winches." Platts was to become good friends with Damant. Tanner and Platts received orders to leave defensive boom duty at Devonport, and sail the *Volunteer* to Portsmouth for refitting under Damant's orders. The ship arrived on February 3, 1917.

The crew was just as important as the ship. Damant first requested fourteen men and one munitions expert who were attached to the *Racer,* a former training ship of the *Excellent* that had been converted for salvage. These men were mostly what were called riggers, who were expert at working the winches aboard the ship. They were under the charge of a foreman rigger named Frederick Little. As for the divers, Damant handpicked men from the *Excellent* whom he considered to be the best deepwater Royal Navy divers in the service. Among them were Leading Seaman Edwin Blachford, Able Seaman George Clear, and Shipwright Ernest Charles Miller.

Damant's principal diver was Miller, nicknamed "Dusty."[*] Aged twenty-eight, he had a long, pale face described by Damant as "dismal." He was a powerful man and an amateur heavyweight boxer, and he possessed a strong patriotic determination to do what he could for king and country. Miller had gained a reputation as one of the most reliable, gutsy, hardworking divers in the Royal Navy. He also exhibited natural leadership abilities and had what was described in his official record as a "strong personality." He was loyal to Damant, and the pair would often box together, forming as friendly a relationship as might be imagined between an officer and a subordinate. In the end, there were thirty-five officers and men aboard the *Volunteer* including the divers. Damant constituted an additional diver as needed.

It took over a week to refit the *Volunteer.* Six special extra-heavy mooring anchors were ordered with the heaviest weighing over six tons. Diving equipment including dresses, boots, helmets, and air pipes were brought aboard. A steam-driven air compressor capable of generating one hundred cubic feet of air per minute was installed along with traditional hand-cranked pumps as backups. A proper plant to deliver the compressed air to the divers was installed, consisting of a reservoir to store the compressed air that extended out to branching pipes that delivered it to divers.

---

* Dusty was a common nickname traditionally associated with the surname Miller in Britain, owing to the flour dust a miller would make while working.

A recompression chamber was also known as the "diver's oven." This was the first chamber used during the *Laurentic* operation and would later be replaced by larger models. Journal of Hygiene *25, no. 1 (1926),* courtesy of Cambridge University Press

One of these pipes also delivered air to a recompression chamber. Sterile and coffin-like, it was usually called the "air chamber" or the "diver's oven." But the presence of the chamber boosted the morale of Damant's divers and suppressed fears of the bends. It allowed for the greater risk taking that might be needed.

There were many unknowns at play. The *Laurentic* had neither been located nor was it known how much damage it had sustained or was enduring from the destructive tides off Lough Swilly. All these factors dictated how difficult it would be to penetrate into the gold's strong room.

Captain Clement Greatorex,* the director of naval equipment and the Admiralty officer to whom Damant directly reported, coordinated

---

* Greatorex would be promoted to rear admiral on April 27, 1917.

the effort. Admiral Frank Finnis, the senior naval officer in Buncrana, was ordered to sweep the channels of Lough Swilly for mines while other ships searched for the wreck. Greatorex contacted the White Star Line for plans of the *Laurentic*. These were sent overnight by train to London from the company's offices in Liverpool and were then forwarded to Damant for study.

For over a week, minesweepers passed up and down the channels of Lough Swilly, dragging their cables on the bottom trying to hook onto the wreck. Commander Geoffrey Unsworth was in command of one of these vessels. He had been out on the lough on the cold night the *Laurentic* sunk, assisting in the rescue efforts. He then had contracted pneumonia. After a stay in a hospital he recovered enough to join the search. Then on February 9 his sweepers caught something.

Word was sent to Portsmouth. Unsworth believed he had found the *Laurentic* lying in twenty fathoms of water. Receiving a telegram to proceed to Ireland, Damant headed to the train station, leaving the final preparations of the *Volunteer* to Tanner and Platts.

Damant arrived in Buncrana and checked into the Lough Swilly Hotel, the same place where Captain Reginald Norton of the *Laurentic* penned his report of the disaster. The hotel became Damant's base of operations as he continued preparations by ordering more specialized equipment such as underwater lamps from Siebe Gorman. He also received a half-model of the *Megantic*, the *Laurentic*'s sister ship, since no such model of the *Laurentic* existed. He also met *Laurentic* survivor Boatswain E. W. Newing who had worked aboard the *Laurentic*. With Newing's help, the plans, and the model, Damant oriented himself to the ways of the ship and how to best get to the gold room. Meanwhile, Damant's divers filtered into Ireland and were put up at the Sailor's Rest in nearby Londonderry.

On February 27 the *Volunteer* arrived at Buncrana ready for action. The next day, Damant led his men aboard the ship and finished preparations by clearing its holds and rigging the mooring gear. All seemed to be as ready as it could be, though the motorized air compressor would not work for more than ten minutes at a time. The divers would have to rely on hand-cranked pumps.

March 1 proved to be as fair a day as any in Lough Swilly at that time of year—there was a heavy sea running, and Damant did not consider the weather good enough to do much work except confirm the wreck was indeed the *Laurentic*. The *Volunteer* cast loose its moorings at Buncrana and steamed out toward the mouth of the sea loch. Looking back, the looming coast of Ireland was jagged, foreboding, and beautiful. In all other directions was endless ocean—a sea that could turn against them at any moment.

For the first dive, Damant opted to go the traditional route and use an open diving boat. After the lengthy process of putting on the diving gear and testing the equipment, the diver stepped down the ladder and into the sea. As the diver sank, he closed his exhaust valve progressively to retain more air in his suit to counter growing sea pressure as he sank deeper into the water. Grasping the line that had been hooked onto the wreck by Finnis's minesweepers, he descended to see what was on the other end.

The water was cold. A soft green glow pervaded, typical conditions in North Atlantic waters. Visibility, when good, was only a dozen to twenty feet at best. Soon, in the wan light the diver saw the shadowy *Laurentic* below him—the topmost part of the wreck was some sixty feet from the surface. From it, tentacle-like lines swayed, pushed up and down and side to side from the powerful swell of the sea. Affixed to their ends were heavy blocks that swung menacingly through the water. These were the *Laurentic*'s falls, the lines that had secured the lifeboats. These lines were extended to their full length of sixty feet. Understandably, there was no man aboard the *Laurentic* to retract the lines to their housings before the ship sank.

The diver sunk past the peril of the falls and then fully appreciated the fallen *Laurentic*. Its bow was pointed in the direction of the Fanad Head Lighthouse, 2.1 miles distant, and its stern toward the open ocean. The ship, once a statement of elegance, refinement, and grace, now lay huge and dead on a cold seafloor. It rested upon its port bilge, the lowest part of the hull. The mast was tilted sixty degrees from the vertical. The diver landed with heavy boots into the forward rigging. Because of the *Laurentic*'s tilt, it was impossible for him to stand on deck. Rather, he clung to what railings he could as the tides pushed and pulled him.

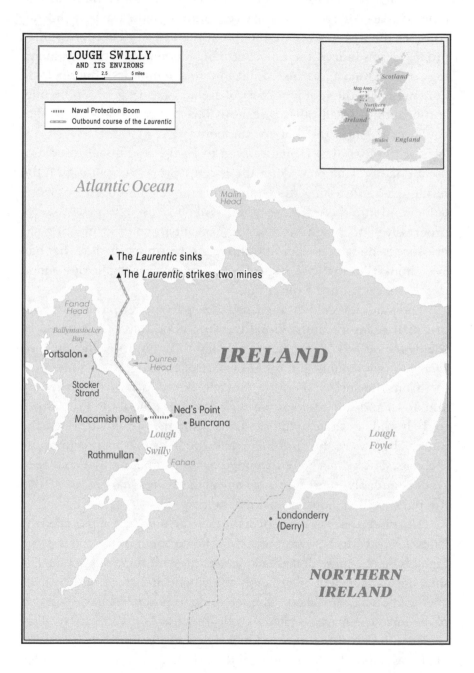

LOUGH SWILLY
AND ITS ENVIRONS

0   2.5   5 miles

······ Naval Protection Boom
▭▭▭ Outbound course of the *Laurentic*

Scotland

Map Area

Northern
Ireland

Ireland

Wales   England

Atlantic Ocean

Malin
Head

▲ The *Laurentic* sinks
▲ The *Laurentic* strikes two mines

Fanad
Head

Ballymastocker
Bay

Portsalon

IRELAND

Dunree
Head

Stocker
Strand

Ned's Point

Macamish Point

Buncrana

Lough

Lough
Foyle

Rathmullan

Swilly

Fahan

Londonderry
(Derry)

NORTHERN
IRELAND

It was not a long dive, and after careful observations he returned to the shot line to begin the decompression process. At the surface, he made a full report to Lieutenant Commander Damant.

Further exploratory dives brought back more information such as the location on the hull damaged by the German mines. With this information, Damant, with the guidance of Boatswain Newing, studied the plans of the *Laurentic*. Each compartment was explained to Damant with all efforts focused on how to get to the second-class baggage room where the gold was stowed. This strong room was roughly in the center of the ship both vertically and horizontally. The problem was there was no way to plumb a line directly to the baggage room. Instead, divers would be required to enter the wreck and work their way through the interior to recover the treasure. Still, it was a rather straightforward job and Damant thought that the work should not take long, barring any complications. He wrote to his superiors, "Given a spell of fine weather I think the prospects are favorable."

This was all the work that could be accomplished on March 1 since the swell was growing deep and a gale was coming. But it was enough. Damant could plan his attack.

17

The Path to the Strong Room

ALL THROUGH THAT FIRST WEEK of March the weather was harsh. The *Volunteer* could not even approach the wreck. In fact, the weather did not settle enough for work until Thursday, March 8. Lieutenant Commander Guy Damant was learning a great deal about the unpredictable weather of Lough Swilly.

Damant needed to perform the operation quickly but methodically. Divers who had to work inside the *Laurentic* needed to have their lines as close to the vertical as possible in order to prevent fouling. Damant selected the starboard entry port as his starting point, a watertight door halfway down the ship's side that offered the most direct access to the strong room. Several days of the operation were used to carefully lay out the mooring gear to hold the *Volunteer* in place since the divers had to repeatedly descend, check the anchorages, then give instructions over the telephone to Lieutenant Tanner to shift the *Volunteer*'s position until it was just right.

On the *Laurentic*, the divers felt a deep oceanic swell that created horizontal surges of water as the crests and troughs of successive waves passed high above. Damant wrote that the divers had to edge "along the high starboard rail, like cats on the ridge of a roof" and cling with their arms and legs to prevent themselves from being swept away.

In the meantime, lines of the falls whipped freely through the water with their tethered blocks hurling inches from the divers' faceplates.

To further complicate matters, the motorized air compressor was still not working. An expert was being sent from Siebe Gorman who could repair it, but in the meantime the divers relied on air from the hand-cranked pumps. It was hard work for the crew of the *Volunteer* who toiled at shifts keeping the air supply steady to the divers.

It was through this slow process that the *Volunteer* achieved the correct position so that on March 12 Damant was ready to penetrate the vessel. Divers went down, and found that the entry port would not open for them. Damant decided to blow off the door using sixteen-and-a-half-pound canisters of guncotton, which was the most readily available underwater explosive. The virtues of guncotton in underwater demolition were noted as early as 1876 with someone writing in the journal *Science*, "In blasting rocks or wrecks under water; gun-cotton is far more effectual than gunpowder.... The effect of the blast, as seen on the surface, is described as surprising: first a shiver and a leaping up of innumerable jets, and then an up-rush of a great water thirty feet in height followed by swirls of mud, large quantities of splintered wood, and dead fishes." The divers set the explosives, laid fuses, and stretched the detonation wire up to the *Volunteer*. Tanner got the ship clear, and Damant exploded the charge. The divers then descended and drove in the entry port, thrusting the door bodily into an interior cross passage. There it fumbled to a rest on some debris, but now it blocked the passage from the inside.

There was no way to remove the door by hand since it was too heavy. It was awkward too, since the door had the same dimensions of the port frame. So divers entered into the dark cross passage and manipulated lines about the door. This was then attached to a hoist while the ocean swell jerked about the line. It took an entire day for the divers to guide the door through the port frame and get it to the surface.

The next day, the divers were prepared to navigate the interior of the *Laurentic*. But they discovered that the release of the door had created a cavalcade of debris in the passage. Casks and cases of stores floated out of the nearby number four hold, surging immediately to the surface or remaining caught behind to obstruct the divers. The men

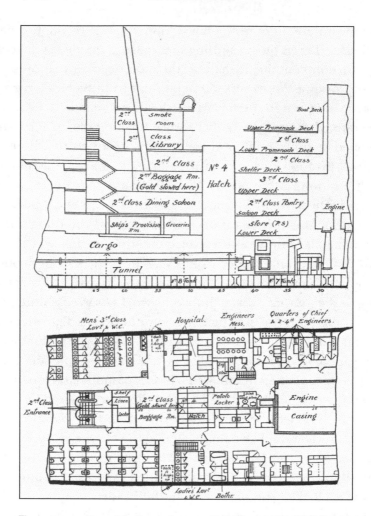

These cross-sections of the *Laurentic* were probably illustrated by G.C.C. Damant and show the position of the gold within the ship. Journal of Hygiene *25, no. 1 (1926): 28, courtesy of Cambridge University Press*

descended with crowbars and pried open cases, unpacking the contents and thrusting them aside or out of the wreck. Damant commented, "Flour in sacks which had been under a head of 70 feet of water for 6 weeks showed the curious property this substance has of resisting immersion: for it was only wetted through a thickness of one or two inches inwards from the outside, the bulk being perfectly dry and sound."

As this flotsam came to the surface, it suddenly dawned on the first mate, Platts, that some of these were not just ordinary stores. The crew had seemed to be a bit overzealous in recovering certain casks over others. Platts quickly found out that these casks contained rum. Suddenly, Platts seized a sledgehammer and smashed open the casks so that the alcohol flowed down the scuppers and into the sea. But that night, there were wild cheers coming from the *Volunteer*'s forecastle.

Platts cleared the lower decks of men and performed a thorough search. In the propeller shaft tunnel he found rows of fire buckets and washtubs brimming with rum. Even a seasoned sailor like Platts could not fathom how the crew had managed to smuggle a cask or two under all the officers' eyes and literally down the hatch. Platts had this rum cast overboard as well.

The clearing of the debris was successful enough that by March 14, divers had burrowed farther down the passage. But here was a new hindrance. A barred iron gate had been installed, which blocked the surest access to the strong room. A guncotton charge on the gate's hinges eliminated this obstacle. Then, after two more hours of shifting heavy cases, the way seemed clear to the gold.

There could not have been anything but palpable excitement aboard the *Volunteer*, even for the normally coolheaded Guy Damant, as Dusty Miller got ready to dive. It was not a sure thing, even with Miller. A hundred things could go wrong—fouled lines, a collapsed passage, or worst of all, a U-boat attack.

It was evening when Miller donned his diving dress and spun down to the *Laurentic*. He eased himself through the entry port and, thrusting his submersible lamp in front of him, ambled along the tilted decks. It was like spelunking a mine shaft, except that the mine shaft was under twenty fathoms of water, and the spelunker, instead of wearing Wellington boots and a harness, bore nearly two hundred pounds of diving gear.

The heavy clank of Miller's diving boots reverberated throughout the dead ship interspersed by the sound of bubbles wafting from his helmet. He passed through the former location of the barred gate. Then slipping and shuffling down the pitched deck, Miller's lamp revealed the steel door of the baggage room.

"I've got to the strong room, sir," Miller telephoned, his voice squeaky from the effects of the compressed air he breathed.

The door was locked—but this was no surprise. That was why Miller brought a hammer and chisel.

It was strange work, being submerged in the bowels of a tilted wreck trying to pry open a nearly horizontal door. Miller wedged the chisel into the door's hinges and swung his hammer repeatedly. After some time, he pried this last barrier loose. Peering into the inky blackness, he set one of his weighted boots forward. The angle of the deck was too steep.

He slid downward and landed right at the foot of the second-class baggage room.

Miller managed the slide well enough, but upon inspection he could see that the compartment showed signs of imminent ruin. There was not much headroom, as the tides and currents of the open Atlantic were warping the ship's bones. The decks above and below had closed together, the stanchions holding them doubled over, and the bulkheads were being torn away.

But Miller had landed upon the prize—a jumble of debris-covered boxes. Each box was made of roughly sawn wood and bore coarse rope brackets for lifting—they were not a model of carpentry. The boxes were a foot square and six inches deep each, but their size belied their weight. Each was about 140 pounds. Even displaced by seawater, the boxes had the apparent weight of approximately 131.5 pounds.

Miller judged the condition of the wreck. It seemed liable to collapse at any time. He needed to work fast and start bringing the gold to the surface. Miller seized one of the boxes and began rigging a sling.

• • •

On the surface, Damant had known that Miller could not simply attach a line to one of the boxes of gold and allow the *Volunteer* to haul it straight to the surface. In addition, the awkward diving suit meant a man underwater could only do a fraction of what he might do unencumbered at the surface. If Damant had measured the lifeline and air pipe that draped into the sea, he would find that he was physically less than three hundred feet from Miller, but in reality Damant was a world away.

Miller loaded the box into the sling, which was connected to a line that weaved through the wreck until it breached the starboard entry port before shooting up to the deck of the *Volunteer*. Miller called to the top through the telephone and had the men pull on the line. He then guided the box to the wrecked gate of the baggage room while giving instructions through the telephone as to when to remove slack from the line.

At one point, Miller was stopped by the lip of a door's coaming, which barred further progress. Miller was forced to heft the box over it. Now he came to a narrow cross passage that tilted steeply upward at sixty degrees for forty feet. The box had to be dragged up the passage. Then there were two more door coamings to get over. Miller had to rest frequently with each exertion, adjusting his exhaust valve, and therefore the amount of compressed air entering his diving suit, before setting to work again.

Meanwhile, for Damant there was little to do but wait and make sure his men adjusted the lines at Miller's request while others kept up the steady rhythm of turning the cranks of the air pumps. Listening to a diver perform work through the hissing and crackling telephone and not being able to directly assist him was an agonizing process, but to send down a second diver into the wreck violated all safety protocols. Another man in the narrow space would increase the risk of the divers fouling their lines and becoming trapped.

By the time Miller and the box reached the entry port, almost an hour had passed. That hour, in addition to the time Miller had spent getting to the strong room, meant that he would require a lengthy decompression process. Clearly, Damant was taking chances with his divers.

Damant's men saw Miller's sling emerging from the cold sea, hugging a wooden crate. The box was hauled upon the deck and then lowered with a thud. The box's label, METAL, was unassuming. There must have been a palpable feeling of exhilaration as it was opened, for it is unlikely that Damant or any of those aboard the *Volunteer* would have seen ingots of solid gold before.

It was quite a motley collection of gold bricks, if motley is the right term for such treasure. They were rough looking and differed in size and shape. Each was stamped with its exact weight and its degree of fineness—most seemed to be 99.95 percent pure. Each were also engraved with the names of banks, firms, or nations. "Banque de France" bricks were packed next to ingots stamped "Rothschild Brothers." Others said "Mocatta and Goldschmidt" while some said "United States Treasury." It was the first victory, and one might imagine that Damant and his men gloated like pirates over the gold. His team had wrested £8,000 of treasure back from the sea. And while there was £4,992,000 more to go, Damant reckoned he could recover the entire hoard in a couple of weeks.

Miller was raised to the surface. He was brought up more quickly than he should have been and consequently suffered acute pains in his joints—the bends. This was somewhat surprising to those aboard the *Volunteer* since Miller was considered relatively immune from the affliction, but Miller's work had been exhausting and he clearly saturated his body with compressed nitrogen. This registered clearly with Damant, perhaps reliving what he witnessed during the salvage of *Torpedo Boat 99*—that all divers, no matter how capable, were merely human. Miller was placed into the recompression chamber.

The next morning came, and Miller was feeling better. So much better in fact that Damant selected him to return to the strong room even though in normal circumstances Damant may have given Miller a rest day. But Miller knew the way, he was the best, and if he was willing to try his luck, so be it. Besides, by this point Damant had no faith that the weather off Lough Swilly would hold in his favor. He needed to get that gold back into the government's hands as swiftly as possible.

Damant's gamble paid off and by the end of the morning Miller had sent three more boxes of gold to the surface. Miller was decompressed correctly this time and had no symptoms of the bends. With that last box, the wind came up and blew northward in a gale. As the *Volunteer* started to rock and roll, Damant gave up his moorings and retreated to Buncrana. There he holed up at the Lough Swilly Hotel and triumphantly penned a report to the Admiralty.

18

The Storm

LOUGH SWILLY SUFFERED THE WORST WEATHER it had experienced since the *Laurentic* sank. One set of salvage moorings that had been carefully placed by Damant's crew had been heavily damaged, and another had torn away completely. But in some ways, the storm was a reprieve for Damant. An expert had come and worked on the motorized air compressor on March 17. He ran a successful test for two hours, running it on kerosene. Damant expected to be able to use the compressor, which would be a godsend to the men who were manning the manual pumps.

Damant reckoned that he would require two to three days of fine weather just to recover the anchors and relay the moorings before he could get inside the *Laurentic* again. On several occasions, Damant brought the *Volunteer* out to the site, but the swell was too great.

During this downtime, Damant took to hiking about Lough Swilly with Boatswain Newing. On one of these occasions, they noticed debris piling up—lots of it. On closer inspection, the pair came upon a pile of parquet floor tiles. In fact, they soon discovered fixtures, fittings, cabin doors, and other items that could have only been deep inside the *Laurentic*. Locals began to carry away all this debris for sale and souvenirs. There was so much of it that an auctioneer was called for and sold the wreckage in lots, much to Damant's disgust. "How much for all that lies on the beach between this rock and that part of a lifeboat?" Damant heard one auctioneer say.

Then the army informed Damant that "three enormous boilers with strips of wood nailed on the outside" had washed ashore under one of the forts. These were the mooring buoys that Damant used to secure the *Volunteer* to the wreck that had gone missing. Damant's team worked for days, soaked by sleet and frozen by snow to recover and repair them. As the days passed, it almost seemed that he would never be able to return to the *Laurentic*. Then he received a telegram from the Admiralty with new orders to head to Sunderland.

* * *

On February 23, 1917, Oberleutnant Herbert Breyer, the *UC-32*'s commander, was running his boat three hundred yards away from the Sunderland breakwater. All hands aboard the U-boat knew the dangers of their service. Death came suddenly either by enemy mine, depth charge, shell, or all too often accident. As a result, an idiosyncratic humor had developed in U-boat subculture. A typical U-boat of two hundred to three hundred feet in length was called a "sardine can" or, more pessimistically, a "tin coffin." Breyer's own boat, belonging to a smaller class of coastal minelayers, was only 162 feet in length and nicknamed a "tin tadpole."

Breyer had been in command of the vessel since September 1916 and had chalked up a little over nine thousand gross tons of shipping sunk due to his actions. While it was a far cry from the record of Germany's U-boat ace of aces, Lothar von Arnauld de la Perière, who had notched up over 453,000 gross tons in his career, it was still creditable. Breyer had already laid three mines, or "pineapples" as his crew called them, off the mouth of the River Tyne. He had fifteen left in the exterior watertight chutes on the forward part of the boat to play havoc with the shipping off Sunderland. Mines were set to be laid at specific depths, which meant that Breyer had to be exact as to where he set them. Indeed, the locations of all the mines were planned and charted in advance, which allowed German vessels to pass through their minefields safely. When a mine was put over the side, it was attached to a sinker that brought it to the seafloor. The sinker held the mine by a water-soluble plug that dissolved after a short period. After it dissolved, the mine, having positive buoyancy in the water, floated upward, attached to the sinker by a tether. This allowed time for Breyer's U-boat to get clear.

Breyer was stationed at the conning tower, overseeing operations. His crew gingerly removed a spherical mine, its horns protruding outward. He kept a lookout for any British patrol boats as the mine splashed into the sea. There were fourteen mines left to go.

But before Breyer could order the *UC-32* to its next position, there was a tremendous explosion, seemingly from under the U-boat itself. The vessel heeled over, and the stern snapped away. The mine they had just laid had released from its sinker too soon, floated up, and struck the boat.

In the U-boat's control room, sailor Oberheizer Reinhard Schirm felt the explosion. The boat plunged into darkness as the sea poured in through the great fissure caused by the blast. The vast amount of water flooding into the boat pressurized the air, which was funneled out through the conning tower hatch. This was further abetted by exploding compressed air tanks. Schirm was blasted upward and out of the boat. He swam to the surface, struggling in heavy leather clothing and seaboots. He kicked off his boots and then worked at his breeches, successfully removing one leg although he swallowed a good deal of oil leaking from the wreck that mixed with seawater. His cold hands could not work his knife to cut his clothing, but he eventually shifted his other leg out. He was frozen and tired. He had not slept in twenty-eight hours.

As Schirm treaded water he noticed the light from a patrol boat approach. He swam to it and then found his hands fumbling with a lifebelt* that was thrown to him. A British sailor offered an oar to allow Schirm to scramble into the boat. Then he heard a familiar voice. "Hullo Schirm, you here too?" It was Oberleutnant Breyer. He and a third man had survived. All were taken prisoner.

The next day, British minesweepers located the wreck of the *UC-32*. Divers were sent down the forty-two feet to the bottom where it lay. The water from the River Wear, however, was thick with silt, and the divers could only feel the wreck. What they did feel, and the bits

---

* "Lifebelt" is the British name for "life preserver" as used in American English.

of debris that they managed to bring up, showed the damage to be quite extensive. The Admiralty decided to call in more expertise and summoned Lieutenant Commander Damant from the *Laurentic* job.

After Damant arrived, he found that location buoys laid by the patrol boat had been swept away. Nevertheless, he quickly relocated the wreck. On March 18, he and his divers descended for a survey to see if it might be salvageable.

One of Damant's divers found the rear door of the starboard torpedo tube open. Damant, not wanting to go away empty-handed, salved a torpedo from the tube (valuable to the Ordnance Department) as well as a "Machinery History" from the flotsam, a technical manual on how the *UC-32* operated. When all was done, Damant noted in a report to the Admiralty that it would be unwise to attempt to raise the vessel because of the fourteen mines still aboard. He suggested blowing them up with a charge. The Admiralty considered the notion and then vetoed it, considering it too dangerous. Damant and his divers returned to Lough Swilly on March 19 with some excellent experience that could prove invaluable for the *Laurentic* operation and become even more important as the war progressed.

• • •

Despite the delays caused by weather, there was cautious optimism at the Admiralty that the work on the *Laurentic* could be completed in a timely manner. Clement Greatorex wrote, "It is considered that with satisfactory weather, there is reasonable prospect of recovery of the whole of the boxes in time."

But the weather was slow to moderate, and it was not until April 4 that work could resume. That day all the salvage moorings were relayed—faster than Damant had originally anticipated. While the next day proved too rough for diving, it was not the case on Good Friday, April 6, when Damant sent down divers to reconnoiter the *Laurentic.* As the first diver descended, it became immediately noticeable that the state of affairs on the bottom had changed. In the initial salvage work, the entry port was 62 feet deep according to air pressure gauges. Now the gauges read 103 feet.

The strong tidal action caused by the storms had crushed the *Laurentic* like an accordion. There were great rents in the ship's plating. But the divers found the entry port accessible. They even wormed their way to the door of the strong room, but they could advance no farther. The deck atop the strong room was crushed to within a few inches of the floor. Figuring that the other side of the compartment might have more headroom, the divers tried to find other means of entry into the room, but each alternate route was blocked by torn and crumpled bulkheads. Damant related the bad luck to his superiors and added that he would keep trying other routes. But the weather worsened again, and he was forced to wait.[*]

The *Laurentic* continued to collapse so that by the time the weather moderated and work was ready to resume, the divers could only get a few feet inside the entry port. The former corridor was

These illustrations show the *Laurentic* as the divers originally found it (left) and what it looked like after the storms. Journal of Hygiene *25, no. 1 (1926), courtesy of Cambridge University Press*

---

[*] By now, Damant knew that intimate knowledge of the interior of the vessel was no longer needed. Since there was no place to accommodate Boatswain Newing on the *Volunteer*, and because Newing had not received any pay since the sinking of the *Laurentic*, Damant discharged him on April 13. Newing returned to work for the White Star Line.

now impassable. The roof deck had collapsed to eighteen inches above the floor deck. Even that space was jammed with ruined steel bulkheads and wreckage.

The most direct way to get to the gold was to somehow widen the passageway. As Damant contemplated how to do this, there was growing anxiety at the Admiralty. Rear Admiral Henry Oliver, chief of the Naval War Staff, wrote to Greatorex on April 24, "I hope that salvage has not been discontinued because there are still over 2,000 boxes of gold in the ship to recover before next winter. The Bank are [sic] always asking me about it."*

There were other distractions. On April 25 Damant was requested to help recover gear that was aboard the *Thrush*, a salvage ship that had wrecked off Glenarm. The *Thrush* had been a barque and commanded by King George V when he was a lieutenant in the Royal Navy some three decades before. Since then, the old ship was given to the salvage section. Damant wrote, "There was a mistaken idea at the Admiralty that wooden ships were best for salvage because their elasticity would stand the bumping which one often gets when lying alongside a wreck in heavy seas. Hence the *Thrush*, which was very strongly built of teak, was hauled out of rotten row, stripped to the hull, given new engines, masts, capstans, workshops, pumps and so on at a cost greater than that of her first building."

Since the *Volunteer* was relatively near it made sense to send Damant. The *Volunteer* headed to Belfast, unloaded it holds, then sailed to Glenarm where Captain Tanner navigated the ship alongside the sharp rocks that had wrecked the *Thrush*. Equipment was hoisted out of the ship and stored in the *Volunteer*'s hold for transport to Belfast. Damant made the trip to Belfast twice before returning to Lough Swilly on April 30, five days lost and the sea miserable again.

---

* The number of boxes is unrecorded, but there were probably considerably less than two thousand. Since there were about 88,000 lbs of gold (44 tons) and each box weighed in at about 140 lbs, and also as the first box was valued at £8,000 out of £5 million total, the number of boxes was probably between 600 and 700. Oliver probably meant to write "bars," not "boxes."

Finally, a break in the weather from May 1 to 4 allowed Damant to work on the *Laurentic* at length. The divers widened the crushed corridor by explosives and used braces and other materials to shore it up. Using munitions inside a collapsing wreck was a precarious business. Above the divers were five decks of ruined ship supported only by luck as constant groaning, creaking, and tremors echoed in their diving helmets. But to Damant it was the most expeditious thing to do.

Then the finicky motorized air compressor went up in flames. Black smoke poured up from the *Volunteer's* hold. Worse still, the compressor was installed near a half ton of explosives. It took ten horrible minutes before the officers got the fire under control. Damant's crew were once again forced to work the hand pumps. Greatorex dispatched a telegram to the Portsmouth Dockyard to send another expert to the *Volunteer* as quickly as possible or send a replacement pump.

But perseverance paid off, and on May 4 the divers reached the strong room again, although it was blocked. More explosives, more removing of debris. Damant calculated that they were less than ten feet from the gold, but as Damant wrote, "Into this ten foot space has been compressed all the structure normally occupying thirty feet or half the beam of the ship, together with what has fallen from above, i.e. wreckage from the starboard side." The divers were relegated to destroying bits and pieces of the wreck at a time, which all needed to be hauled out. "The process is extremely slow," Damant wrote.

But steadily, the way was widened until a diver squeezed into the gold room. He got himself into position, casting the light of his underwater lamp about the compartment. Damant, waiting anxiously by the telephone for the diver's report, heard a voice crackle, "The gold's not here, sir! It's gone. The deck is full of holes."

19

"Give Me More Air"

THE VIOLENCE OF STORM and tide had torn the *Laurentic*'s steel, ripping great rents in the deck of the strong room. Everything in the compartment had been swallowed, including the gold boxes. The gold, far denser than other metal in the wreck, had a natural tendency to tumble downward. Now the boxes were out of reach, buried deep in the port side upon which the ship rested. There could be no other feeling but frustration for Lieutenant Commander Guy Damant. The salvage that he had initially thought would take a couple of weeks would now take far longer—just how long remained to be seen.

Damant meditated on what was to be done. The corridor-tunnel could collapse at any moment, and the way was so narrow that it was too awkward to remove the large pieces of deck plates and bulkheads that were piling on the gold cache. The only way to get at the treasure, Damant decided, was to excavate vertically through the wreck, by blasting a hole straight down through the starboard side toward the approximate location of the gold.

Over the following weeks, Damant dived to the wreck to plan where to place explosives followed by divers who laid guncotton charges as he directed. It was confusing, since the ship was crushed and lying on its side. To keep themselves oriented, the divers used the mainmast, which was in line with the baggage room, as the main landmark. After the divers decompressed, guncotton was exploded, which created a black fog in the water from silt and debris that made it all but impossible to see for an hour. It was only when a modicum of visibility returned that a diver returned to the wreck, attached the destructed materials to a sling, and hoisted them up to the *Volunteer*.

The power of the explosions killed and stunned the teeming sea life. Herring, mackerel, cod, and all other kinds of fish carpeted the *Laurentic* while others floated dead to the surface. Damant, supremely curious, noticed that only certain species of fish died while others went about their business unaffected. He concluded that only fish with swim bladders were killed, since the concussions of the blasts disrupted the gas in their bladders. He filed the phenomenon away as something for future research.

The smorgasbord served by Damant's demolitions was eagerly snapped up by sharks, particularly dogfish, a small species that was abundant off the Irish coast. After an explosion, the dogfish came in schools, gorging on fish. While not great whites, they were still a nuisance. Damant would write, "I and other divers had to fix charges right in the midst of them. After firing, however, it was never possible to find a dead dogfish: on the contrary they could be seen rising to the surface almost in the foam of the explosion, and tearing at the bodies of the freshly killed teleosteans." Miller, while working on the wreck, often offered his reinforced boots to the aggressive creatures who bit at them eagerly.

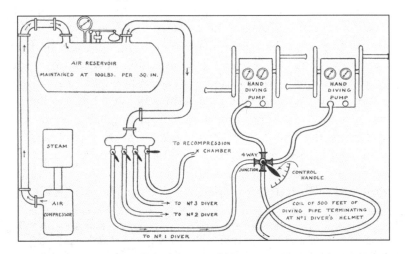

This illustration shows how compressed air was delivered to the divers. *Journal of Hygiene* 25, no. 1 (1926): 38, courtesy of Cambridge University Press

While the divers were now free of the hazards of collapsing tunnels and all the water above them was open, the workaday grind was coupled with new dangers.* For speed's sake, Damant purposely cut short decompression times until minor symptoms of the bends occurred.

Damant had made note of phenomena that enhanced his knowledge of decompression illness and how it subsequently affected the divers. Since he deliberately cut the times on Haldane's decompression tables to what he deemed was the absolute minimum, he observed differences in cases. For example, divers who slung plates for hoisting had to screw or unscrew with their fingers tight shackle pins attached to the plates to get the job done. In many of these cases, divers complained about decompression illness pains in their forearms.

Men who worked hard imbibed more compressed air. As a result, their bodies became more saturated with nitrogen than others. Such had been the case with Miller when he brought up the first box of gold from the wreck. Other hazards involved clearing off the deck plates and debris. Damant wrote:

One may understand the situation by visualising one of those cranes so often seen towering over the sites of buildings in course of erection. Imagine now a dense fog (representing the intervening sea) which prevents the men at the crane and on the ground respectively from seeing anything of each other; add the complication that the crane instead of being fixed relatively to the ground is afloat, and that besides being subject to lateral displacements of several yards under the influence of winds and tides it has the habit of jumping vertically at irregular intervals as the swell passes under it. Again, let us have a furious wind (to represent the tide) which gets hold of any slack line such as the crane wire it is desired to lower to the diver and streams it out

---

* There was some good news for Damant at this time. On May 10 a mechanic arrived from the Portsmouth Dockyard and finally got the motorized air pump in good working order. Also, for its part the Admiralty tried to give Damant more flexibility to the job and established a hundred-pound account with his bank in order to pay small accounts.

nearly horizontal; let the weight to be lifted be five tons of jagged plating which has to be slung and guided up between overhanging decks and structures by one man who is in a clumsy diver's dress, and whose range of vision is about five feet, who can only communicate by telephone, and who depends on a vulnerable rubber air pipe with a tendency to twine itself round the lifting wire at some mid-water point equally inaccessible to himself and those above.

Damant continued, "All the conditions for an accident are present, and a high standard of attention and discipline is needed to prevent one. That alone does not suffice, however."

• • •

One afternoon in early May, Edwin Blachford donned his diving suit and climbed down the ladder of the *Volunteer*. With him, aside from the normal tools, he carried a large canister of guncotton. Sliding down the shot line, he landed on the beaten rubble of the once elegant *Laurentic*. This was what the divers called the *working area* or *working position*. Near his leaden boots was a sling attached to a steel wire that spun up and out of sight to the surface over a hundred feet above. It was strained tight since the sling was struggling to hold open a heavy deck plate.

Deck plates had proved to be the most difficult sections of the wreck to remove. If only a few rivets remained holding a plate to the wreck, it held firmly even against the strongest pulls of the *Volunteer*'s derricks. It was only after multiple charges were set off on top of them and all the connections were severed that they could be hauled to the surface. However, Damant had discovered that deck plates and similar structures came apart efficiently if the explosives were placed beneath them and detonated while the joint was under stress.

Blachford got on his hands and knees and crawled right under the deck plate. He sought to place the guncotton at the joint where the plate was attached to the rest of the ship and the stress was greatest.

(Left) Deck plates being removed from the *Laurentic*. *Courtesy of the National Archives, London, ADM 116 1741*

(Right) Diver Edwin Henry Blachford. *Courtesy of the Historical Diving Society, UK*

Blachford gave directions to the surface through the telephone connection. "Lower my pipe and line a little."

He reached forward and attached the explosive to the joint. Its detonation wire drooped through and up to the surface. "Take in the slack of the firing circuit."

Meanwhile, Damant oversaw the proceedings on deck. There was probably monotony about the work as the *Laurentic* had lost its golden luster of excitement and had become a slog of diving, explosions, diving, dead fish, diving, removing debris, and repeat. Even the winch, strained as it was hauling up the deck plates, would have been something he had seen many times.

Just then, there was a snap from the winch as the wire that pried open the deck plate flew into the air. It spun out and fell slack on the deck. A shackle on the derrick had broken. Those present could only imagine the great deck plate slamming upon Blachford and trapping him beneath it.

A palpable silence fell on the deck of the *Volunteer*. To that point, there were neither serious injuries nor deaths during the operation.

A voice suddenly cracked through the telephone. "Give me all the air you can, sir."

There was no time to congratulate Blachford on not being dead. Damant ordered the men to increase the diver's air.

Blachford's voice piped through the telephone again. "That's right, give me more yet, and get another diver down here as quick as possible."

Diver George Clear, who had hooked up the wire that had held the deck plate, had just finished decompression and was only partially undressed. Quickly, men started to suit him up again. But as for Blachford's request for more air, Damant hesitated. The air pressure flowing into Blachford's diving dress at that moment was getting high enough to rupture the suit. He did not know why Blachford would want more air. Damant needed more information.

Damant sent a query down to Blachford through the telephone, but the only response that came was roaring air. It was too loud for Damant to make anything of what the diver was saying. He ordered the air supply to be eased somewhat, so as to better hear Blachford.

After the gust of compressed air died away, Blachford's voice slowly and purposefully crackled over the telephone.

"Give me more air."

With all things being equal, Damant figured that to send more air into the suit would simply destroy Blachford's diving dress. Damant would not do it.

By now George Clear was ready. He was handed a fresh wire that had been rove into the derrick. This was attached to a new sling. Following Blachford's air pipe, he made his descent.

Clear found the spot where his comrade was trapped. With quick action, he attached the sling to the plate. The crane aboard the *Volunteer* pulled, and the deck plate slowly hinged open like a clam.

Blachford slid out, his suit in perfect order. It had been nine minutes since the wire first snapped. He was hauled up, unruffled.

Damant asked Blachford why he kept asking for more air. Blachford replied that when the deck plate came down on him, he thought that inflating his suit would relieve the pressure on his back. When

Damant pointed out that overinflating the suit might burst it and thus drown him in his helmet, Blachford was taken aback, having not considered the notion at all.

Upon reflection of the incident, Damant wrote, "It may be objected that undue risks were being run, that no divers should have been below while hoists were being raised to the surface, that charges should not have been put under plates in the way described, but laid on top and repeated again and again till disruption was effected, and so on. The answer is that such procedure would have increased the time required for any particular piece of work fourfold. The gold was being sought, not for any selfish purpose but for National needs in war-time by a fighting Service, and the divers recognised that chances must be taken for the sake of quickness, and were proud to take them."

· · ·

Fine May weather yielded work for six of seven days between May 16 and 22. More plating and bulkheads were exploded and removed. They were now driving through the heart of the *Laurentic* by descending into a large aperture they had blown through the decks. They were clearing out the ship's innards. With each deck plate removed, the divers found furniture, bedding, and paneling. Provisions that had been stowed in the ship's hold bled freely into the sea, and there seemed to be an infinite amount of lumber beneath all that ruined steel. All of this needed to be pulled out by hand and loaded into heavy perforated hoppers, which were painted white so that they could be easily seen in the depths of the sea. Again and again, debris was hoisted to the surface where it would be dumped off-site.

It was during this phase of the work that on the afternoon of May 22, Dusty Miller spotted a red-colored brick on the wreck. Then he saw another and another. The red was merely a trick of the diffraction of light in the water. Miller had found the gold again, which had broken out from its boxes and was now strewn in the rubble in a seemingly concentrated area. With the excitement of a person who just found sunken treasure, he telephoned his finding to the *Volunteer* and began loading the bucket. By the end of his dive he had recovered ten ingots. By the end of the day, divers had recovered twenty-two gold bars.

Relief is the word that was used by Damant to describe the feeling he and his men felt at that moment. Miller had worked at 115 feet for ninety minutes, and he was eager to surface. Damant, for time's sake, attempted to decompress him in forty minutes. Miller should have taken at least eighty-seven minutes to stage decompress. He paid the price and was stricken by the telltale sign of diver's palsy with sharp pains in his joints. He was sent to the diver's oven and could only watch the elation through the thick glass porthole of the chamber. But Miller would recover from the bends yet again.

The weather the next day was too rough for work, so Damant sailed to Buncrana where he landed the gold. The ingots were examined by Treasury officials. The weights and numbers that were stamped into them were recorded. They were sent under guard by rail to Belfast where they were stowed in the Bank of Ireland's vaults. Clement Greatorex telegrammed congratulations to Damant and his men. Damant, resting at the Lough Swilly Hotel, could not have done anything but smile as he sent back thanks. There was still a long way to go, but they were on the right track.

When they returned to the wreck, Damant followed the trail of where Miller had found gold and determined where to excavate. Caution mixed freely with excitement. Damant did not want to use explosives near the treasure from fear that blasts would hammer the ingots deeper into the wreck. Work slowed to a crawl since he could not dismember the *Laurentic* efficiently. However, the concentrated effort coupled with another spell of fine weather paid off. On June 8 nine more ingots were discovered.

By this time the divers were becoming quite familiar with the various types of gold bars in the wreck. The most valuable were the so-called Rothschild variety, which had the finest gold content. These weighed a bit more, about thirty pounds for a single bar, and their value was estimated at about £2,000 each. The least valuable bars were from the Bank of France. These bars had a copperish color without as fine a gold content. They were considered to be worth about £1,600 each. As divers found the bars of gold and put each into the hopper they reported over the telephone, "One in the bucket!"

• • •

Since the declaration by Germany that it would resume unrestricted submarine warfare on February 1, 1917, the policy had proved to be highly successful from a military point of view with hundreds of thousands of tons of Allied shipping sunk. And the British could seemingly do nothing about it. At the start of the war, the German Empire had at its disposal a single class of oceangoing U-boats armed with torpedoes. However, after the Belgian coast fell into German hands, it developed smaller classes of short-range U-boats that could operate effectively against nearby British shipping lanes. In particular, there was the UB class, an attack craft, and the UC class, a minelaying class. As the war progressed, these vessels grew larger and more sophisticated with the third generation of the UB type tripling its predecessors' size and giving it an operational range of ten thousand miles.

U-boats were therefore active all through the British Isles, and one of their targets was the shipping lanes off Lough Swilly. If Damant was growing obsessed with sunken gold by chasing down rabbit holes, he would have been equally concerned with the likely appearance of a U-boat, which could easily sink the slow and heavily moored *Volunteer*.

Some of the most active U-boats around Lough Swilly were the minelayers. In response, the Royal Navy sent minesweepers to regularly clear the channels. These small ships usually worked in pairs by laying out a long wire between the two ships. The wire, which formed a bight, was dragged at the appropriate depth by a device called a water kite or paravane. This weighed down the cable and provided tension. The wire could either cut a mine's mooring cable allowing it to float to the surface or catch the cable and drag the whole mine along, or simply set off the mine. Often the minesweepers would themselves be damaged or destroyed by the mines—there was a high mortality rate in that branch of the Royal Navy.

While Damant and his divers were busy working at the salvage, minesweepers two miles distant caught a mine, which was accidentally

Drifting German contact sea mine. Note that the horns on this mine were removed, and this photograph was probably taken during a training exercise. © *Coll. Fr. Philips*

exploded by sweeping wire. While two miles might seem a considerable distance, sound travels farther and faster in water. What is more, it is far more powerful.[*]

The concussion of the exploded mine gave a hard and violent shock to Miller. He was apparently all right, but Damant called off operations. Damant instituted a rule that diving work was to be suspended while the minesweepers were working within a five-mile radius. This was still not enough as another diver took a blow when a mine was exploded six miles away. Damant complained to the Admiralty concerning the matter, but it was never fully resolved.

---

[*] The human ear generally experiences pain from 130 decibels. A jet engine produces about 140 decibels of noise. Gunfire can reach up to 155 decibels. While there is no simple way to calculate decibels of the same noises underwater—since that would depend on temperature, water pressure, and other variables—it is always much more powerful. An increase in 62 decibels is not uncommon for a sound transferred from the air to water. The power of sound waves underwater had already been seen by Damant's team after all the fish were killed by their use of explosive charges.

The men of the *Volunteer* witnessed a great convoy assemble for weeks. The ships included newly built vessels from the shipyards along the River Clyde. As they departed Lough Swilly for the United States in late June, they sailed in three tight columns surrounded by destroyers. However, a coordinated U-boat attack, presaging the famous "wolf packs" of the Second World War, played havoc with them.* The remnant returned helter-skelter into Lough Swilly. Damant recalled, "For days afterwards the tide used to sweep masses of wreckage, capsized lifeboats and occasional bodies past us as we worked on the wreck."

As for the U-boats, none attacked the *Volunteer*. Damant thought that they were lucky. He wrote:

> The Germans knew nothing about the *Laurentic* or what we were doing out there. If they had we should not have lasted long. Submarines had been sighted and attacked close to our mooring buoys more than once while the *Volunteer* was absent. Perhaps they thought that she was the focus of some sort of trap and avoided her. They kept laying mines in the neighbourhood and two or three of our minesweepers whose Captains I used to play billiards with in the evenings were blown up with all hands.

Aside from worry over U-boats, the weather had stabilized and the fickle motorized air compressor had not broken down. In fact, Damant received an upgraded one from Siebe Gorman on June 16. Throughout that month, the divers removed debris and regularly found gold. But picking out the ingots one at a time from thousands and thousands of tons of debris made it apparent that the operation was going to last some time unless they discovered a concentrated hoard.

This was seemingly the case on June 20 after the *Volunteer* hoisted away a large piece of bulkhead. The divers discovered 220 gold ingots in the rubble and a large quantity of florins.** They found more in

---

* U-boat tactics during the First World War normally relied on single U-boat action instead of the famous wolf packs of the Second World War in which multiple submarines would assail a convoy in a coordinated attack.
** Coin worth two shillings.

Neutralized German sea mine taken on board a French minesweeper. © *Coll. Fr. Philips*

subsequent days, and on June 25 landed 265 gold bars. An assured Damant reported, "There is reason to believe that other large quantities are close at hand."

Damant's confidence was shaken, however, when he learned that Dusty Miller was to be reassigned. Miller had just been promoted from shipwright to carpenter. Because of this, he was to receive a new assignment. But Miller was the one who first brought up the gold boxes and the one who rediscovered the gold on May 22. To Damant, he was a good luck charm. Miller, despite being banged up from exploding mines and contracting the bends multiple times, was eager to carry on the work.

Damant penned a letter to the salvage section head, Captain Christopher Metcalfe, on July 4, writing of Miller, "By his energy, knowledge of ship construction, and power of identifying the different decks and bulkheads in their present shattered condition he has succeeded in finding gold more often than the other three divers combined." Damant pleaded, "It is very urgently desired to retain his services here if possible as the knowledge of the structures near the strong room which he has acquired during the gradual breaking up of the ship is invaluable and cannot be replaced. A newcomer would be hopelessly lost among the distorted and unrecognisable shapes of twisted beams and plating." Metcalfe passed on the request to Greatorex who made Damant's case to the second sea lord. Miller was allowed to stay on.

To motivate and reward the work, on July 14, 1917, Greatorex proposed that the salvage party should share a gratuity equaling one eighth of one percent of the value salvaged as incentive. Greatorex noted, "These operations require the greatest perseverance on the part of the divers ... , as the depth ... at which these men are diving is far greater than most commercial divers will attempt." The Treasury approved the plan, and it was to go into effect August 1.

By mid-July, Damant and his divers were picking the bones of the area where they had found the large gold cache. While there were still some gold bars scattered about the rubble, it was clear that the rest had dropped through more rents in the decks. Studying the plans of the *Laurentic*, Damant guessed that the gold may have fallen down through what was once the second-class dining saloon or owing to the way the ship rested on the ocean floor, slid deeper to port. Resolved, Damant began to open the wreck in both directions.

The seemingly infinite supply of debris continued to hamper them. "The stuff is small and has to be loaded into a hopper by hand and hoisted clear," reported Damant. "The wood is all broken up small and is waterlogged, and is mixed up with rivets, upholstering, fragments of sharp metal, and so on."

During this stage of the operation, Damant instilled a discipline among the divers so as to optimize work. No diver was allowed on the bottom for more than one hour so that divers could decompress in a relatively short forty-five minutes. Cases of the bends were limited, and those that did occur were quickly treated within the recompression chamber. Damant felt "confident that by patiently going on the present lines and lifting two to three tons of debris daily the bulk of the specie will come to light."

But few bars of gold were found. Deeper and deeper Damant and his divers delved into the *Laurentic.* At first, they excavated parts of the upper and main decks on the port side until they hit stone and shingle on the seafloor. It soon became apparent that the decks had actually slid off the wreck and were just lying on the sediment.

Repositioning the divers, Damant worked the men in the main body of the wreck. Deck plate after deck plate was hauled out. To hasten the process, Damant changed his choice of explosive from guncotton to gelignite. He had thought the guncotton charges were too bulky, prone to misfire underwater due to the strong water pressure, and inefficient—they did not produce the same explosive power at that depth as they did in shallower water. Gelignite was moldable, easily handled, and safer.

As the divers dug deep, the skeleton of the *Laurentic*'s fore and aft shot up like cliffs around them. The place where the gold had been stowed was in what was called a *well deck*—that is, it was lower than the decks fore and aft of it where the passenger accommodations were. And above loomed the *Laurentic*'s mainmast. Originally, it was an excellent landmark to determine where to excavate, but now it fouled the divers' lines and threatened to topple at any moment. Damant, who did not want to waste time dealing with parts of the wreck that did not have gold, ignored it as long as he dared. But it was proving to be too dangerous and at last he cut it off with explosives. It rolled onto the seafloor where it pointed at the area where the divers worked.

The *Laurentic* fought back against these new intrusions. In mid-August the towering superstructure around the pit of the working area had lost its stability. At last, two decks worth of plating slowly but irreversibly slid into the working area, covering three hundred square feet.

It took a couple of weeks for Damant and his men to get through the newly laid plates, and by September the divers were again picking up a few gold bars. Damant thought that they were making steady progress and would soon reach the main hoard. But even Damant, as determined as he was to raise the *Laurentic*'s gold, would have been justifiably distracted when a telegram arrived from Nell's sister.

He was now the father of a baby girl, Eleanor Brook. Damant could not anticipate when he would see her. Perhaps it would be several months, since he kept stressing to the Admiralty that it was important to continue the work until at least October before winter weather battered the wreck again and perhaps piled silt upon it.

But to Damant's surprise, the Admiralty sent new orders on September 2. Work was to be suspended. The *Volunteer* sailed for Queenstown where it unloaded its specialized diving equipment. The ship was reassigned for mooring work. Damant and his party had recovered 542 gold bars since first arriving at Lough Swilly. The estimated value of the gold in 1917 currency was £836,358.

Recognizing the labor put into the work, Greatorex recommended promoting Damant to acting commander. The Admiralty, for indeterminate reasons, did not promote him at this time but instead offered the Board of Admiralty's appreciation and gave him a £200 bounty in addition to a portion of the one-eighth percentage of the value of the gold, which in total was just over £992. Damant's share of this was £190. Damant was granted leave on September 19, 1917, and he returned to his home of Thursford in East Cowes where he met his new daughter, who was soon nicknamed *Baboo*. It was the first time he had slept in Thursford since the start of the war. He found it bright and spotless.

As happy as this time may have been, Damant was puzzled as to why the Admiralty had called off the operation. There were 2,669 ingots still embedded in the wreck. With persistence, he was sure he could recover almost all of them.

PART III

20

Schooling in Salvage

ONE DAY IN LATE SEPTEMBER 1917 Lieutenant Commander Guy Damant found himself at the famous Savoy Hotel in London for lunch. The luxury hotel attracted the most fashionable people, and its enormous restaurant was one of the finest in London. Damant's companion was impressive, too. Captain Frederick Young was soon to become the official head of the salvage section, and almost as a denouement to the adventures on and inside the *Laurentic*, he had invited Damant out for a meal. Young reveled in the opulence of the Savoy. They were surrounded by head waiters, managers, and stewards. One took Young's coat, another his hat, and a third his gloves and walking stick. Settling himself upon a plush seat, Young proceeded to order the most expensive food and wine on the menu.

Despite the scene, Damant could not help but feel disappointed, depressed even. The recent American entry into the war had mitigated the need for the *Laurentic*'s gold. The United States would now help back the credit of the Allies as well as keep up the steady source of matériel needed for the Western Front. The gold, while important, had to wait due to other pressing war needs—Damant's mission had been deferred. Damant was to return to gunnery duty.

Young listened to Damant's complaints and considered that the talented officer was in fact underserved teaching ballistics at HMS *Excellent*. Young said that he should join the salvage section on a more permanent basis. Following the lunch, Young exerted his influence

Sir Frederick Young. *Desmond Young, Ship Ashore: Adventures in Salvage (Jonathan Cape, 1932).*

at the Admiralty, and it was as good as done. Damant was therefore ordered on October 1, 1917, to report to the HMS *Vernon* for instruction. The *Vernon* was a facility at Portsmouth composed of several ship hulks dedicated to training and research for submarine warfare. Damant was to be fully familiarized about mines and submarines—essential elements in the recovery of sunken ships.

While Lieutenant Commander Damant had been diving upon the *Laurentic,* Britain was suffering unprecedented losses from Germany's U-boat campaign. From January to April 1917, the Central Powers had sunk 2,360,000 tons of Allied and neutral shipping. Ninety percent of the work had been done by U-boats. This figure must be compared to the total of four million tons sunk since the start of the war in 1914. In April 1917 alone, the Allies suffered their greatest shipping losses of the war: 869,103 tons carried by 373 ships. Of these ships, 354 had been sunk by U-boat action.

Historian Arthur J. Marder wrote, "The British had suffered serious mercantile losses earlier in the war. These had come mainly from enemy surface craft. But in 1915 and 1916 the submarine, which had been a fragile thing at the beginning of the war, had developed into a desperately dangerous instrument of destruction. It was evident as 1917 opened that the whole issue of the war would depend on the success or failure of the new unrestricted campaign."

First Sea Lord Jellicoe wrote that Germany's U-boat campaign was "the gravest peril which ever threatened the population of this country as well as of the whole Empire." This was not a hyperbolic statement. The Imperial German Navy was close to driving Britain out of the war.

Twenty-two German U-boats had been lost over the course of 1916, and another two in January 1917. Of these, four had sunk by accident and two by Russia. At best, the Royal Navy could hope to destroy only two U-boats per month. Meanwhile, Germany began its unrestricted campaign in 1917 with about 142 submarines and was producing more. While the U-boat campaign lasted, which was until the end of the war, the German navy averaged about forty-six U-boats at sea at any given time—targeting almost entirely British shipping.

From the start of the war the Admiralty had put its hopes in arming merchant ships, but this proved ineffective since after the unrestricted war began, U-boats were far more likely to attack submerged with their torpedoes rather than at the surface with mounted guns. The British tried using mines, but these often broke adrift from their sinkers and floated up to the surface. Moreover, they were not reliable. In 1917 it was estimated that only one third of British mines actually exploded. So desperate were the early months of 1917 for Britain that the Admiralty entertained all sorts of suggestions to fight the U-boats, including the use of sea lions to locate them.*

---

* The sea lions had been trained to listen underwater for different sounds, for which they would receive fish as reward. They were so successful that the animals

Germany's success came at a price, however. The United States was provoked into entering the war on the Allied side. In the meantime, the Admiralty slowly developed more effective antisubmarine measures. Better mines, developed by copying German models, resulted in a reliable mine known as the H2 that was available in quantity by September 1917. The British created vast underwater minefields so that by the end of the war it was estimated that the Royal Navy had laid 116,000 mines, not to mention another 56,000 laid by the other Allies.

In addition, guns designed to shoot munitions that would explode underwater were mounted on surface ships as well as the refinement of the depth charge, an explosive canister that detonated at a set depth. Hydrophones were further developed to listen for the sound of a submarine's propellers as it moved underwater. Indicator nets, which were nets connected to buoys, were produced *en masse*. When the buoys moved, it revealed a possible U-boat underwater.[*]

The Admiralty also debated one proposal which stuck in its craw—adopting a convoy system for merchant shipping in which ships traveled in groups protected by armed escorts. Convoys were used successfully during the Napoleonic Wars over a hundred years earlier, but by the time of the First World War convoy was viewed as an antiquated technique that was not applicable to modern naval warfare. Opponents argued that a convoy would allow the U-boats to find packs of targets; they asserted that merchant ship captains did not have the seamanship to sail in the tight formations that convoys required. Some said that there were not enough fighting ships to assign to escort convoys. But most of all they disliked the convoy system because it was seen as a defensive measure. The Royal Navy should be used to hunt and destroy the U-boats, not babysit convoys.

---

had become quite fat. However, when tested in the open waters of the Solent, the animals could not tell the difference between the noise made by a surface ship versus the sound made by a U-boat's propellers. Also, the animals apparently found enough fish in the Solent to satisfy themselves without needing to overexert seeking out propeller noises. The experiments were abandoned.

* These indicator nets were often studded by mines since U-boats had net cutters that made the net in of itself rather useless.

Jellicoe, who had been appointed first sea lord mainly to address the U-boat threat, had developed an antisubmarine division at the Admiralty. While not absolutely opposed to convoy, he was slow to adopt it, and then it was done haltingly. But the effects were obvious. Ships that traveled in convoy were far more likely to reach their destinations than those that traveled alone. The future head of the German Navy during the Second World War, Karl Dönitz, was a U-boat commander in 1918. Writing of the impact of the convoy:

> The oceans at once became bare and empty; for long periods at a time the U-boats, operating individually, would see nothing at all; and then suddenly up would loom a huge concourse of ship, thirty or fifty or more of them, surrounded by a strong escort of warships of all types.... The lone U-boat might well sink one or two of the ships, or even several; but that was a poor percentage of the whole.

Because Britain was slow to adopt convoys, the measure at first was merely a bandage on the mounting losses. In addition, merchant ships were not required to sail in convoy so there were still plenty of targets for the U-boats. Even after the adoption of convoy, nearly two hundred thousand tons of British shipping was sunk in September 1917, which grew to 276,000 tons in October. Even in the final phases of the war, there was continued anxiety over the U-boats, leading First Lord of the Admiralty Sir Eric Geddes to write, "I am getting very concerned, as are we all, at the reduction in killing power of our anti-submarine methods." In fact, the Admiralty anticipated a new great U-boat offensive. By no means was the U-boat war won, and the Admiralty expected greater shipping losses. Since vessels were being sunk at a greater rate than they could be replaced, the country needed men who could recover these ships and cargoes. Damant was a perfect choice because of his diving expertise.

• • •

Oberleutnant Reinhold Saltzwedel had a hawkish look about him that reflected the predatory nature of a U-boat ace. He had been in command of five different U-boats of the coastal classes, the UB and UC groups. In these, he had wreaked havoc upon the enemy, sinking 111 ships racking up a total of 172,824 gross tons of cargo sunk. Certainly Saltzwedel was proud of his accomplishment, and so too was the German Empire, decorating him with the second- and first-class Iron Cross, entering him into the Royal House Order of Hohenzollern, and bestowing him the highest honor in the German Empire, the Pour le Mérite, known informally as the "Blue Max" owing to the color of the award's cross.

On December 2, 1917, Saltzwedel commanded the *UB-81*. This was a third-generation coastal attack craft that had already achieved success in sinking the *Molesey*, a 3,218-ton steamer that was carrying a cargo of phosphate. Saltzwedel and the thirty-five men under him were now at depth, stalking the sea traffic that passed south of the Isle of Wight. As he looked through his periscope for a new target, he could see St. Catherine's Lighthouse to the north.

While each class of U-boat varied in size and purpose, their layouts were generally similar. A standard U-boat of the German navy during the First World War was composed of a series of compartments that were separated by watertight bulkhead doors. At the surface, these doors would be open, allowing an observer to see the entire length of the vessel in either direction. Most forward in the boat was the torpedo room, which was the business end of the submarine. Here, men would load torpedoes into one of up to four tubes. The standard torpedoes aboard a U-boat ranged up to almost twenty feet in length and weighed over a ton each.

The next compartment aft was the battery room. This compartment was divided into an upper and lower half, with the lower half filled with massive lead-acid accumulators, battery cells that provided electrical power to the boat while it was submerged. When surfaced, these cells were recharged by generators attached to diesel engines located farther aft. A walking deck separated these cells from the upper half of the compartment, which contained berthing and messing compartments for the officers and crew.

Aft of the battery room was the control room. This compartment contained the controls necessary for steering, diving, surfacing, and adjusting ballast. Also, here could be found the chart table and everything needed to safely navigate. Adjacent to the control room was a small radio room used to send and receive operational orders while surfaced. Directly above the control room was the conning tower, a separate watertight compartment that housed the boat's periscopes and equipment for aiming torpedoes. Here a man could be stationed when surfaced and pass information and orders below.

Aft of the control room was the engine room, which contained the diesel engines used to drive the boat on the surface. The crankshafts of these engines were connected to a combination electric generator and motor in the next compartment aft, called the motor room. These generators were used alternately to charge the batteries after a long run submerged and to provide propulsion via electricity provided by the batteries up forward. A series of clutches on each shaft allowed the crew to line up propulsion or battery charging as needed. At the very aft end of the motor room was a single torpedo tube, which enabled attacks in both directions.

German U-boats were at the cutting edge of naval technology during the First World War, being highly effective and dangerous to not just their victims but also their crews. Even as Oberleutnant Saltzwedel stalked ships south of St. Catherine's Lighthouse, there was a sudden explosion in the *UB-81*'s stern, followed by a cascade of water. His U-boat had struck a mine.

The crew rushed forward, abandoning the rapidly flooding engine and motor rooms, sealing them off with the watertight doors and by shutting isolation valves. They gathered in the control room with Saltzwedel, and he used the remaining high pressure air in the banks to blow the forward ballast tanks. This brought the submarine's bow up so that it lay at a 53-degree angle in almost 92 feet of water. Since the length of the boat was 183 feet, this had the effect of bringing the bow to the surface. The men removed the torpedoes from the tubes and three of them climbed out to attach tackle in order to haul other men out. Seven more were lifted up but three retreated back into the submarine since the weather was bitterly cold. The others, chancing it, stayed on the surface, and shot signal flares and flashed searchlights knowing full well only the British could rescue them.

Six hours later, the sea had picked up and the wind raged. The men on the bow of the *UB-81* stood their miserable vigil wet and shivering. The rest of the men were now huddled into the torpedo room. Then a vessel came into view. It was a British patrol boat, the *P32*. It chugged along in the rough sea dead ahead at the *UB-81*, seemingly oblivious to the U-boat's existence.

Closer and closer it came. Then with a great crash the *P32* plowed right into the U-boat's bow. The men who were outside the U-boat splashed into the cold sea. They were the lucky ones, since the submarine's torpedo tubes were open and water quickly flooded the vessel. Only six survived the collision. Saltzwedel was not one of them. The crew of the *P32* claimed the collision was an accident on account of the rough weather, but some of the German survivors thought otherwise.

A few days later, the Royal Navy found the wreck and marked the site with twenty-five-gallon oil can buoys.

· · ·

Lieutenant Commander Damant, having finished training at the *Vernon*, was first ordered to survey and report on various shipwrecks around the coast before he was directed to raise the *UB-81*. If he could do it, then it would be a boon to the Royal Navy since it would give invaluable information on German equipment and weapon design. Furthermore, if the job could be done quickly, the documents inside the U-boat could be useful for Naval Intelligence. To Damant, it was a new and exciting kind of mission.

The prospects of raising the U-boat were daunting—the wreck was in open water with a strong tide, and being December, it would mean work under harsh and frigid conditions. What made matters worse was that because it was a secret mission in a heavily traveled shipping lane, Damant was prohibited from remaining on the spot after dark or laying permanent mooring buoys. He wanted to have a team of men he knew and trusted. He could think of none better but those who had worked with him so reliably on the *Laurentic*. Specifically, Damant got George Clear and Edwin Blachford assigned to him, and also possibly Dusty Miller.

The initial plan was to pull two nine-inch sweeping wires under the U-boat's hull, and divers would ensure that they were positioned correctly. These would be pinned by the divers to the wreck. The wires would then be attached to winches on salvage ships at the surface that would raise the vessel. From there, it would be easy enough to tow the boat to the deep dock at Portsmouth where it could be fully ransacked and studied. The risk to this proposition was that the boat would sink during transit to Portsmouth—Damant had considered beaching the vessel on the nearby Isle of Wight to at least do temporary repairs, but in the end he felt it would compromise the secretive nature of the operation.

But problems occurred before this eventuality. It was often too stormy to get to the wreck site. Then on those days that Damant could get to and work on the U-boat, he found that the sweepers had trouble getting lifting wires beneath it. While Damant and his men had great experience working inside wrecks, they knew little about actually raising an entire vessel. Damant decided it would be best if he requested some help from Captain Young. Young sent Lieutenant George Davis, another salvage officer who was much more experienced in recovering vessels, and in October had directed the lifting of another U-boat, the *U-44*, thus winning valuable materials for the Naval Intelligence Department.

Davis arrived on December 16, but bad weather hampered all operations. When divers could descend they wore extra layers of clothing, but the ambient frigidity of the sea still sucked the heat out of their bodies despite these efforts. By early January, Damant and Davis were only able to get one lifting wire beneath the *UB-81*. Then there were the marker buoys. These would get constantly ripped from the wreck from the conditions or cut by the busy shipping traffic through the English Channel.

If there was one positive element to the adventure it was that Damant had moved his base of operations from Portsmouth to Sandown Bay on the Isle of Wight. On December 24, 1917, inclement weather prevented any productivity, and he snuck away and bicycled home for Christmas. He spent the holiday with Nell and Baboo over a dinner of roast pork. They headed to Nell's mother's house for tea where all the family's babies were assembled. Baboo did not like the crowd, and her cries led to a general cacophony of baby screams. Damant, loading his bicycle with apples and cakes, retreated back to his duty in the dark.

The repeated problems prolonged the job so much that on January 21, 1918, Davis was detached from Damant to work on another wreck. Finally on January 25, after a spell of rough weather, Damant returned to the site to find that the marker buoys had torn away once again. Damant had the tugs under his command sweep the area repeatedly to find the wreck. It is hard enough to find a surface vessel wrecked on the bottom, but U-boats are notoriously difficult to locate since they were built in a smooth shape in order to make them hydrodynamic. This had the side effect of making it difficult to hook them with sweeping wire. As January ended and February began, Damant still could not locate the *UB-81*, although they did find another U-boat wreck. Old and of little value, they left the submarine where it lay.

At last, on February 5, the Admiralty admitted defeat. Rear Admiral Edward Phillpotts, the director of naval equipment who had replaced Greatorex in October, called off the salvage. Citing the weather, Phillpotts thought Damant, the twenty men under him, and the two lifting vessels on standby would better serve the Admiralty on other jobs. The *UB-81* still lies at the bottom of the English Channel as of this writing.

So Damant's U-boat salvage expedition was a failure. However, there were two lessons to be learned. First, salvage as a whole took too long for military purposes since as time passed, the knowledge of new U-boat design became less valuable. Also, from an intelligence point of view, whatever documents that might be acquired from a U-boat by direct salvage would be at best historical artifacts by the time it was raised. Second, it was difficult to keep such operations secret. Even the smallest U-boats were almost one hundred feet long, and if they needed to be beached, camouflage could only do so much.

Even as these obvious problems were mulled over by the Admiralty, Damant was sent to look for other U-boats. He explored possible cases in March 1918, but Damant found that the wrecks were either not in a salvageable condition or the sea surrounding the wrecks made recovery impractical.

• • •

Aside from seeking U-boats, Damant was also assigned to salvage lost ships. His first major job was to recover the liner *Comrie Castle*, a 5,167-ton troopship that had been torpedoed in the English Channel on March 14, 1918.

He arrived soon after the sinking and interviewed the captain. Damant noticed that the captain constantly trembled. After speaking with Damant for a while, he excused himself to his cabin, ostensibly to compose himself. Ten minutes later, he stumbled out, his face covered in blood. Damant jumped toward him, but the captain, supporting himself against the door with one hand and stroking his bloodied cheeks with the other, said, "That's better. I always feel fresher after a nice shave."

Damant's task was to raise the *Comrie Castle* by patching the damaged areas and pumping the holds free of water so that it could be raised, towed, and beached for full repair. This was the kind of straightforward salvaging work that Captain Frederick Young's core of officers had been doing throughout the war.

But the pumps he used to clear the holds could not bring the water down, nor could he find the leak in the bulkheads. What made matters stranger, if not more dangerous, was that the *Comrie Castle* had an apparatus that used phosphorus in order to generate a smoke screen. The chemical had broken loose after the torpedo strike and sloshed all over the deck, spraying everything, including clothing. It seemed harmless until it dried, when the phosphorus would spontaneously combust, especially if brushed.

After about four days on the job, Damant fell thirty feet through a hatch into the water-filled hold below. Damant recalled, "On each of the two lower decks through which I fell, men were working close to the hatch aperture. I remember seeing their startled faces and rigid attitudes as I whizzed past. The mate carried me up the vertical ladder across his shoulders." Luckily, Damant had no serious injuries, but he took a couple of days to recover. Commander G. J. Wheeler, an experienced salvage officer, took over and successfully raised the vessel. Damant wrote, "I don't think that I should have succeeded, being too ignorant of such work."

● ● ●

At midnight on March 24, 1918, sixteen ships in eight columns proceeded in darkness through the English Channel. About them was an
escort of six British destroyers while the captain of the convoy sloop
Syringa, one mile ahead, shepherded the formation to keep the ships
from blundering into one another as they conducted zigzag maneuvers. All was dark except for some navigation lights. The only obvious
illumination came from the St. Catherine's Lighthouse on the Isle of
Wight some twelve miles distant to the east-northeast.

One of the convoy ships was the *O. B. Jennings*, an American tanker
of over ten thousand tons owned by the Standard Oil Company. The
ship was weighed down to its maximum with a valuable cargo of not
just oil but also highly flammable naphtha.

At half past midnight the captain of the *Syringa*, on the bridge,
observed a flash of light on the starboard bow. This was followed
by two more flashes. He judged that the light was perhaps twelve
miles off. All things considered, he suspected a ship may have been
torpedoed. He gave this slow thought, and at 1:15 AM, directed a
course change to the convoy to head north-northeast to take effect
at 2:15.

Orders were signaled out, but not all ships received the message.
As a result, some made the course change while others did not. The
convoy became divided into two groups, with the *O. B. Jennings* being
one of the ships to maintain the original course and others, such as
the oil tanker *War Knight*, following the new heading.

The captain of the *Syringa* saw what happened, immediately per-
ceived the danger, and tried to correct it. But in the confusion the
O. B. Jennings cut across the bow of the *War Knight*. The *War Knight*
slammed into the *O. B. Jennings* abreast of the bridge on the starboard side.

This was where the naphtha was stowed.

A tremendous fireball lit the sea and leaped from the *O. B.*
Jennings to the *War Knight*. The *War Knight*'s deck was seared and
thirty-six men were incinerated. Burning, some of them managed to
fling themselves into the sea. But the sea had become a hell of fire
and water since the fireballs soared into the sky and fell into the
ocean, setting everything ablaze. The *War Knight* stopped dead in

the water burning and burning while the *O. B. Jennings* limped on in a circle to port.

Most of the crew of the *O. B. Jennings* were not near the explosion and were able to escape to the lifeboats. In the meantime, destroyers dashed through the flames and picked up badly burned survivors who would not dare launch a lifeboat into the burning sea. One intrepid sailor leaped from a destroyer aboard the *War Knight* to enable the ship to be taken in tow.

Slowly, the *War Knight* was towed away in the hopes that somehow they could extinguish the flames and preserve its valuable cargo. But then the ship struck a mine. The *War Knight* was hauled into shallower waters where it would at last sink, unsalvageable.

Meanwhile, the *O. B. Jennings* burned even as the rescue tug *Seahorse* latched onto it. The smoldering ship was towed into Sandown Bay on the Isle of Wight. The Admiralty called for the salvage section and Young sent in Damant who arrived on March 26 to assist Commander Herbert Malet in the work. They stayed aboard the salvage ship *Linnet* while they waited for the fires to die.

But two days after the collision, the *O. B. Jennings* was still on fire. Oil leaked from the ship and coated the beaches of Sandown Bay. Finally, when the flames seemed to have mostly subsided, Damant went aboard the vessel and walked the hot decks. His boots burned as he and his men used fire buckets to put out the remaining flames.

Damant returned to the *Linnet,* pleased at the good work he had done. He went to his bunk and fell asleep. Then at one in the morning a huge explosion nearly knocked him out of his bunk. The *O. B. Jennings* had become a mass of flames—worse than before. "Pitch black, greasy smoke drifted across the Island for a week or more," wrote Damant. "The watchers of Cowes smelt its smell. Can you imagine the filth one had to work in, in a flooded oil tanker? Every deck was inches deep in black slippery fuel oil. As the tide rose this was lifted till it coated the underside of the deck above, and all the bulkheads and stanchions, from which it dripped like treacle on ones head."

This treacle dripped all over Damant as he worked on the wreck and ruined his coat, trousers, and cap. Even more disturbing were the seemingly random explosions that rumbled throughout the ship. More days elapsed with no end in sight to the fires. After burning for ten days and seeing no other recourse Malet asked a torpedo boat to partially sink the vessel with its guns.

This worked and after another four days the fires were under control. The salvage team connected pumps to the undamaged tanks in the after portion of the ship and withdrew eight thousand tons of naphtha from the vessel. The holes in the ship were patched, the ship pumped, refloated, and then given permanent repairs. Damant stayed with the operations until April 20, and eventually the *O. B. Jennings* was made ready to return to the United States. Malet and Damant were commended by the Admiralty for "an excellent piece of salvage work."* Damant put in a reimbursement to the Admiralty for just over six pounds sterling for his ruined clothes.

---

* It was on this voyage home that the *O. B. Jennings* was permanently sunk by a U-boat.

21

Codes and Ciphers

THE BRITISH GOVERNMENT, PARTICULARLY PRIME Minister Lloyd George, was growing tired of First Sea Lord Sir John Jellicoe. His reluctance to implement a convoy system and the lingering distaste of not winning an obvious and outright victory at Jutland resulted in his surprise dismissal on Christmas Eve, 1917. His deputy, Vice Admiral Sir Rosslyn "Rosy" Wemyss, then became first sea lord.

With what contemporaries described as a "fighting face with a monocle set in it," Wemyss turned out to be one of the most popular senior officers in the Royal Navy. Charming, aristocratic, courteous, and tactful, Wemyss was a great storyteller, but he was also a very capable administrator. Unlike Jellicoe, he was a decentralizer who gave greater liberty to the various divisions of the Royal Navy to do their jobs. He embraced the convoy strategy, and also backed the expansion of the British Naval Intelligence Department to fight the U-boats.

British Naval Intelligence during the First World War was considered a model to other covert services. Originally, there was a Naval Intelligence Division but also a separate secret cryptology branch known as Room 40, so called for the space in the Old Admiralty Building it occupied and grew out from.

Room 40 was started as an almost amateurish operation when the Admiralty sought the assistance of the director of naval education, Sir

Alfred Ewing, in an attempt to crack German codes. Ewing, who had an interest in puzzles, quickly realized that the intensely complex German codes and ciphers were out of his depth. He enlisted academics such as historians and linguists to work on the codes and ciphers. At the same time, British intelligence of German transmissions grew apace with the expansion of wireless telegraph interception operations. The Germans were seemingly unaware of, or at best unconcerned, that almost all of their messages—naval, diplomatic, consular, and commercial—were being intercepted by the British. Perhaps the Germans were confident in the codes and ciphers they used to mask the content of the messages—but they did not know about Room 40.

The code breakers of Room 40 first had to learn the difference between a *code* and a *cipher*. A message sent in code requires a codebook that both the sender and receiver possess which is used to translate the message. This acts as a lexicon that includes words, numbers, dates, and phrases which has its corresponding code opposite it. A codebook was divided in half, the first half alphabetized by the plain word or phrase that the sender wanted to transmit, called *en clair*, and the other half sorted by code so that the recipient could decode the message. For example, Germany used a three-letter code, O-D-I to represent *Musterung auf der Gefechsstation*—muster at battle stations.

In contrast, a cipher transposes or substitutes a letter or number for another in a systematic way. For highly secretive messages, a coded message would be ciphered, sometimes more than once. The receiver of the message would have to first decipher the message using a key, which would give the message in code. Then the receiver consulted a codebook to find the meaning of the communication. For example, the code O-D-I might be ciphered to 3-F-7 where the O is represented by 3, D by F, and so on. Ciphers could be quite complicated with multiple symbols or letters standing for a single letter or symbol.

Room 40 was aided by the acquisition of three important German codebooks in 1914. There was the *Signalbuch der Kaiserlichen Marine* after the Russians captured the German cruiser *Magdeburg*, the *Handelsverkehrsbuch* taken from the *Hobart*, and the *Verkehrsbuch*. These codes were not only used by the German Imperial Navy but also by merchant shipping and diplomatic attachés. While it is true that the Germans did cipher their codes, early in the war they changed the codebooks infrequently. The *Signalbuch der Kaiserlichen Marine*, the most secret of the codebooks, for example, remained in force until May 1917. In addition, German use of codes was sloppy and haphazard with them often announcing on wireless (picked up by British intercepts) that the cipher keys were changing. When a ship did not possess the new key, the captain sometimes sent a message requesting that the transmission be sent in the old cipher. By comparing old ciphers to new ciphers with the same message, it made the process of cracking them easy for Room 40.

In May 1917, Naval Intelligence took over the management of Room 40. The director of the division was Rear Admiral William Reginald Hall. Charming and magnetic, he had two penetrating eyes that reminded one writer of a peregrine falcon. One of those eyes would flash from time to time due to a facial twitch. He was nicknamed "Blinker" as a result, but to friends he was merely Reggie.

Hall had a successful career until the start of the war when declining health forced him ashore. There, a retirement would have

Admiral Sir William Reginald "Blinker" Hall (1870–1943), 1917. © *National Portrait Gallery, London*

waited others, but he was chosen to become the Director of the
Naval Intelligence Division. As a line officer, Hall was known to care
deeply for the welfare of his men, and those who served under him
in the Intelligence Division were quite loyal to him. Still, Hall was also
quite ruthless, and he proved to be remarkably adept at espionage.
He was not above any skullduggery and took delight in the use of
double agents, disinformation, bribery, and blackmail. An American
attaché described Hall as "a perfectly marvelous person but the coldest-hearted proposition that ever was—he'd eat a man's heart and
hand it back to him." One story that Hall often related involved a
justice who had given a light sentence to a German spy whom Hall
helped catch. The judge gave the lenient sentence on the grounds
that the spy was merely passing on information as to the location of
factories in Great Britain which were *not targets of military importance.*
Hall was so outraged that he sent a report back to Germany in the
spy's name giving the location of the judge's country house as the
site of one of those factories. Later, the judge found himself at a
dinner with Hall and lamented that his house had been bombed by
German Zeppelins. He barely escaped with his life.

Hall said, "Well, it was not a target of any military importance,
was it?"

This anecdote, which was collected by Room 40 historian Patrick
Beesly, was probably apocryphal, but Beesly was quick to point out
how revealing it was that Hall himself was fond of telling the story.

Even though Hall did not control Room 40 at the beginning of the
war, since it was a separate organization, he was privy to much of its
collected information. The Admiralty was aware, in virtually real time,
of the movement of Germany's High Seas Fleet as well as the coded
messages that German diplomats would transmit overseas. Room 40
was able, for example, to warn the Admiralty of the movement of
the German fleet precipitating the Battle of Jutland. However, even
though this basic information was given to the Admiralty, many of
the highest ranking officers distrusted Room 40 and would often not
accept the code breakers' interpretation of it. This was due to the
prejudice of Royal Navy professionals against the code breakers, who
were mostly of civilian stock. As a result, the information given to

Admiral Jellicoe by Room 40 during Jutland was neither fully trusted nor used. In consequence, Jutland was a tactical victory for the Royal Navy but not the great war-changing triumph that the British craved.

Likewise, sometimes the information given by Room 40 to the Admiralty was purposefully *not* used. Patrick Beesly contended that the Admiralty knew of dangers being posed to shipping due to the first wave of unrestricted submarine warfare in 1915. He argued that the British government, who knew of the movements of U-boats via Room 40's intelligence, did nothing to save the *Lusitania*, which had been targeted as a ship carrying munitions to Britain. The *Lusitania* had Americans aboard and Beesly contended that the Admiralty purposefully neglected to impart important information to the ship since they were trying to bring America into the war on the Allied side, implicating First Lord Winston Churchill. The fury over the sinking of the ship nearly did bring the United States into the war, but Germany changed their policy of unrestricted submarine warfare at that time and postponed American entry. There is little reason to doubt Beesly, who had a long career in naval intelligence and thoroughly examined the documents at the British Archive.

A major impetus to the American entry into the war was another Room 40 *coup*, a decode of a January 1917 telegram from Arthur Zimmermann, the German foreign minister, to his ambassador in Mexico. The telegram instructed the ambassador to inform the Mexican president that Germany was going to resume unrestricted submarine warfare and would try to keep the United States neutral. However, if the United States declared war on Germany, they offered Mexico an alliance in which they promised to help restore lands that had been ceded to the United States at the conclusion of the Mexican-American War in 1848.

After Blinker Hall saw the message, he was delighted and managed to publicize the information without compromising Room 40's secrecy. Even better, Zimmermann publicly acknowledged the truth of the telegram. The telegram sparked outrage in the United States which, in conjunction with the renewal of unrestricted submarine warfare, led the United States to declare war on Germany on April 6, 1917. After Blinker Hall was given full control over Room 40, the operation as a whole became more efficient, with Hall's network of spies in the Naval Intelligence Division feeding information to the code breakers.

Another important development was the appointment of Rear Admiral Roger Keyes, the Royal Navy's Director of Plans, to the command of the Dover Patrol on January 1, 1918. Naval historian Arthur J. Marder summed up Keyes as "one of the most attractive of men, warm-hearted and full of boyish enthusiasm—a born leader with few brains." But even Keyes, who admitted he had a "thick head," also declared, "I do believe I have the knack of getting the right people about me and making good use of them." Keyes was one of the more dashing naval figures of the First World War. In April 1918, he was tasked to execute a plan first concocted by Jellicoe to block up the German U-boat bases in Belgium. The submarine bases at Zeebrugge, Ostend, and Bruges in Belgium, were connected by two canals. Keyes was to take several aging cruisers whose holds were filled with concrete and scuttle them across the canals' entrances. This Keyes did in two bloody actions after which eight Victoria Crosses (the most eminent award given for gallantry in combat) were awarded as a part of two hundred total medals. However, the plan did not work since the ships were scuttled in the wrong places or only partially blocked the entrances. The U-boats remained active although the Admiralty trilled about the thrilling victory, comparing Keyes to Lord Horatio Nelson. Even though Keyes got more publicity for the raids, he served the purposes of the war more concretely by intensifying the antisubmarine defenses across the English Channel.

The Strait of Dover was considered to be the most critical sea passage in the British Isles. For U-boats it was far more efficient to cut through the English Channel rather than take a 1,400-mile round trip around Scotland to access the shipping lanes in the Irish Sea and the western approaches. Because of the critical nature of the passage, a separate command, known as the Dover Patrol, was created specifically to guard the strait. In order to bar passage to the U-boats, the Royal Navy laid the Dover Barrage, a vast minefield. To further control the Channel, patrol craft monitored the waters and minesweepers cleared away German countermines. But for the first few years of the war, this proved ineffective as the U-boats passed relatively unscathed.

Then Keyes took over. In 1918, he introduced massed patrols and lit up the waterways between the narrows of Folkestone and Cap Gris Nez using searchlights and flares. The purpose was to force U-boats to travel submerged through the waterway and thus into deepwater mines which were technically more effective than their predecessors. In addition, in 1918 the United States began to lay its own "Northern Barrage" of mines along the North Sea from the Orkney Islands to Scandinavia in order to further contain German U-boats. These measures proved to be effective enough, coupled with a decrease in German U-boat construction, so that by 1918 there was a net reduction in the number of U-boats in the German fleet.[*]

In early 1918, the needs of Blinker Hall's intelligence operation and Keyes's successes in sinking the U-boat coalesced. Hall had worked throughout the war to make an efficient intelligence gathering operation, especially in regard to the movements of U-boats. Without this knowledge it was impossible to plan any antisubmarine campaign. Information was harvested from a number of sources, including tracking U-boats's wireless signals, deciphering, secret agents, surveying German dockyards, reports of sightings, and interrogating prisoners. Hall even sent men to search German corpses found on downed Zeppelins. Now Hall had something else in mind.

Lieutenant Commander Guy Damant was called to London for an interview with Admiral Hall. Hall explained to Damant that he had relied on an agent in Berlin to smuggle copies of the German cipher keys to his code breakers. However, there had been no word from him for some time, and Hall feared that he had been caught. The spy, who may have been an office janitor, was undiscerning and extremely brave. He walked into German naval staff rooms and pocketed anything important, and sometimes even unimportant. Once he sent a package to the Admiralty containing an Admiral's fur gloves, a cinema program, and his wife's ration books.

Even without the cipher keys, Room 40 was still able to figure out the German codes, but it prolonged the process because Germany

---

[*] The German Admiralty had such confidence in their U-boats that they purposely delayed orders for construction of new submarines. This was a costly mistake.

had tightened up its intelligence and was changing ciphers every few weeks. Good and relevant intelligence was critical since the end of the war was still in doubt. On March 3, 1918, Germany signed a final peace treaty with the newly formed Soviet Russia at Brest-Litovsk which was quite favorable to Germany. This freed up German forces on its eastern border, which the kaiser turned toward the Western Front in France for a spring offensive in which they hoped to quickly defeat the Allies before the United States could fully deploy troops to Europe. All early signs showed this new offensive was quite successful.

Hall explained to Damant that he needed a new source of intelligence, in particular a way to obtain the cipher keys. Knowing about all the fresh U-boats littering the English Channel owing to efforts of the Dover Patrol, Hall realized that materials he wanted were *inside* the U-boats. If divers could swiftly obtain these documents, that would assist the entire intelligence network and thus win the war.

Damant knew that diving had been done to investigate U-boat wrecks since at least 1915, with civilian and Royal Navy divers even going so far as sketching wrecks. However, nothing worthwhile was obtained until May 16, 1916, when the *UC-5* was salvaged whole by Captain Frederick Young of the Salvage Section. The U-boat had run aground and was beached near a Harwich pier. Although most of the material aboard the U-boat was already destroyed by the Germans, what remained proved valuable to Naval Intelligence. Damant understood, remembering full well when in March 1917, held back from work on the *Laurentic* by the gales about Lough Swilly, he had helped obtain a torpedo and a "Machinery History" from the *UC-32*. Then that summer and into mid-October, Lieutenant George Davis raised the *UC-44*, thus providing more important materials to the Admiralty.

Hall had already sent a proposal to the director of naval equipment, Rear Admiral Phillpotts: form a secret diving squad that would be solely responsible for working on U-boat wrecks with the objective of recovering intelligence *inside* the wreck while it was submerged. Two officers and four divers would suffice for this "special service." The team could be based centrally and given training on U-boat construction, torpedoes, and mines. The squad could then be sent out on short notice to wreck sites where an Intelligence Division liaison would give the squad as much information they had on the specific U-boat. This would allow the divers to work with "speed and knowledge."

Phillpotts agreed, and recommended Damant and Miller to head up the effort with Damant in general charge. Their work in the tight interiors of the *Laurentic* at great depth made them the obvious choices. Without the distraction of being called away to other salvage operations like the *O. B. Jennings*, Blinker Hall anticipated great success. The whole plan was approved by First Sea Lord Rosslyn Wemyss.

Admiral Hall stressed the urgency of the work to Damant. They needed to get inside freshly sunk U-boats, outward bound if possible since homeward bound U-boats would have ciphers that were about to expire. A ship would be put at Damant's disposal, and he could use his *Laurentic* divers.

Damant was eager. "This was an exciting job and right in my line of experience and one in which I would have the help of men whom I had trained and knew."

22

The U-Boat Hunter

GUY DAMANT SET UP HIS HEADQUARTERS in Portsmouth, and with Miller assembled a team of *Laurentic* veterans including George Clear and Edwin Blachford. There were new additions such as Petty Officer Albert Balson and Leading Seaman Percy Frater. Partially in acknowledgment for Damant's past services and of his new responsibilities, Damant was promoted to the rank of acting commander and made a full salvage officer.

For this work, Damant was given the *Moonfleet.* The steel tug, at one hundred feet in length and 145 tons, was originally built as a fire ship. The engine room had enormous fire pumps and there were water guns on the deck. For Damant's purposes the water guns had no value, but the ship was fast and handy. It was also tiny—there was no place for the officers and men to berth so they would necessarily have to lodge ashore. Also, the *Moonfleet* was too small to hold a recompression chamber. Damant would have to rely on Haldane's decompression tables and experience to safely bring divers back from the bottom.

Damant's first case was to investigate a U-boat he had surveyed before being called away to the *O. B. Jennings.* When he and his men returned to the wreck site in April, he found that the marking buoys had disappeared. After a lengthy search they located the wreck, and

Miller reconnoitered the site. His report was not encouraging. Due to the U-boat's position, its general location in a busy sea lane, and adverse sea conditions, it was not practical to salvage the wreck. As for getting inside, this too was impossible since the hatches were too small for divers in their bulky gear. Lieutenant George Davis, who had worked with Damant on the failed attempt to raise the *UB-81* the past winter and was present, pronounced the situation impossible.

But Damant sensed an opportunity that was only possible because of his work on the *Laurentic*: "An alternative to diving in these cases would be to open up the wreck by explosives and try to secure material by diving." But Damant was called off this job to hunt fresher wrecks.

Damant explored cases that he termed "mare's nests." In many instances, British antisubmarine forces would report a sunken U-boat—especially when they saw wreckage float and oil bubble to the surface. But in some cases the Germans would discharge oil and prepacked wreckage through the torpedo tubes on purpose. The Royal Navy would thus assume that the U-boat was destroyed and launch no further attack. The U-boat would then escape. In order to confirm a sinking, the local senior naval officer would send minesweepers to find the wreck. These would drag the bottom until they caught some obstruction. Then they would send hurried word to the Admiralty that they found a U-boat. Damant and his men would be dispatched as soon as they were available.

Damant received new orders to report to Dover. The *Ocean Roamer* had seen an explosion near the Varne watch buoy. When the ship arrived, oil and wood were floating on the surface. Although the location was not in one of the British minefields, it was obvious something suspicious had happened. Sweepers were called in and located an object underwater. Divers went down. It was a recent U-boat wreck.

Damant arrived aboard the *Moonfleet* on the evening of May 20, 1918. The next day, he went to the wreck on a diving boat with Commander Cooper from the Naval Intelligence Division as well as his divers. As the little boat made its way out to the site, Damant could see a lightship to the west-northwest. This warned vessels off from the Varne shoal, an almost six-mile-long sandbank along the Strait of Dover that was a danger to vessels. Damant found that the buoys left by the sweepers were in place. A simple measurement of the lead line spoke of fourteen fathoms at low water with a sandy bottom. Visibility underwater was good.

Damant sent Miller down. The diver clambered over the side ladder and into the water. In moments, he had located the wreck lying among long weeds at the bottom of the channel. It was one of the coastal attack submarines, a second-generation UB type.

Miller surveyed its periscopes, one abaft and one before the conning tower. The boat rested on her starboard beam ends, and she was listed such that the port diving planes, both fore and aft, were buried in the sand. On the bow, there were painted eyes. This was a symbol of good luck, but to a British diver working on this kind of assignment it may as well have been the eye of the devil. It was taken to mean, "I see and conquer." Protruding from the wreckage was a human arm.

Going about the wreck, Miller secured mooring wires to the boat's stem and stern. There was no number that he could find painted on it that could identify the vessel. It had been seriously

UB-class U-boats were small coastal attack crafts. The boat in this photograph is the *UB-10*, a UB type I design. Note the painted eyes on the bow of the vessel. *Courtesy of Tomas Termote*

damaged aft on the port side. The outer plating was driven in, forming a long and ugly gash, fifteen feet long and twelve feet wide, which flattened out toward the boat's rear. But there was no clue as to what happened to the U-boat until Miller sighted a spherical object lying next to the submarine. One of its five horns was so bent that it was doubled over. On it there was branded a number, 832. It was a British mine.

Apparently, the U-boat had been cruising at depth and, unbeknownst to its captain, had run afoul of mooring wires from a couple of British mines. The submarine towed the mines a good distance away from its original minefield as its screws reeled in the tethering cables. Closer and closer the mines were drawn in until at last one struck the U-boat's stern. The resulting explosion immediately destroyed the U-boat and brought it to the bottom. The second mine, while damaged, was unexploded and intact.

Miller noticed the hatch on the conning tower was partially open.

He accepted the easy invitation. Miller opened the hatch fully and squeezed his legs in. He could get no farther. There was no way he could squeeze the rest of the way down in his diving gear. As he fumbled in the dark of the conning tower his legs bumped into something.

It was a body—perhaps two.

Miller could only have been expecting this—certainly the entire crew of the U-boat was dead inside. To do anything substantive, the bodies needed to be removed. He grabbed a body and pulled it partially out of the hatch. By the uniform, Miller could see it was an officer. He tied a line to it in order to haul it to the surface.

Just then the current began to run hard. This tugged at his air pipe and lifeline, inhibiting the work. Miller grabbed the officer's hand and removed an engraved gold ring. Then, with a call to the surface, he began the lengthy decompression process.

When Miller got to the deck of the *Moonfleet*, he gave Commander Cooper the ring. Perhaps the Intelligence Division could identify it and the owner.

Owing to tide conditions, Damant waited until the evening for slack water. The brief period of time between tides was the best moment to conduct diving operations since the water was still. When the seas were ready, Damant sent down George Clear to finish Miller's job and remove the body from the conning tower hatch.

It is an awkward job to do almost anything requiring manual dexterity in a diving dress, and to add the additional handling of a corpse requires not a little sangfroid. This Clear possessed to enough of a degree that he removed the body after some fumbling in the dark. It was set to a line and hoisted to the surface.

On the deck of the *Moonfleet*, Damant and Cooper inspected the body. He was shot twice—once in the head and once in the stomach. The finger next to the ring finger was heavily bandaged. They buried the body at sea.

After the *Moonfleet* went into port that night, Admiral Hall telephoned and ordered that somebody who got a good look at the face should come at once to Whitehall. Miller went and met with Hall to describe the body. Hall ordered that a photo taken recently of a group of U-boat officers posing outside their quarters in Kiel be sent up to him. After it arrived, Miller pointed to a man in the back row of the photograph. He had his hand on the shoulder of an officer seated before him. The finger next to the ring finger was stiffly bandaged. "That's him."

Admiral Hall looked through some papers and found that the man was Oberleutnant Fritz Gregor and had been the commander of *UB-33* since September 1917. He sunk fifteen ships since he took command. Hall, pleased that they could identify the U-boat, said to Miller, "Go on and get the signal books."

As to why Gregor was shot, Damant and his team could only conjecture. After the U-boat struck the mine it would have sunk quickly. Anybody toward the stern would have been killed quickly either by the explosion of the mine or the onrush of water. It seemed that Gregor planned to escape by releasing compressed air inside the conning tower until the internal air pressure was greater than the pressure of the seawater surrounding the U-boat. The hatch would pop open and Gregor would be ejected to the surface. Apparently, one of Gregor's

The *UB-20* was a UB type 2 boat and similar in design to the *UB-33*. *Courtesy of Tomas Termote*

crew saw this and knowing that the end was near, decided to shoot the captain either for not doing the noble deed of going down with his command or maybe because of some personal animosity.[*]

Damant made a report to the Admiralty to go over the available options. One choice was to raise the boat entirely. Damant thought that the wreck was in a good position for this since they were only a few miles away from a safe anchorage. However, Damant was quick to point out that because the diving planes were buried deep in the sand it would inhibit getting the lifting wires under the vessel. If the wires were placed outside the planes, then they would be liable to slip off. Damant reasoned that if he were to try raising the U-boat then there was quite a good chance of the stern breaking off because of all the damage there—not to mention that his men would have

---

[*] The British returned Gregor's ring to his widow, an Englishwoman who lived in Newcastle upon Tyne.

to get rid of the unexploded mine. Damant characterized the entire job as "long and doubtful."

Damant then gave a pitch for what he really wanted to do—blow open the U-boat with a large explosive charge. "This would open up the boat well and countermine the unexploded mine.... Further charges could be used as necessary," Damant wrote. "It is purely speculative whether material of value would be recovered in this way but from experience of charges used in *Laurentic* I should expect some success." He awaited orders.

There was some debate between the Salvage Section and the Naval Intelligence Division as to how to proceed, but after two days they gave Damant permission to use explosives. Damant ordered three hundred pounds of gelignite and underwater detonators. The earliest day that was fit for diving was May 25, 1918. By the afternoon slack water, he was ready to blow open the *UB-33*.

Damant specifically wanted to remove the conning tower. Since this was right above the control room, it would provide direct access to this most important compartment. Because the gelignite had not arrived yet he chose to use TNT. Miller was loaded up with forty-five pounds of the stuff and sent over the side.

Miller found the wreck as he had left it. Since Clear had removed the body a few days prior, it was easy for him to stuff the conning tower with the explosives and attach the detonation wire before decompressing to the surface.

Once Miller was aboard, Damant had the *Moonfleet* get as clear from the wreck as possible, stretching out the detonation wire. There must have been some consideration on Damant's part that he hoped he knew what he was doing as he pressed the detonation plunger.

The water frothed to the surface and then stilled. The *Moonfleet* shifted back to its station over the *UB-33*. The next diver found that the water was full of sediment and oil. In the limited visibility he could see and feel that the conning tower seemed to be blown loose although it still needed to be removed.

The next morning confirmed this, as well as the status of the unexploded mine, which had been launched two feet forward in the blast without exploding. It was safely out of the way. Using winches from the *Moonfleet*, Damant removed the conning tower. These were picked for parts before being dumped off-site.

There was now a hole that allowed for access to the control room. But the space was still so narrow that Damant needed to set off more charges to enlarge it. This required several days of work. A diver, in most instances Miller, went down, set charges, and came up. Then the *Moonfleet* got clear, detonated the explosives, came back, moored over the wreck, and divers descended to inspect the work.

It was on one of these occasions when Miller was assessing the wreck that he heard a whirring noise in his helmet.

He called through the telephone to see if the *Moonfleet* was working its engines.

"No," they replied.

Still hearing the noise, he dropped to the side of the U-boat and began to search. As he walked forward, the sound seemed to grow louder and louder. He soon found the source in the foremost torpedo tube, where a live torpedo was thrust halfway out of the tube. The explosion had set off the motor of the torpedo. Fortunately, jammed as it was in the tube its motor was burning out of its own accord.

On May 29, the last charge was fired to enlarge the opening. Miller descended to the wreck one more time. Slipping through the hole, he entered the control room. The only light came from his submersible lamp that revealed the bodies of German officers, weightless in the sea.

Miller shifted bodies and wreckage—searching. In a later interview, he would describe the inside of these U-boats. He saw more scenes of murder, like that of Gregor, but also suicide. There were letters home. "I shall never forget the expression of horror upon some of their faces or the mutilated heads of those who had blown out their brains," Miller recalled.

Then there was the sea life that had wormed its way into the wrecks. Crabs and lobsters were disturbed by Miller's presence, and conger eels, some seven to eight feet in length, fed on the dead.

"They give one a bit of a shock," Miller said.

Miller searched the U-boat for something small and seemingly inconsequential. He struggled for several hours among the closely packed wreckage and bodies to reach the wireless cabinet in the control room. Damant was impressed and thought that Miller worked with "the greatest energy and determination." At last Miller found it, a locked steel chest. He pried it loose from the wreckage and sent it above.

Within the box were the latest signal books, cipher keys, and minefield plans—a bonanza for Naval Intelligence. These were immediately taken by Cooper to the Admiralty. As for Miller, Damant recommended him to be recognized for his "zeal and ability."

Damant, egged on by success, was eager to continue probing the *UB-33*. He needed to remove more debris and bodies. He wrote, "I consider that much material might be recovered from her in a reasonably undamaged state." To help with the work, he urged the Admiralty to outfit the *Moonfleet* with a small recompression chamber—something that would never happen.

Damant received a telegram with new orders on May 31:

VERY URGENT.

Operations on VARNE are to be suspended.

Lieut Commdr Damant with diving party & gear to proceed immediately by train & report to Vice Admiral East Coast Immingham for urgent service.

Moonfleet to proceed as soon as possible to Immingham.

23

Underwater Espionage

THE URGENT WORK AT IMMINGHAM turned out not to be a sunken U-boat but the wreck of an old steamer—another mare's nest. But it was the beginning of a summer in which Commander Damant and his divers engaged in one of the most hazardous and least known branches of espionage during the First World War. In later decades, he and his men would enter popular imagination as the "Tin-Openers," a group of divers who helped win the war by obtaining valuable intelligence in grim and dangerous conditions.

Damant despised any publicity concerning this or any of his other work, and there is no doubt in my mind that he would have disliked the appellation "Tin-Openers"; he probably would have preferred "special section." For the rest of his life, Damant never spoke publicly of this covert work except in a draft of his unpublished memoirs. However, shortly after the war, Miller was interviewed about his experiences by the *Saturday Evening Post.* The result was exaggerated tales of action and adventure under the sea where Miller was said to have dived on no less than sixty U-boats—an impossible number. But the *Saturday Evening Post* article, "A War Secret," mostly corroborates in substance, if not in detail, the Admiralty records as well as Damant's own account. Notably, Miller never named his fellow divers, either because he considered it bad form to publicize the names of his fellows or because he wanted to augment his own accomplishments. The former is more likely. The author of the article, pandering to his audience, makes Miller out to be an aquatic superhero. It is true that Miller was remarkable, and he was the best of the special section—winning a Distinguished Service Cross for his efforts—but he was one of several divers. Of the others, little is known about any of them except for their deeds. In this regard, Edwin Blachford and George Clear predominate in the records and remained with Damant throughout.

Most of the action occurred in the English Channel, specifically in the area of the Dover Barrage, though the work took them as far afield as Scapa Flow. All the wrecks were of the smaller coastal classes, either UB or UC boats since these were the most active in those waters. Most of the time, Damant's team took a train to a new location, beating the *Moonfleet* by a day or two, and began work on diving boats. Damant wrote:

> Bundling pumps, gear, and some dry clothing into lorries and trains, traveling all night, we would reach some bleak port with nothing to eat and nowhere to sleep. As it would be days before our own ship could get round from the other side of England we had to cram into some trawler and go out to the scene. Often the obstruction had disappeared, often it would turn out to be the ancient wreck of a sailing ship or jagged rocks. Twice it turned out to be a real submarine but one which must have been sunk long before and was now encrusted with barnacles. Such wrecks continue to emit patches of oil and are attacked over and over again by newcomers to the area.

By the time the war was over, Damant's team had surveyed or explored at least fifteen different wrecks with roughly half that number supplying intelligence materials. This number does not include separate wrecks explored by Miller or worked on by other officers in the salvage section. But most other officers in the salvage section were engaged in trying to salvage U-boats and were not seriously diving on them. While it would be confusing to list every U-boat that

SIGNIFICANT U-BOAT WRECKS
DIVED ON BY G.C.C. DAMANT'S SALVAGE SECTION

0   50   100 miles

DATA ON U-BOATS TAKEN FROM INNES MCCARTNEY

▲ Sunken U-Boat
═══ Mine fields

Shetland Islands

NORTHERN
BARRAGE

NORWAY

Scapa Flow
▲
UB-116

Inverness •

North Sea

GERMAN
and
BRITISH
MINED
AREA

IRELAND

BRITISH
MINEFIELDS
▲
Whitby • UC-70

Irish Sea

Liverpool •
Immingham •

GREAT
BRITAIN

NETHERLANDS

Harwich • ▲UC-11

London •

BRITISH
MINEFIELDS

Plymouth •   Portsmouth •   Dover •   Ostend •
                              Folkestone •   Bruges •
▲   *Isle of*   BELGIUM   GERMANY
UB-74   *Wight* ▲ UB-81

English Channel   *Cap Griz Nez*

LUX.

▲
UB-109 ▲
          UB-55 ▲
              UC-64
▲
UB-33   *FRANCE*

Damant's squad investigated, an esoteric exercise at best, the summer and autumn of 1918 was episodic.

By the late spring of 1918, Germany's spring offensive had failed and the gains in territory it had made in April were being steadily rolled back. The Allies were now planning a massive counterattack that would lead to the end of the war. At sea, the U-boats were still doing grave damage to Allied shipping with almost three hundred thousand tons sunk in May, but this figure was far less than the nearly mortal wound the U-boats inflicted in 1917. In May 1918 the Royal Navy had more success in sinking U-boats, eighteen total, than it had since the start of the war—it was widely reported that German morale was flagging. Now it was a matter of pressing the U-boats through the coordinated use of convoy and antisubmarine measures so that the Allies would not lose their advantage. For this to work, every cipher key, every code, and every German transmission needed to be known and translated by Hall's code breakers in Room 40.

● ● ●

After Damant's great success in recovering the documents and other materials from the *UB-33*, the Admiralty pressed him for more. Indeed, there were even discussions to begin a course at HMS *Excellent* for the specialized type of salvage work that Damant and his divers did. Without new trainees, the Admiralty decided to split Damant's group in two, figuring that more cases could be investigated. Miller, whose singular talents were so well regarded that the Admiralty considered him pseudolegendary, was assigned in early June to assist Lieutenant George Davis, who was working on a U-boat wreck and needed experienced divers. Apparently, divers Albert Balson and Percy Frater joined Miller for the assignment. To remind Davis of Miller's status, the Admiralty sent a telegram to him: "You will understand that Mr Miller is an officer whom it is only intended to use for very important work and that every consideration should be shown him."

Miller's assignment with Davis had to do with a report that came from the armed yacht *Lorna*. Before the war, the *Lorna* was often seen during Cowes week. Now it had a more serious business. The ship had been protecting vessels in Lyme Bay, near Portland, when on the evening of May 26, 1918, the captain sighted a periscope. The periscope was not pointed at the *Lorna* but focused to the west where a merchant ship was coming into the view. The U-boat showed no sign that it was aware of the yacht's presence even as the *Lorna*'s captain brought his vessel within 150 feet on the U-boat's starboard side.

The *Lorna* crept up on the submarine until it was within ten feet. Suddenly, the periscope dipped under the sea. The *Lorna* then went full speed ahead and clipped the U-boat's conning tower. The ship dropped a depth charge set to explode at fifty feet. Moments ticked by before a froth of water sprayed to the surface. The *Lorna*, circling to starboard sent down another depth charge. There was another explosion followed by froth. Debris and oil slicks percolated to the surface.

The captain of the *Lorna* guided his vessel into the debris field. It was clear that a U-boat was down there, but he wanted to ensure that the submarine was not playing some sort of trick. The *Lorna* rolled a third depth charge into the sea. Just then, voices with distinct German accents could be heard from the water.

"Kamerad!"

"Help!"

There was nothing that could be done. The depth charge exploded, throwing four German survivors into the air.

Three of the Germans died immediately. The fourth, badly wounded, was hauled aboard the *Lorna*. His sailor cap, labeled UNTER-SEEBOOTS ABTEILUNG, was still fast to his head.

The U-boat was the *UB-74* commanded by twenty-seven-year-old Oberleutnant Ernst Steindorff. It was a week out of the German submarine bases in occupied Belgium and had already sunk three ships on this cruise. The lone survivor claimed that his captain had failed to keep a mindful watch since he was hungry to attack more prey. He died of his wounds three hours later.

A search was immediately conducted and a local diver found the *UB-74* a week later. It was resting on an even keel at twenty-one fathoms. The depth charges caused a riveted seam to fail catastrophically, opening up a forty-foot-long and three-inch-wide hole in the pressure hull in the vicinity of the torpedo tubes.

The Royal Navy was interested in this wreck for several reasons. This was the third generation in UB-class submarines with new weaponry. The Germans had developed a new type of long-range gun fitted on its U-boats as well as torpedoes equipped with an experimental magnetic system, which would detonate the weapon just as it was passing under the keel of a ship, making it far more destructive.

Naval Intelligence sent orders not to raise the U-boat but to explode the forward hatch so that divers could access the officers' quarters. This was done by divers overseen by Lieutenant Davis. The work of gaining access and using charges to widen the hole was made easier by the good visibility even at that depth, although there was a current that seemed to constantly run and played havoc with the divers' air pipes and lifelines. On June 6 the hole was wide enough for divers to enter the wreck. But all they found were bodies and signal cartridges. As these were shifted, the divers tried to penetrate farther aft to the control room. But here they were stymied—the way was blocked by debris. They did not have the experience to go deeper.

Blinker Hall took a personal interest in the work. As a result, Miller was sent to assist Davis on June 11. Upon diving, Miller noticed that the U-boat's gun was longer than others he had seen. It was a nice piece of workmanship with an intricate sighting mechanism. This was probably the gun that the Admiralty wanted to study. It was severed from the wreck with a charge of gelignite. Lines were slung onto it and it was pulled slowly off the U-boat and towed to shallower water. There, it was hauled ashore by tackles, loaded onto a truck, and sent off under guard to the Naval Ordnance Department.

In the meantime, Miller began to work inside the wreck probably with Balson and Frater. Many contorted and mutilated bodies were found throughout and had to be removed. Documents were found periodically by Miller and the other divers, including a diving logbook and crew lists. It was a long slog, but after multiple dives he reached the control room. There were documents as well as a wooden box that contained a magnetic pistol. This was apparently an example of one of the experimental devices being tested in the U-boat's torpedoes.

Miller would stay on with Davis through August before returning to Damant.

* * *

Commander Damant's next viable case came on June 26. He had received word from the senior naval officer at Harwich, a port town in Essex, England, north of Dover, that a patrol boat had witnessed an explosion. The boat went to the spot and found a German officer flailing in the sea. It was the *UC-11*'s commanding officer, Oberleutnant Kurt Utke.

Utke claimed he was fifteen meters below the surface when his U-boat suddenly suffered a violent explosion. As the *UC-11* rapidly filled with water, he managed to open the conning tower hatch and get out—he was the only survivor. He informed his interrogators that he had already completed his mission by laying all the U-boat's mines. He had been homeward bound.

The day after the sinking, Damant arrived to find that sweepers thought they had hooked on the U-boat. The next morning, June 28, he went out on a diving boat (he had come ahead of the *Moonfleet* with Blachford and Clear) and found that the sweepers had caught upon the sinkers and mooring wires of some old German mines. Suspecting that this was related to the *UC-11*, Damant continued the search assisted by experts who used electric underwater metal detectors. They soon found the wreck, and Damant dove to survey it.

The spring tides, after a new or full moon when the difference between high water and low water was greatest, did not allow much time to work underwater. But Damant was able to gather enough information on the wreck to form a plan. The *UC-11* was rather small, about 111 feet in length, and had been damaged with a large fracture just behind the conning tower. Since it was a minelayer, it had six chutes toward the bow. Each one of those chutes could contain two mines.

Damant surmised what had happened. The U-boat had fouled in the mooring wires of some old German mines. It may well have been mines the submarine itself had laid on prior missions. The Admiralty, for its part, sometimes let old mines be, with Blinker Hall's unit sending out misinformation that the seas had been swept clean to set as a trap.

UC-class U-boats were small coastal minelayers. The *UC-5*, pictured here, was a UC type I boat and similar in design to the *UC-II*. You can see grates over the chutes where mines were loaded. *Photograph courtesy of the Library of Congress Prints and Photographs Division, LC-B2-4257-2*

There would be little value in trying to raise the wreck since the design was outdated, but it was probable that there was viable intelligence inside of it. While at high tide the depth of water was not too great—thirteen fathoms, and there was no apparent way for a diver to enter the boat. The hatches, as usual, were too narrow. More disturbing was that all the mines were still in their chutes—Utke had lied when he said he had laid them all.

The most expeditious way to get inside the wreck was to use explosives as Damant had done before. But doing so might

inadvertently trigger all the mines and destroy the U-boat plus whatever else was in the area. Seeing no other way, Damant requested
permission from the senior naval officer in Harwich to use explosives. The officer in turn contacted Admiral Hall, who promptly
gave his approval.

Damant sent down his divers to stuff the conning tower hatch with
one hundred pounds of TNT. They sealed it shut, decompressed to
the surface, and boarded the little diving boat. The circuit wire was
run out from an ad hoc reel made of handspikes. They got as far
away as possible and then Damant pressed the detonator.

The resulting spume of water did not seem to be any greater
than what might have been expected from a hundred-pound charge.
The next morning, July 1, Damant sent Clear and Blachford down
to see what had happened. They found that the conning tower had
become separated from the U-boat, but it had fouled into the new
opening—the mines were still unexploded in the chutes.

Damant decided to double down. The process was repeated.
Damant prepared a light charge of gelignite and dived. He set the
explosive, fastened the priming wire, decompressed up to the boat,
and removed his diving gear. The idea was that he would run the
circuit out to its full extent of seven hundred yards before setting
off the charge.

Damant drifted away on a strong tide with his divers. But when
he was scarcely one hundred yards away the reel holding the detonation wire jammed. They could not stop the drift of the boat, and
the strain would cause the wire to part from the explosives. If that
were to happen they might lose days of work, so Damant pressed
the detonator.

The charge went off as planned and the explosion was what
Damant expected. Then three seconds later a tremendous secondary
explosion boiled through the water. Spume spouted from the sea and
a rolling wave headed directly at the boat, threatening to capsize it.
While Damant was out of his diving dress and could swim, Blachford
and Clear, both wearing their heavy diving boots, would certainly
drown.

The wave lifted up the rowboat, men and all, and then lowered it back to the sea—it did not overturn. "A bit of luck, that," Damant would later recall.

Debris started surfacing. Some of this was fished out, and to Damant's delight there were undamaged papers, which Naval Intelligence used to reconstruct two useful charts. By the afternoon, when it seemed safe enough, Damant sent Blachford and Clear down to the wreck. It was evident that this second charge had set off the mines, but it wasn't apparent if all of them had exploded.

Blachford and Clear entered the now-accessible control room and began to recover documents. As they worked, they heard banging noises, as if an object was hitting the wreck. This frazzled the divers who imagined mines going off at any moment. They returned as quickly as they could and presented Damant with more papers to send to Blinker Hall.

Damant wrote in wonder, "The results obtained show that most violent explosions can take place within a few feet of papers without destroying them." But he would not send down more divers until he got orders.

● ● ●

Damant shortly got a new assignment on July 3, 1918, the *UC-64*, another minelayer.

This boat had gone down from a mine explosion in twenty-two fathoms of water, again off Harwich. When Clear and Blachford surveyed the wreck, they found it listed forty-five degrees to port. It was camouflaged with splotches of different colored paint and its bottom was black or red—the divers could not tell by the light. Damant sensed opportunities in the forward and aft hatches that, while awfully narrow, were wider than in previous cases. To make matters trickier, all the U-boat's mines were in the chutes, and they were in an *active* minefield. Damant and his divers fully realized that their closest kin might just have the opportunity to cash in on the £500 indemnity the Admiralty promised if any of them lost their lives.

The *UC-19* was a UC type 2 boat that was similar in design to the *UC-64*. *Courtesy of Tomas Termote*

Damant considered the situation and was nervous. If he were to blow open the hatches to make space, he might set off the mines just as he did on the *UC-11*. In his initial report, Damant hesitated. It would be much better to work with one of the coastal attack U-boats that did not have so many mines. "I don't think prospects of getting papers good on account of mines, and if a UB boat of recent date is found it would be better to switch over to her."

But the Admiralty ordered him to proceed, so Damant set Clear and Blachford to work. They wiggled into the wreck through the forward hatch and came to the battery compartment, which was also a living compartment for some of the U-boat's crew. Here, the bottom deck was driven up by ten feet, forcing tons of debris to jam together, including the smashed accumulators from the U-boat's batteries. Most distinct were the corpses—many were enmeshed in their hammocks.

Blachford and Clear needed deeper access into the wreck, and Damant, still fearful of the mines, ordered them to remove the debris by the handful. Damant estimated that without explosives this process could take a minimum of four weeks to get results.

When this assessment got to Blinker Hall, he quickly scribbled on the report, "Explosives must be used." This was quickly vetoed by the director of naval equipment, who knew just how dangerous this would be.

Finally, Damant, pressed for time, decided to risk it anyway and employed a light charge of gelignite to cut off the conning tower in hopes of accessing the control room. Luckily, this went without incident and by July 29 they enlarged the hole. After a couple of days of removing debris and bodies, Blachford and Clear entered the control room on August 1.

The floor of the control room, like that of the battery, had been pushed up and the bulkheads were forced inward, giving little space. Blachford and Clear continued to search, but they could not find any materials of intelligence value, only a purse from one of the bodies. At last, Damant gave up hope of finding anything useful in the wreck and moved on to new cases.

· · ·

In August, Damant encountered wrecks that were either too old to be of intelligence value or too impossible to work with. For example, he reported on August 11, "Explored fore part of wreck up to control room bulkhead which is shattered. Found everything blown into small pieces, only fragments of bodies. Bedding and clothing rotten and fell to pieces when handled. No chance of anything important." The only saving grace in this case was that Damant managed to salve the U-boat's gun for the Department of Naval Ordnance.

There were breaks from the labor of a sort. As the *Moonfleet* sailed to a new case on a beautiful summer day, the men amused themselves by taking target practice at floating mines. "With a rifle, hitting the body of the mine would make a small hole which might possibly cause it to sink in several hours time," wrote Damant. "But if you hit one of the protruding horns, the mine exploded and bits would sail into the air looking no more dangerous than scraps of paper carried by a wind … that is when viewed from a distance…. If they came near, one could hear the vicious whistle with which they cut the air. One's desire to score bullshorn was countered by fear of being too close if one did."

Some wrecks had mysteries, such as the *UB-55*, which they dived on off Dover on August 14. Damant thought it promising enough to try to blow open the forward hatch for his divers. But when he set off the charge, there was a heavier than expected explosion. He had inadvertently set off the bow torpedoes. But his divers recovered material, including a deck gun, papers, and keys. Curiously, on this wreck one of the drowned Germans was wearing a leather suit and not a uniform. There was no record of why this might be, but he may have been a German spy that the U-boat was to deposit on a remote shore. Damant wrote of some of the other strange cases he found, "Guns, bodies, mysterious electric boxes (one turned out to be a harmless gramophone) were hoisted up as well as their latest torpedoes and masses of books and papers. In one odd case we found two U-boats telescoped into each other, one freshly sunk, the other a wreck of some months standing."

When a U-boat hit a mine, it typically only struck one out of a group of twenty or so. This meant that when Damant arrived at a case there were usually another nineteen live mines floating in the nearby sea. Damant recalled, "One used to wonder, when dropping anchor over a new case whether, on its way to the bottom, it would happen to strike one of them. Then there was the chance that the diver on his way down would touch one with his lead soled boots. One could see nothing but blackness looking downwards while descending but, once on the bottom, looking upwards, a mine or two could often be seen swaying gently overhead."

All the divers in Damant's special section were volunteers and had personal loyalty to Damant. At times, Frederick Young attempted to transfer divers out of Damant's command to go on other salvage duties. This eventually led Damant to object to Young, "The divers are not paid as Salvage Divers and volunteered for this service on the understanding that they would be kept together as a whole under myself."

All this time enemy U-boats were active in the area—so were British antisubmarine forces. Damant wrote of one unknown wreck they were diving on, "On several days the divers were severely shaken by the explosion of depth charges during attacks on enemy submarines within a short distance. On one occasion the shock was so great as to bang down the hatch on top of a diver who was working inside a submarine. He had great difficulty in forcing it up again to get out." In this case, the diver must have been Blachford, in light of Damant's subsequent correspondence, but no further details of the episode have been revealed in the historical record.

On August 29 Damant received word from an excited Admiral at Whitehall that a U-boat had been freshly sunk off Folkestone by a mine. The water was shallow. It should be easy. "Don't tell me that it is old wreckage," said the Admiral, "for I have eight live prisoners out of her." The *Moonfleet* arrived at the scene the next morning.

Blachford and Clear found the wreck at fourteen fathoms on a sandy bottom. This was the largest and latest of the *UB* types at over 181 feet long, the *UB-109*. It was listed thirty degrees to starboard with severe damage to the engine room where the U-boat fell into a shapeless wreck. The boat was cut cleanly in two, about twenty-five feet abaft the conning tower. To Damant, the damage to this wreck was more severe than in all the other cases he had seen. But the conning tower and forward hatches were open and were wider than hatches on previous cases. Because of this, and the generally good condition of the wreck forward, there was no need for explosives. Upon entry into the forward compartment of the wreck, Blachford and Clear noticed that the water was unusually warm, even hot. The wreck was so fresh that seawater was still mixing freely with the sulfuric acid from the U-boat's batteries, heating the water.

All about the divers was a murky blackness only resolved by the illumination of their lamps. This showed bedding, loose debris, and bodies. Blachford and Clear quickly got to work passing the deceased through the hatch and clearing out bedding. Each body was searched for identification, and notebooks were taken for scraps of information before the bodies were buried at sea. All sorts of potential valuables were passed up to the surface. These were taken by a motorboat to shore where a car would rush them to the Admiralty.

It was in this way that two flat tin boxes were recovered by the divers. In them were charts that showed passages through the defensive minefields around the German coast. The charts indicated that the defensive minefields had changed, and one exit by which U-boats had been using and the British had been watching with four destroyers had been closed up with fresh mines. This freed up the destroyers for other work.

A third flat box was found, but as it was being passed up one of the divers dropped it. A search for it proved to be in vain. Damant, however, was determined to find it. So he obtained one of the other two boxes that had been sent to the Admiralty. Then Damant wrote, "Waiting for a day and hour when the tidal stream would be exactly the same as at the time of the loss, I stood over the [U-boat's] hatch and let my box fall over the side and, as it disappeared into the distance, jumped down after it. I had previously arranged for the air pipe to be paid out quickly and the boat moved after me, so was able to keep in sight of the drifting box. As I had hoped, it led me straight to the lost one, caught among some rocks. I sent it up in triumph." Despite Damant's cleverness, the box proved empty.

The real objective of the divers was to work aft in the *UB-109* toward the captain's quarters. It was there that confidential documents would be locked up. Once this was achieved, they could then pass into the control room where more materials could be found. Adjacent to it, was the wireless cabinet where signal books and cipher keys were stowed.

To get to these compartments, Blachford and Clear had to squeeze through five different openings in their diving dresses: the forward hatch, the bulkhead door between the forward living quarters and the officers' quarters, a narrow partition between the officers' quarters and the captain's quarters, a watertight door to the control room, and the door of the wireless cabinet. During the prolonged journey, they had to continually remove debris and bodies while ensuring that their air pipes and lifelines did not get caught or cut in the wreckage.

The divers found sets of the newest Zeiss binoculars, the best of their kind. But acid from the U-boat's batteries had corroded the binoculars beyond repair. Other things were more useful, such as buttons from German uniforms that some friends of Damant converted into cigarette lighters. Damant noted, "The lighters looked very attractive but never worked after the first day." As a souvenir, Damant presented to Nell a linen tea towel with the German imperial seal upon it.

On August 30 the divers reached the captain's quarters. This portion of the U-boat had remained intact. To all the divers' amazement, a large mirror sat unscathed upon the door of the captain's wardrobe. Damant went down and studied his reflection in it by the light of his lamp. It was here they also found some intelligence materials. On August 31, the divers passed into the control room where they recovered more documents, including a chart revealing that the U-boat was tracking convoys. On September 1 the divers entered the wireless cabinet where they recovered the cipher keys and codebooks. Then after two days of no work due to bad weather, Clear and Blachford recovered more materials. But the well was running dry. On September 6 Damant suggested moving to new quarry. Hall was pleased and arranged for a hundred-pound bonus to all of Damant's divers.

A new case was waiting for Damant. The *UC-70* had sunk on August 28 off Whitby, but because of Damant's investigation of the *UB-109* it had to wait. In the meantime, the approximate location of the wreck was buoyed for him. On October 4, Damant arrived, not on the *Moonfleet*, but on the yacht-turned-salvage-vessel *Corycia*. Damant had complained about the lack of space in the *Moonfleet*, so the Admiralty, which by then highly esteemed Damant and his divers, gave him a new ship. The yacht provided more comfortable quarters for the divers. Damant berthed in the owner's cabin, which had a private bathroom. Even better, the yacht still had its civilian crew that included a steward and chef who provided the same sort of food the yacht's owner might have expected during the pageantry of Cowes Week. But this was not a pleasure cruise. Aside from the necessities of war, Damant was in pain, suffering from a form of neuralgia. He also had dental troubles, and a local dentist extracted most of his teeth.

However, the docks at Whitby allowed ample room for the *Corycia* to stay alongside the dock, which meant that Damant did not have to stay aboard even though his quarters were admittedly more opulent.

The *Corycia* was a private yacht that was converted into a salvage ship during World War I. *Courtesy of the Royal Yacht Squadron*

Nell, leaving Baboo with her sister, came to Whitby, and the couple stayed at a luxury hotel that was nearly deserted.

It might have been a vacation of sorts except that Nell contracted Spanish influenza. The disease, far more deadly than normal strains of the flu, grew to pandemic proportions. Five hundred million people were infected worldwide, resulting in fifty to a hundred million deaths. Nell developed pneumonia two days after contracting the illness. The hospital was short-staffed, but Damant was able to get the doctor to assign two nurses to her, day and night. He was convinced it was this that led to her eventual recovery.

As Nell fought off the flu, Damant received verbal orders from Admiral Hall that he was to obtain papers from the wireless cabinet of the *UC-70.* Naval Intelligence impressed the high priority of this mission, and Damant ordered a lockable desk to store the secret documents.

After two days of searching, divers located the wreck at fourteen fathoms. The boat was lying at a list of seventy degrees on its port side. The damage to the hull was not too great—the depth charges that sank it inflicted far less injury than a mine would. Even better, the forward, conning tower, and engine room hatches were all open. Damant supposed that the crew were alive when the U-boat sank to the bottom and had made efforts to try to escape. The first body they encountered was in the conning tower and wore no uniform but a leather suit. The underclothes showed his name was Dobberstein. He was the commanding officer of the vessel.

The next day, Blachford and Clear were sent down, with one operating by the hatch and the other working inside the wreck. This way, one could pass debris to the other as well as allow the man on the outside to monitor the inside diver's lifeline and air pipe.

It was during this process of clearing out the debris that Blachford and Clear found several iron cases, heavily padlocked. They resembled other confidential boxes that they had brought up from other U-boats. These were brought to the surface and opened with cold chisels.

Inside were sausages and cans of other food. As the divers continued their work, they even found a bag of potatoes, securely locked. Oberleutnant Karl Dobberstein was reputed to be tough and rationing was clearly enforced. One man subordinate to him who had been taken prisoner by the British claimed that he was "a most brutal officer and very much disliked by the crew."

On October 11 Blachford and Clear had reached the wireless cabinet, where two bodies blocked access. They shifted these out to the hatches and sent them to the surface. Damant's men attached weights to the bodies and as they did so saw that one body's throat was cut.

The wireless room was cleared of materials, which were sent with an intelligence officer to Whitehall. Also recovered for study were wireless instruments and ammunition. The intelligence recovered by Damant's team was apparently of the highest caliber. When Blinker Hall read Damant's report, he made an annotation on the report, "Read with interest and admiration."

Damant continued to search the wreck until the end of October, but did not recover anything else of significant value. Then on October 29 he received a priority telegram to travel by rail to Scapa Flow with two divers and equipment. This was a high-priority case. In fact, Blinker Hall had promised Damant a Distinguished Service Order, a vaunted decoration given for meritorious service in combat conditions, for the work he was to do.

The war was in its final phase. On September 15 the Bulgarians asked for an armistice. On October 20 the Ottomans followed suit. Seeing the writing on the wall, Admiral Scheer recalled all U-boats operating against merchant shipping. With the other top officers of the German Admiralty, Scheer began to plan one last naval blow against the British Fleet for honor's sake. Scheer wrote that it was "impossible for the Fleet to remain inactive in any final battle that may sooner or later precede an armistice. The Fleet must be committed. Even if it is not to be expected that this would decidedly influence the course of events, it is still, from the moral point of view, a question of the honour and existence of the Navy to have done its utmost in the last battle." Also, a naval victory might grant Germany a better position at the negotiating table. An action was planned for October 30.

But the plan never went into effect. Large numbers of German sailors failed to report back from shore leave. Throughout the High Seas Fleet, mutiny broke out to varying degrees, including insubordination, shouting for peace, and cheering for President Woodrow Wilson. Scheer later commented, "The idea had taken root in their minds that they were to be needlessly sacrificed." Operations were called off.

It was in this atmosphere that Damant and his divers drove across the moors to catch a 1:00 AM mail train at York. They arrived at Edinburgh in the morning and by the evening reached Inverness, where an automobile was waiting for them. The car whisked them on a long drive over the Scottish heather to the village of Scrabster, which they reached by midnight to find beds and a hot meal aboard the destroyer HMS *Marne*. The ship ferried them to the great naval base at Scapa Flow on the morning of November 1.

When Damant arrived he was surprised to find his old friend and mentor Andrew Catto already working on the wreck. Catto was somewhat hurt at being overridden by his former apprentice, but Damant noted that Catto was "a decent man and we got on without friction."

The U-boat in question had been caught in a trap. A line of mines connected by wire was cast across the entrance of Scapa Flow for some three to four miles. A watcher from an observation station ashore could set off all the mines with a touch of a button when he saw indicator lights being set off from loops of wire set below the sea. In most cases, lights went off when regular traffic passed into Scapa Flow, and throughout most of the war, the watchers had nothing exciting to report. But on the night of October 28, 1918, the watchers saw an unexpected indicator light go off. Then, when the moment was right and the U-boat nosed forward far enough that the lights attached to the mines started to blink, they hit the button. The resulting explosion woke residents in the countryside for miles. Then, just to make sure the job was done, destroyers came out and discharged multiple depth charges on the spot until oil bubbled to the surface.

By the time the Royal Navy was done with the U-boat, it was battered and flattened. Letters in the pocket of one of the bodies gave the identification of the boat as *UB-116*. Multiple bodies and wreckage were removed as divers made room to squeeze toward the wireless cabinet for the materials therein.

What impressed Commander Damant most about this wreck was that all the bodies had new, clean clothing, both civilian and military. There were also textbooks, dictionaries, grammars, and kit bags packed. They were outfitted as if they were not expecting to return to Germany. Stranger still, Damant remarked that every body aboard belonged to a German officer.

Damant presumed that the officers were "inspired with the idea of striking a last, desperate blow for their country. They had [no] hope or intention of returning to Germany where revolution and mutiny had broken out but intended, if not killed, to give themselves up after doing all the damage they could. This unusual luggage was intended for their use in captivity."

Admiral Hall ordered that the operation should remain as secret as possible. To complicate matters, there was a Presbyterian minister ashore who had heard rumors of the U-boat and wanted to hold a service for the slain Germans. In order to prevent this, Naval Intelligence ordered that no bodies should be raised to the surface. Damant had the bodies searched and buried at sea, all completely underwater. He observed, "The Scapa water was very clear and transparent, all round her [the wreck] on the white sandy bottom lay the bodies of the unfortunate crew of officers with sinkers lashed to their heads and feet."

Shortly after, Damant received orders to report to Vice Admiral Sir Herbert King-Hall. The vice admiral had nothing to do with the type of operations Damant was involved in, so it puzzled him as to what the flag officer wanted. Damant found King-Hall seated at his desk surrounded by a semicircle of grim-faced secretaries, flag officers, and one black-clothed civilian. This last person was the Presbyterian minister.

The vice admiral said to Damant, "I have been shocked to hear that you have been guilty of revolting barbarism.... Conduct of which the most degraded savages would be ashamed and of which, thank God, I could never have believed a Naval Officer would have been capable.... In some mad frenzy you have allowed or encouraged your men to insult and mutilate the bodies of those poor Germans who were doing no more than their duty."

Damant asked for details and learned that the minister had reported to the vice admiral that he had been told in confidence that the German bodies had been "skewered together in bundles like larks on a spit!" In order to ensure that no one discovered the mutilation, Damant had weights tied to the bodies. Upon questioning the minister, Damant found out that he had gone to a canteen where one of the divers was having tea. The minister then asked the diver why no bodies had come ashore. The diver replied that "weights had been secured to them," and the bodies were buried at sea—which was considered to be an honorable burial. The minister apparently misheard "secured" as "skewered" and, sufficiently horrified, imagined the rest.

Vice Admiral King-Hall, who had not known about Damant's orders, was duly informed. The vice admiral ended the affair with handshakes and apologies. The minister was, according to Damant, "hounded back to his Manse with curses and [his conduct was] reported to the Moderator of the General Assembly of whoever was his spiritual boss."

Meanwhile, on the *UB-116*, diver Blachford struggled for two days toward the door of the control room in an ever-diminishing space as he forced himself farther aft. He could see the door to the compartment hanging loose, but the deck above was forced down to no more than a crawl space. Sliding and wriggling, he edged closer to the door, and saw protruding from it a pair of arms. Clutched in a corpse's dead hands was a square package, weighted and tied with copper wire. Blachford seized it. This package proved to contain all the codes and ciphers of the *UB-116*. That night, the codebooks were sent ashore and transmitted by telegraph to Naval Intelligence.

Damant concluded that the captain of the U-boat, determining that he was inside Scapa Flow and unlikely to return to Germany, had ordered the codebooks sent overboard. The person who clutched the codebooks must have been in the act of bringing them to the torpedo tubes to send overboard when the mines exploded.

The codebooks were recovered on November 9. Two days later, Damant was looking for more intelligence material when there was a tremendous clamor throughout the Grand Fleet at Scapa Flow. "Sirens blowing, bells clanging, drums beating and improvised bands in fancy dress marching round and round the docks," wrote Damant. "The armistice had been signed. The war was over. The cipher books mattered nothing."

At Whitehall, members of the Board of Admiralty gave speeches and commendations to the men and officers of the Royal Navy. Throughout the fleet, Commander in Chief Sir David Beatty allowed a celebration by "splicing the main brace" at 1900—that is, one tot of rum additional to the daily ration would be issued to officers and men. The last time that had been done was at the coronations of Edward VII and George V.

As for Commander Damant, he headed to London to celebrate. On November 16, he met Nell, and then, after being given leave, the couple rushed home to the Isle of Wight. Thursford was clean and warm. Baboo was "all jumps and activity." It was a very happy time.

• • •

Of his divers, Damant felt that Edwin Blachford and George Clear were in the gravest danger because of their work in active minefields. He recommended them for Distinguished Service Medals and for Blachford to be promoted from Leading Seaman to Petty Officer. This was done in 1919.

But to Damant's disappointment, he never received the Distinguished Service Order that Admiral Blinker Hall had promised him for the work at Scapa Flow. In fact, after his leave at home, Damant visited the Admiralty and found that Hall had resigned, filled with apparent disgust at Prime Minister David Lloyd George and the armistice terms.

Some months later, Damant received a letter from his brother Jim that began "Dear O.B.E." Damant had been bestowed an Order of the British Empire, a newly minted order of chivalry that was created by King George V in 1917. Jim had apparently seen it announced in the newspapers. While it was created with the intent of honoring noncombatant contributions to the war effort, it was soon divided into military and civilian divisions. Damant, who was inducted into the military division, was dismissive of it, if not contemptuous. "I had been awarded one of these newly invented decorations," he wrote, "but already they were being so freely distributed as to have become a subject for jests."

The Admiralty had no further use for Damant, and they advised him that he had best get himself demobilized. But Damant was not done yet—not by a long shot. "There was another string to my bow," he wrote. That string was the *Laurentic*'s gold.

PART IV

24

"Every Prospect of Success"

AFTER THE ARMISTICE, THE ADMIRALTY found itself just as busy as when the war was still on. The Royal Navy took over vessels of Germany's High Seas Fleet for internment and disposal, which included surrendered U-boats. By December 1918, 134 submarines had been transferred to British control. Furthermore, the Allies had to remove all the mines that had been strung throughout the seas. While each of the Allies was given responsibility for certain sectors, the British were responsible for the lion's share of the work, which amounted to nearly eighty thousand mines. All of these had to be swept up and disarmed.

In the general jubilation of the end of the "war to end all wars," the Admiralty saw no reason to keep the salvage section as a permanent fixture since there could not possibly be another war of such scale in the future—besides, it was not cost-effective. The Admiralty sent a notice to shipowners and underwriters stating that on May 5, 1919, salvage operations would revert back to private firms aside from a few outstanding projects. The section divested itself of equipment. Diving dresses, hundreds of miles of rope, submersible pumps, and all those things necessary in salvage operations were sold at cost. Pumps that once were worth £1,900 sold at an over 90 percent discount. Salvage vessels were to be paid off and decommissioned.

The chief work left for the section was clearing the wrecks that were scuttled at Ostend and Zeebrugge during Admiral Keyes's raids. Ostend needed to be dredged and its docks repaired. Similar work was needed at Zeebrugge, which also included salvaging additional crafts that had been scuttled into the waters by the retreating Germans. Frederick Young was in charge of these operations, which would ultimately take two years to complete.

Young was disappointed even though he was made a commodore, and he was to be eventually knighted for all his work. He had reverted from being the head of the salvage section back to his former title as naval salvage adviser. Young received no thanks from Lloyd's of London, the Ministry of Shipping, or any of the shipowners or underwriters for the work he did in saving their vessels. Young's son, Desmond, would later write of his father, "The only complaint I ever heard him make was that Commander Kay [one of Young's assistants] and his other officers had not even a medal to show for four years incessant work, which, though little was known of it at the time or afterwards, was a not inconsiderable contribution towards winning the war."

In July 1918, Young had been asked by the Bank of England when the salvage of the *Laurentic* would recommence. Young wrote to Damant at the time and asked about the outlook for recovering the *Laurentic*'s gold.

Damant wrote back with measured enthusiasm. "At the time of suspending operations in September 1917 gold was being recovered at the rate of about £50,000 pounds worth weekly and the prospects were good. It is possible that serious silting or further break up and dispersion of the wreck have occurred since then. I should expect to recover one or two millions worth in another season's work." Damant contended that if he had the appropriate equipment and ship he could easily resume operations on May 1, 1919, not thinking that the war would be over by that time.

After the armistice, Damant fought to remain in the salvage section and not demobilize so he could return to the *Laurentic*. He could not get a straight answer from the Admiralty if he was to continue or not. He wrote, "It was rumoured that private salvage firms, also left in the air by the sudden ending of the war, were fighting to get that job and the rich pickings it carried: dirty work, it was said, was in progress behind the scenes." Meanwhile, Damant obtained permission to keep his *Laurentic* divers together aboard the *Corycia*.

With the question of who would continue the *Laurentic* job in abeyance, Damant kept himself occupied by working on different salvage operations. He completed the salvage of a German U-boat that had surrendered in Chatham in January 1919. Unlike his prior work, this was a great spectacle in full public view. After Damant deposited the U-boat at the dock, it was swarmed with souvenir hunters. His next job was at Boulogne, where he perfected his French as he spent three weeks searching for a sunken submarine off Cap Gris Nez. He could not find it. Between jobs he returned to Thursford where he commuted by ferry to the *Corycia* at Southampton to tend to the vessel. When workers for the ferry company went on strike, he fitted up his yacht, *Tessa*, and sailed over on it, sometimes taking Nell aboard. The couple enjoyed tea as they crossed the Solent.

Now that the war was over, Damant thought the *Laurentic* situation was promising since more salvage equipment would be available. His chief desire, aside from actually getting permission to continue the work, was to obtain a better salvage ship to enhance operations. The *Corycia* was unsuitable for all the heavy lifting and winching that needed to be done. But he wanted to keep the *Corycia* as a supporting ship for he and the divers to berth in. But much as in 1917, the remaining salvage ships were tied up with projects. The two he had been eyeing, the *Bullfrog* and the *Holdfast*, were being used by Young in Belgium and were unavailable. But Young was not particular and wrote, "Any steam craft or lighter that could take lift over the bows should be sufficient for *Laurentic. Kymos, Bellinda,* or *Danehurst* would do."

But Damant wanted the *Racer*. He knew the ship well since it had been a training vessel for HMS *Excellent*. In the early years of the war it received a complete overhaul and had been converted to a salvage ship. Those that served on the *Racer* in her various missions during the war thought fondly of her, with one crewmember writing:

> *She isn't much to look at, and she ain't so very big,*
> *She ain't no "forty-knoter," nor got no fancy rig.*

Though her name ain't in the papers
Still—She's done her little bit,
For, when other ships were in the soup,
She was IT.

HMS *Racer* had eight submersible electric, steam, and compressed air pumps and a recompression chamber for the divers. The device, much like the one used on the *Volunteer*, was a small affair eight feet in length and four and a half feet in diameter and could hold two men lying side by side. There were controls inside and outside so that a man inside could manage his own compressed air in the chamber and could run it up to forty-five psi if necessary. Even though there were larger air chambers, the *Racer* did not have enough deck room for a bigger device. But there were some improvements from prior models. Those inside could vaguely see what was happening on the deck through a thick glass window, and there was also an air lock which allowed small things, such as cups of tea, to be passed inside.

The *Racer*, constructed in 1884, served as a training ship for HMS *Britannia* before being converted into a salvage vessel during World War I. *National Museum of the Royal Navy, 2007/47*

Young, however, could not give Damant the *Racer*, either. It was due to be decommissioned. Instead, Young promised him HMS *Moor*, a mooring lighter very similar to the *Volunteer*. It was a new construction and was slated to be ready in late June. In the meantime, Young instructed Damant to conduct a survey of the *Laurentic* in order to assess whether the work could continue.

But the *Moor* was unsatisfactory to Damant. It was too small and similar to the *Volunteer*. Besides, late June was too far into the salvage season. Since Young was no longer officially in charge of the salvage section, Damant decided to bypass him. On May 1, 1919, he wrote directly to Rear Admiral Edward Phillpotts, the director of naval equipment. Damant contended that if he had to use the *Moor* he would lose at least two months' time because the first month would be taken up by preparations such as laying moorings and "other, unproductive work." He warned that the Admiralty should not expect to get the same results as they got in 1917.

The Admiralty heeded Damant because of the high esteem that he and his divers had earned from their war contributions. On May 7, the navy canceled orders for the *Racer* to pay off and made it available to Damant at Southampton. The ship would be commanded by Lieutenant Harold Jones of the Royal Navy Reserve, but the general command of the operation was entirely Damant's.

Damant's action irritated Commodore Young, who, while no longer in charge of the section, still had enormous sway at the Admiralty. Damant should have at least conferred with Young. But even though Young was annoyed with Damant in particular, the commodore also exhibited frustration with the *Laurentic* operations in general. The *Laurentic* salvage was always outside the direct oversight of the salvage section even though it was expected to support the mission. Again, Young instructed Damant to conduct a survey of the *Laurentic* using the *Corycia*. Damant demurred, writing that he needed to have the appropriate vessel to do the job. Young's ire was further aroused, and he huffed back that Damant was "now wasting valuable time" and ordered Damant to conduct a survey with the *Corycia* while the *Racer* was being prepared.

Damant then provided a fuller response in a telegram:

I consider it impracticable to get a preliminary survey apart from
main operation. Wreck is known to be collapsed and useful information can only be got by minute examination of one special area.
To carry this out I would require the same mooring as are now
being prepared for the main operations. Owing to depth of water and state of wreck it would be altogether unsafe for divers to
attempt to hold *Corycia* in position with her own anchors which
would almost certainly foul wreck and be lost.

But Young felt that Damant should do the survey anyway and
ordered him to just use a diving boat from the navy's base at Buncrana to do the survey. Damant complied and sent a request for a
vessel. But there were none available that met Damant's requirement
to be at least thirty-two feet in length. In the end, Damant used the
Corycia. On May 26 he left East Cowes to meet the ship and headed
to Lough Swilly. He arrived four days later.

Damant and his divers made a brief survey of the *Laurentic* on
May 31, 1919. Much to Damant's relief, the wreck had not changed
much since 1917. He reported, "A fair amount of plating and debris
has settled down which will have to be blasted away and hoisted
out but so far as it is possible to judge the main operations can be
undertaken with every prospect of success."

It is unclear, but it seems that Young never got Damant's survey
or Damant sent it directly to Phillpotts. Regardless, Young was not
supportive of continuing the *Laurentic* operation through the Royal
Navy. He sent a message to Phillpotts on June 14 regarding the *Laurentic.* Phillpotts summarized:

The Naval Salvage Advisor at Ostend [Young] has been communicated with and now considers that further salvage operations should
not be carried out by the Admiralty as the salvage section is now
closed except in so far as the Salvage Operations on the Belgian
Coast are concerned. He suggests the owners of the bullion, the
Bank of England, should be informed accordingly and make their
own arrangements as to further salvage operations. Commodore

Young further suggests that a suitable firm to undertake this work is the Liverpool Salvage Association, Exchange Buildings, Liverpool.

But the Admiralty was ready to go through with the work with Royal Navy divers and Phillpotts told Young as much. Young sent a telegram to Phillpotts stating that the position of the *Laurentic* "does not in my opinion warrant heavy government expenditure when in all probability outside tenders no cure, no pay could be obtained."[*]

The Liverpool Salvage Association, which Young recommended, was the organization to which he was the chief salvage officer. Naturally, this leads one to conclude that Young sought to take over the gold salvage for personal gain. Young was known as a liberal spender that lived a high lifestyle. However, this premise is debatable. Young's original contract when he became the Royal Navy's salvage adviser was that he was to work on navy ships only. However, in the course of the war, the section took on more and more merchant ship salvages. Since his contract was never amended, this meant that he could legally claim a salvage award on every merchant ship and cargo he had worked on since the war started. This was not an inconsiderable sum. Young's son, Desmond, wrote that a solicitor who knew of the matter told him of it and added, "The case would have to be settled out of court. But the values involved are so enormous that I feel confident I could get him at least £250,000,[**] perhaps more, without difficulty." Desmond claimed that when he spoke to his father about this good fortune he told his son, "I have no wish to make money out of my country's misfortunes—and I have no intention of trying to do so." Desmond wrote, "At least it could not be said of him that he was one of those hard-faced men who look as though they had done well out of the war."

While admittedly Desmond would be writing with a faithful son's bias there is no reason to reject his father's motives. The Liverpool Salvage Association was one of the best in the business and made its money chiefly through fees and commissions rather than a percentage

---

* A no-cure, no-pay agreement is a common type of contract in which the salvage company takes on full financial and physical risk for the job and only receives a percentage of the proceeds of the recovered materials as payment.

** Between £7 and £8 million in 2016 currency.

of the value of what was salvaged. Besides, Young had been considering continuing the *Laurentic* work through a salvage company as
early as August 28, 1918, when he had a conversation with a repre-
sentative from the James Dredging Towage and Transport Company
of Southampton. The company submitted an offer to Young pro-
posing that their firm should take over the work. James Dredging
would supply stores, craft, insurance, coal, a ship, and equipment.
The company was to bear full financial burden and risk. Then after
proceeds were recovered, they would deduct out-of-pocket expenses
and divide the rest equally between themselves and the government.
Young wrote that they would consider their offer, but there was no
follow-up in the historical record. Still, the whole notion of Young
recommending his own organization to conduct the salvage with a
no-cure, no-pay agreement does not quite sit right ethically.

But Young's suggestion was just not dismissed out of hand. The
commodore was highly respected at the Admiralty. The whole matter
devolved to the likelihood of Damant recovering more gold. Phillpotts
asked Damant what he thought of his chances. Damant resubmitted
his survey results and boldly underlined the sentence that contained
"so far as it is possible to judge the main operations can be undertaken with every prospect of success."

The debate went to higher levels at the Admiralty and a query
was made to the assistant secretary for financial duties, Sir Vincent
Baddeley. The forty-five-year-old Baddeley was a careerist who had
steadily worked his way to the upper echelons of the Admiralty's
bureaucracy. He started in the War Office as a clerk in 1897, but
two years later transferred to the Admiralty. From there he became
the assistant private secretary to the first lord of the Admiralty before
being promoted to principal private secretary. Early in his career he
had been involved in revamping the Royal Navy's education program.
After serving four first lords of the Admiralty, a service he would
always consider the highlight of his career, he was promoted in 1911
to principal clerk of the Admiralty and made a companion to the
Order of the Bath. Sir Vincent had a stiff exterior and had gained a
reputation for being demanding, precise, and difficult. In his position,
he was responsible for the financial controls in the Royal Navy and

held the purse strings tight. Also important was his role as a member of the Treasury Emergency Committee, which had been established during the war to expedite financial matters. In almost four years of war, the committee held over six hundred meetings that dealt with twelve thousand matters.

Sir Vincent's contemporaries contended that his tough exterior came from his love of the Royal Navy. But he had a gentler side and was known by friends and intimates for his fundamental kindness. In fact, he ran a flat for younger bachelors who had entered the civil service.

In his query to Sir Vincent, Phillpotts noted that the salvage of the *Laurentic*'s gold might be costly with multiple ships involved. Support was iffy, with one Admiralty official writing that the "Bank of England may be easily able to make arrangements on some satisfactory basis with a private salvage firm."

Sir Vincent's response was first a correction. The gold did not belong to the Bank of England but rather the government. Then he turned to the matter of who should be responsible to the salvage—the answer was clear. The work should be carried out by the Admiralty because it was the government's gold. But Sir Vincent wished to check with Sir John Bradbury, who was the permanent secretary to the Treasury and the most senior civil servant in that department. Bradbury too thought the work should proceed and that the cost of operations should be born by the Treasury. Bradbury noted that the Treasury was "anxious that the fact that this gold has been lost should not become public property, at any rate for some time to come."

The Treasury, while agreeing to pay for the operation, was still concerned about finances. In order to figure this into their calculus, Phillpotts contacted Young and Damant to work out the figures. The costs to operate the *Racer* and *Corycia*, as well as the costs for the diving party, stores, crew, equipment, and pay for the officers, were estimated to be £125 per day. In light of the potential reward of millions in gold, this was a risk that the Treasury was willing to take. Therefore, they gave their approval for the Admiralty to continue the work using Royal Navy divers.

25

The Return to Lough Swilly

THE *RACER*'S ARRIVAL AT LOUGH SWILLY on June 25, 1919, marked
the beginning of the end to a long-deferred job. The *Racer*, although
an older ship, had been refitted and was better suited to salvage work
than the *Volunteer*. What is more, Commander Damant had at his
disposal more divers than he did in 1917. Not only did he start with
his veteran team of Miller, Blachford, Clear, Balson, and Frater but
he also had gone to the *Excellent*, asked for volunteers, and obtained
four more divers.

Miller, as he had been during the war, was to be Damant's second
in command. The bond that the two had forged during the conflict
was complete and Damant completely trusted him. He would later
write of Miller, "With a sardonic wit he could talk to anybody and
persuade officials in the dockyard to disgorge all the anchors, boats
and so on which we needed in a hurry, moreover he was adept at
the involved paper work of accounting for the expenditure of such
stores.... He possessed all the qualities which I lack and loyally exer-
cised them on my behalf."

But there were problems. George Clear departed the team early
on, seeking employment as a commercial diver at higher pay. Damant
did not grudge Clear the opportunity, and even provided a reference
for him, no doubt remembering all the dangerous work he performed

inside the U-boats. Also, the *Racer* was still on the list of ships to be disposed of as part of the postwar demobilization. Damant urged the Admiralty to let him keep the *Racer*, he could only hope that they would listen. In addition, Damant, who had been working as an acting commander, was denied the ability to retain the rank and reverted to a lieutenant commander on the retired list.* Then, of course, there was the question of whether they would find any gold at all. If they were not successful, the work could be handed over to a private salvage company.

Yet one more issue of possibly the greatest importance to the success of the mission was the political situation in Ireland. There had been a long history of suppression and disenfranchisement of Ireland's Catholic majority in what could only be characterized as bigotry. In the years preceding the First World War, there had been a growing movement for home rule, whereby Ireland would govern itself within the framework of the British Empire, like Canada or Australia. It was only the Protestant-dominated northern province of Ulster that did not support home rule and wished for Ireland to stay completely in the United Kingdom. One's political stance on the issue of Irish home rule correlated almost entirely with denomination.

A law providing for home rule was put on the statute books in September 1914. But the war crisis resulted in delaying the implementation of the new governmental structure. This delay in turn radicalized many Irish partisans, who coalesced about the political party Sinn Féin or other paramilitary groups that concluded that the only way forward for Ireland was complete independence. Throughout the war, Ireland was a pressure cooker that at times went off. During Easter week in 1916, for example, the British Army suppressed an insurrection by Irish nationalists in the so-called Easter Rising.

In December 1918 Ireland held its first postwar general elections. Sinn Féin won a landslide victory and ousted moderate Irish political parties that had supported home rule. These newly elected members of Parliament refused to go to London and formed their own separate

---

* On the other hand, Damant was paid year-round by the Admiralty even though the salvage season was during the warmer months of the year on the assumption he was planning the operation and would be available for an emergency salvage since there was no longer a salvage section.

parliament in Dublin, declaring independence on January 21, 1919.
That same day, hostilities began when a detachment of Irish paramilitary volunteers ambushed a 160-pound shipment of gelignite from
a Royal Irish Constabulary (RIC)*–escorted wagon outside Tipperary
that was bound for the Soloheadbeg quarry. The incident was the
beginning of the Irish War of Independence, sometimes called the
Anglo-Irish War or the Black and Tan War.** It was never a full-scale
conflict but a guerilla war of ever-increasing violence. Marauding was
common, especially for materials that might help the Irish rebels.

Damant was fully aware that the gelignite that he used for breaking
apart the *Laurentic*, not to mention the wreck's gold, was a prime
target for brigands and pirates. It was for this reason that Damant had
ordered an entire ton of the explosive rather than smaller shipments.
Damant reasoned that because of "the special difficulties connected
with transit of explosives in Ireland it is desired to avoid frequent
renewals of stock." While this raised eyebrows at Whitehall, the request
was ultimately granted.

It was also for fear of Irish nationalists that Damant rarely brought
the *Racer* and *Corycia* into harbor. As long as the weather was right,
the *Racer* and *Corycia* spent their evenings in Ballymastocker Bay, an
inlet on the western shore of Lough Swilly about four and a half
miles south of Fanad Head. The two ships watched the long golden
coast, its beauty contrasting the violence occurring throughout the
country. Still, connections with civilization had to continue, and the
Corycia would sail regularly to Buncrana to pick up mail and stores.

A year and a half had passed since operations were abandoned
in 1917, and time was needed to prepare for the renewed effort.
There were mooring operations. Anchors were laid tight and strung
with a series of weights called "clumps" that totaled up to seven tons.

---

* The RIC was the police force that represented the British government in Ireland.
** "Black and Tan" referred to the ad hoc uniforms of mixed khaki and dark green
that British recruits, who were sent to strengthen the RIC in 1920, wore. The Black
and Tans, often unemployed war veterans, were known for their brutality and often
targeted civilian Irish in reprisal for Irish Republican Army attacks. The Black and
Tans were also supported by an auxiliary division. These "Auxies" became more
infamous in their brutality than the Black and Tans.

Laying the mooring took several days of work with divers constantly checking to make sure everything was perfect.

When all was ready, the divers finally and fully surveyed the wreck in detail to see what the wild weather off Lough Swilly had done. Damant remembered all too well how the ship had been crushed within weeks of his arrival in 1917. However, when divers landed on the wreck on July 3, 1919, Damant was pleasantly surprised. They easily found the working position, a deep thirty-by-twenty-foot pit framed fore and aft by towering superstructure. There was little silting. It seemed to be merely a matter of resuming the work from where they had left off. "There is no doubt as to the position of the gold, and it is only necessary to go on digging out the debris … to expose it," Damant wrote to his superiors at the Admiralty.

Getting to the working position was difficult for a diver. The shot rope to the wreck was always left on overnight and attached to a buoy so that it could be easily picked up in the morning. The men aboard the *Racer* made sure to give it plenty of slack since the strong tidal action at Lough Swilly jerked at the line and threatened to sever it on the wreckage. The additional slack also ensured that the line would almost always foul in the *Laurentic*, which made the job of the day's first diver especially onerous since he had to free the lines.

Diver Ernest Crouch, a newcomer to the *Laurentic* who had been a diving instructor at HMS *Excellent*, wrote that the strong tide made reaching the working position difficult:

> You landed on the wreck [and] found yourself about forty feet high on the starboard side of the ship. As she was lying on her port side, you had to make the best of your way down to the bottom of the hole…. Having nothing to catch hold of, one hand had to be very careful or else you would have [fallen] into another compartment and lost yourself. There have been times when we had to jump to the bottom so you used to pull down sufficient air pipe to enable you to reach the bottom then jump keeping your air outlet closed. It used to be a bit risky but [it was] a nice sensation feeling yourself falling slowly through the water and watching everything about you. It seemed minutes before you landed, but it was only seconds.

There was a rhythmic beauty to their labor. At 6:45 AM the *Racer* greeted the day by raising its anchors and sailing for the wreck site; it was followed by the *Corycia*, where Damant and the divers berthed. After arriving at the site, the diving party transferred from the *Corycia* to the *Racer* and moored for the day. By 9:00 AM, the first divers descended to the wreck and checked the connections. Then divers worked for an hour at a time setting off explosives and removing debris. Damant thought an hour underwater was enough at twenty fathoms, but he hoped to have them stay under longer as they gained experience. At 5:00 PM work ceased, and the moorings were cast loose and attached to marker buoys. By 8:00 PM both the *Corycia* and *Racer* returned to Ballymastocker Bay.

All this work, as it had in 1917, was interrupted continuously by the oceanic swells and the usual rough weather. On average, Damant supposed that they could work the wreck only one out of three days. When weather was good, he worked both watches and on Sundays. Damant drove the men hard, determined to produce results.

And Damant was pleased, especially in the *Racer*. "I find that I can do far more work per day than could be managed with the *Volunteer* in 1917," he wrote, "this owing to the general convenience of the ship and her equipment and the valuable assistance of her Staff, workshop, and auxiliary machinery."

After almost a month of work, on July 20, 1919, Ernest Crouch found the gold again. There were five ingots that alone were enough to pay for over half the salvage season. Subsequent days brought more gold so that by the end of July, the divers had recovered 206 ingots. While encouraging, and a fortune just in itself, there were still 2,463 out of the original 3,211 bars still embedded in the wreck.

The gold was only making itself apparent in ones and twos. There were hardly any traces of the bullions' original wood boxes. Damant anticipated that at any moment they would pull up some deck plate and reveal the main hoard. Still, with gold coming up, he knew that he had proved that the Royal Navy could do the job. "How happy I was!!" Damant wrote, "Our efficiency was proved, our position consolidated and the fear of some intrigue for handing the job over to some one else, swept away."

Salvage team with a diver during 1919 season. Notice the box for coins found on the wreck and the gold bars. Ernest "Dusty" Miller is standing on the far right. Guybon Damant is third from left. *National Museum of the Royal Navy, 2007/47*

But as August passed, the gold appeared less frequently. Where before the layers of deck plates were the main obstacle, Damant became impeded by a mass of rubbish that swished about the working position. As current and tides swam back and forth it washed in debris from the higher framing superstructure and covered what Damant's crew had just dug out. These little bits of cement, metal, and wood all needed to be removed by hand. Since Damant was forced to use continuous charges of explosives to break up the larger pieces of the ship, this resulted in concussions that shook still smaller material into the pit. Damant used explosives so routinely that certain safety measures, such as getting the ship clear of the work, became lax.

On August 8, Damant set off an eighty-pound charge. The *Racer* quivered and suddenly the engineer, ashen faced, ran onto the deck. He claimed that water was pouring into the engine room. There were four to five feet of seawater in the bilges. If the water continued to rise, it would put out the ship's fires and the *Racer* would be sitting in the middle of the sea prone to sink. Meanwhile, a diver noticed splintered planks sticking out of the ship's bottom.

But, geared as it was for salvage, the *Racer* had plenty of pumps. These were put to good use as the water was drained from below decks, and upon further examination they found that the water was coming from the ship's condenser, which had been cracked. Additional leakage was coming from cracked casks and other stores. The splintered planks the diver saw were actually debris from the *Laurentic* floating toward the surface.

Damant wrote, "In harbour that night we cleared these out and my good angel Miller at last found the seat of the trouble in a disused sea cock which a diver was able to plug from outside while we made a proper internal repair." Damant reported the affair to the Admiralty and promised to make sure the *Racer* got well clear of explosions in the future.

It was frustrating for all hands as the gold grew scarcer. Damant was convinced that they were right by it, but the debris made the job a horror. Damant thought the work could be sped up if he had an underwater pump that could suck up the little bits of wreckage that he assumed covered the gold. He sent a letter to the Admiralty and contacted salvage companies to see if there was any such piece of equipment that could help them.

As Damant struggled to find a technological solution to ease the work, the divers toiled by hand, filling hoppers with loose debris. As in 1917, the surrounding superstructure loomed higher and higher as they dug, threatening to collapse. Diver Crouch compared the working area to "a very dark hold when you looked up, and you could see all the ship side plates and deck plates on the move with the motion of the swell.... On nearly every occasion the diver went down in 1919, he got foul as there was so much obstructions overhead." Damant, however, would not stop the work to deal with these obstructions since they were, as he thought, so close to the main gold hoard. As August passed, the weather grew ugly again, allowing for only intermittent work.

Despite these difficulties, Damant was optimistic and reported to the Admiralty on August 27, "I expect to get considerably larger quantities of gold when weather allows of 5 or 6 consecutive days diving. At present the frequent gales carry away marker buoys and shift rubbish about in the wreck so that on resuming several hours of diving time are lost in restoring the arrangements."

It was at about this time that Damant started to receive inquiries from newspapers. In early August, somebody in Buncrana had tipped off reporters that a major gold salvage was underway off Lough Swilly. The press wanted details. They wanted photographs. They wanted interviews. A naval charity that had heard of the salvage requested that a faux bar of gold, if not a real one, be donated to their organization. The *Racer*'s boatswain, Henry Howell, who may have been the source of the leak, requested permission from the Admiralty to publish an article on the gold salvage.

Damant, however, would not entertain any sort of publicity, so the newspapers published articles based on their own limited understanding of the situation. The *Irish Times*, after noting incorrectly that Miller was in charge of the operations, proclaimed on August 18, "It is thought that all the gold is likely to be recovered during the week-end, as full advantage was taken of the spell of fine weather." The *Evening Telegraph and Post* declared, "While treasure-seekers in Tobermory Bay have been salving scraps of old iron and ballast stoves from the rotting hulk of the gay galleon of the Armada,* the Admiralty Salvage Corps have quietly and effectively been working to more practical purpose on the wreck of one of the galleons of the greatest Armadas of the 20th century. Over a million pounds of ingot bullion have just been recovered from the *Laurentic*."

While an eventual leak of the operation was inevitable since there were so many people involved in the salvage, Damant was still appalled and continued to deny all requests for an interview. As long as he was to be in charge, there were to be no reporters on the *Racer* or *Corycia*. He wrote to his superiors at the Admiralty stating, "I think it would be wise to do as little as possible to call attention

---

* Tobermory Bay on the Isle of Mull in Scotland has a legend that a ship from the Spanish Armada lies laden with gold somewhere on the bottom of the bay.

to these operations as there is a possibility of attempts being made to corrupt divers and others; and the landing and transit of the gold is not without risk." All that summer, Damant had observed that the *Racer* was exposed and isolated off Lough Swilly with few weapons to guard itself.

The Admiralty agreed with Damant and would not divulge any information concerning the *Laurentic* to the press. This, however, did not prevent reporters from continuing to use their imaginations or citing overinflated figures—one article claimed that £3 million had been recovered. But eventually, without any other information, reports of the *Laurentic* became infrequent, although they would percolate to the surface from time to time.

Damant, however, was more than willing to suffer a visit from his old friend Professor J. S. Haldane and his son, who were very much interested in the work and wanted to see how the method of staged decompression was holding up in the field. The answer was that it was holding up very well. There had been only a few instances of decompression sickness, and Damant strictly enforced proper safety measures. While observing operations, Haldane asked if any of the divers had been blown up from the wreck. Damant answered no.

Just at that moment a diver came shooting up out of the water. His diving dress had overinflated and the man within was unable to control it. Fortunately, the diver was clear of the ship, since if he had struck the *Racer* or one the mooring buoys, it would have torn open his diving dress and the weight he bore would have sunk him straight to the bottom. Diver Ernest Crouch, who witnessed the exchange with Damant and Haldane and the subsequent blow-up, called it "a very strange coincidence." The diver was pulled out, his suit checked, the problem cleared, and then sent down to the bottom to stage decompress.

September began with a roar, and on most days the exposed position of the *Racer* did not allow for work to be done. Even when it was comparatively calmer, the swells rolled the *Racer* violently. And debris kept refilling the working position. Damant, ever optimistic,

A diver demonstrating a blow-up in an experimental diving tank at HMS *Excellent*. When a diver experiences a blow-up, air from the diving dress cannot escape. The diver is unable to reach his valves and is helpless. *Report of a Committee Appointed by the Lords Commissioners of the Admiralty to Consider and Report upon the Conditions of Deep-Water Diving, 1907.*

wrote to the Admiralty, "There is no difficulty that could not be overcome in a few days of such settled weather as one experiences earlier in the summer; the present slow progress is entirely due to meteorological conditions."

With the weather deteriorating, diving operations concluded on September 9, 1919. Moorings were taken up and stowed underwater in Ballymastocker Bay. They had recovered 315 bars valued at a little over £484,209. They also recovered about twenty pounds in coins, which were defaced and warped by the use of explosives. The cost of the operations for 1919 was £12,018, about 2.5 percent of the value of gold they had recovered. "I consider that the rest of the gold recoverable could be salved at the same proportional cost," Damant wrote.

Damant was quick to point out that it was far more cost-effective to have him do the work as an Admiralty operative rather than outsource it to a private salvage firm.

As with the 1917 operations, the Treasury consented to allow for a one-eighth of one percent bonus for the team, which amounted to £575, after tax, to be divided among the men. Shares were not equal and given out under the advice of Damant. For example, by the Treasury's calculations an able-bodied seaman would receive just under four pounds and a diver almost thirteen pounds. Divers made an extra six shillings and eight pence for one dive a day and sixteen shillings for two dives a day. Diver Ernest Crouch noted that this was "very good pay but working in that depth the civilian diver would receive about a pound each dip also a big percentage of what was salved." Crouch estimated the divers were receiving about one shilling for every bar salved. Damant never claimed a share for himself, but the Treasury insisted on granting him a £110 bounty. Considering that the divers earned eight and a half pounds per week and Damant fourteen pounds per week, it was a nice bonus, but not one that would change his lifestyle.

At the end of the season, the gold was transferred entirely to the *Corycia*. The Admiralty, fearful of landing the gold in Ireland, directed Damant to sail directly to Liverpool. He therefore took the gold-laden ship and sailed through the old naval boom to anchor off Buncrana. On September 12, the evening before he was to sail to Liverpool, Damant had the *Racer* leave the safety of the boom to anchor in Ballymastocker Bay to prepare for the voyage to England. Damant ordered to have the yacht ready for full speed by daylight. Night settled upon Lough Swilly, and the *Corycia* swayed gently in her anchorage as Damant slept in his bunk.

At midnight there came a shouting from the deck. A watchman was hailing somebody. Damant roused himself and headed on deck. On the sea, there was a large, open boat with eight or nine men in it. They shouted over the water that they were fishing.

Damant thought it strange. He had often anchored in the bay, and it was almost always desolate. He had never seen anybody, let alone a large boat, fishing in the bay. Damant decided to let it be, and was about to turn in to his bunk again when another open boat appeared.

Damant roused all hands, and arms were served out. He then sent a message to the engine room asking how long it might be before the *Corycia* could build full steam. To his relief, the engineer replied they could do half speed at once and build up to full steam in a half hour by forcing the fires. Meanwhile, a third and fourth boat appeared. The *Corycia* was being surrounded.

Damant ordered the *Corycia* to weigh anchor and head out to sea, leaving the so-called fishing boats to their own devices. The *Corycia* swiftly sailed through the ring of boats. Fortunately, there was no gunfire, just suspicion. Damant later wrote that he could never prove an attack was imminent, but commented, "I never again saw boats fishing or pretending to fish there.... The spectacular capture of all that treasure was exactly the sort of thing the rebels aspired to. Enquiries among the natives ashore, made in later years, were fruitless, no one would speak of anything connected with the rebellion which was only natural as informers were shot out of hand."

The *Corycia* sailed to Liverpool on September 13. When the ship arrived safely at the dock, Damant was greeted by a man in a bowler hat who had a lorry at his disposal. Sailors loaded up the truck with what the man wrote down on the bill of lading as "an unknown quantity of gold in 25 boxes." They quickly drove off into the city, leaving Damant at the dock pondering if the man was genuine. But since no complaints came from the Treasury it must have been all right. And it was. A military escort took the gold and transported it to Lime Street Station. A special train then brought it to London and the Treasury.

Some more good news came. At the urging of Damant, the *Racer* was taken off the disposal list by the Admiralty. The salvage ship was sent to Portsmouth to get new pumps installed that could help finish the salvage work. The divers, meanwhile, returned to the *Excellent* and were slated to return in the spring. With high hopes, Damant returned home to Nell at Thursford to plan for a triumphant 1920.

While there were still 2,354 bars of gold left somewhere in the wreck, Damant had no doubt that they would get it. "I consider that a full season's work in 1920 would enable the rest of the gold in the wreck to be recovered," he asserted in a report. "The prospects of doing so are extremely good as there is little more blasting work to be done and advantage could be taken of this winter to prepare a pumping plant capable of discharging the rubbish and sand under which a quantity of gold is still lying."

However, a newspaper reporter managed to speak with some of Damant's team and wrote, "The general view on board the Admiralty salving steamer *Racer* from which the divers descend is that all the bullion will not be recovered by the next two or three years."

Damant was given a long leave by the Admiralty. It was a lovely autumn. He and Nell often fished from the *Tessa* in the Solent. Although Damant thought that Nell "looked very sweet in a suede jersey and grey skirt," and they caught dozens of whiting and flatfish, his thoughts were ever turned toward the next spring when he would return to Ireland and finish the work.

26

Invincible

AFTER THE *RACER* DEPARTED LOUGH Swilly in September 1919, the violence in Ireland had escalated. On September 7 Unionist reprisals against Sinn Féin and the Irish Republican Army (IRA) began in earnest with two hundred British soldiers burning and looting buildings in the town of Fermoy. A few days later, on September 12, the British government outlawed the Irish parliament. In order to counter British intelligence, Irish leader Michael Collins formed a covert team to carry out assassinations of RIC members and British operatives. Called the "Twelve Apostles" after their original number and later referred to as the "Squad," they carried out their most famous attack in Dublin on the morning of November 21, 1920, when they assassinated fourteen people, including British army officers, an RIC officer, and other affiliates. That afternoon, British police forces and the Black and Tans arrived at a Gaelic football match in Croke Park, Dublin. Their orders were ostensibly to search the men in attendance but the result was a massacre that left fourteen dead and over sixty injured. November 21 became known as Bloody Sunday in Irish history and became a rallying cry for Irish freedom.

Even before Bloody Sunday,[*] violence was mounting and disruptions throughout Ireland were the norm. During the winter of 1919 to

---

[*] This is but one of several "Bloody Sundays" in Irish history.

1920, the director of naval equipment, Rear Admiral Edward Phillpotts, worried about the *Racer's* vulnerability. He went so far as to suggest that the whole *Laurentic* operation be turned over to a private salvage company. Sir Osmond de Beauvoir Brock, the deputy chief of naval staff, concurred and suggested contracting out the work and merely providing a guard of marines. But Sir Vincent Baddeley persuasively argued that the Admiralty needed to take responsibility. He asserted that when it sunk, the *Laurentic* was an armed merchant cruiser with a Royal Navy officer in command. It was agreed that the Admiralty would continue to carry out the operations while the Treasury would resume paying for it.

For security, the Admiralty insisted that all men assigned to the *Laurentic* salvage needed to be from the Royal Navy as opposed to civilians that were from the Royal Fleet Auxiliary (RFA) or the Royal Navy Reserve (RNR). Sir Vincent Baddeley wrote, "Taking into consideration the proximity of the *Laurentic* to the Irish Coast, the fact that vessels will be working in and out of Irish ports, and the conditions existing in Ireland, I am strongly of the opinion that the work should be carried out entirely by men working under the Naval Discipline Act." The Naval Discipline Act required that men in the RFA and RNR be treated as if they were in the Royal Navy for the duration of the war. But with the war over and demobilization underway, these men were no longer subject to the law.

This resulted, despite Damant's protests, in the removal of several personnel from the *Laurentic* and included the *Racer's* commanding officer, Harold Jones, a man with whom Damant got on well. A new commanding officer of the *Racer*, a Lieutenant Y. C. N. MacMillan, was interviewed by Damant and, although not his first choice, was found suitable.

Despite the objections, Damant was worried about security, too. Damant wrote to Phillpotts on November 1, 1919, recalling the threat of the "fishing boats." "During the operations this summer it was evident to me that a raid carried out by a few of the large local open boats attacking simultaneously from different directions at night could hardly fail to carry the ship and secure her contents." He requested rifles, hand grenades, and two Lewis guns—a light machine gun of

American design that was widely used during the First World War. Phillpotts responded that rifles would be sufficient.

However, Phillpotts received a new appointment as president of the Royal Navy's Ordnance Committee and was replaced on May 1, 1920, by the fifty-three-year-old Rear Admiral Edward Francis Bruen. Bruen had commanded the battleship *Bellerophon* at Jutland and his correspondence gives the impression of an exacting, but fair, command. Damant ended up getting the Lewis guns and rifles but not the hand grenades.

Treasury officials noted that the cost of operations in 1919 was more than double the expenses of the original salvage of 1917 by an estimated £5,000 to a specific £12,018. In 1917 Damant had been forced to do the job on the cheap because of the war. Back then, he did not have a proper salvage ship, enough men, or reliable equipment. Still, Treasury officials were impressed that the cheapest salvage season happened to recover the most gold. To save funds, Damant proposed disposing of the *Corycia*, which cost about £200 per week to operate. In its place, Damant suggested that the Admiralty hire a drifter, a type of small boat generally used for harbor work, to assist the *Racer*. The drifter's owner would be responsible for its upkeep and crew while the Admiralty would supply the coal. It would be a less expensive means to help the *Racer* with mooring, fetching stores, or simply retrieving the mail. While this meant that the divers and Damant would need to berth on the *Racer* instead of the more hospitable *Corycia*, it was a plan that could be managed. Damant's proposal was adopted in principle, but the Admiralty opted to assign the naval drifter *CD 1** with a Royal Navy crew to the operation. This small, eighty-four-foot boat displaced 101 tons and had been built for the Royal Canadian Navy during the war but afterward had been taken over by the Royal Navy.

For the 1920 salvage season, there were fifty-six officers and crew manning the *Racer* in addition to twelve men in the diving party, which was composed of the divers and their attendants. With Damant as the officer in general charge of the operation, there were sixty-eight souls on the *Racer* while the *CD 1* had eleven. While somewhat crowded

---

* *CD* stood for "Canadian Drifter."

on the *Racer*, the 167-foot ship had been built for a maximum complement of 126.

Despite removing the *Corycia*, Damant estimated that the cost of operations for 1920 would run to £12,750, slightly higher than the £12,018 expended in 1919. Some of this additional cost had to do with equipping a new dredging pump for the operations. Damant, realizing that the higher cost might prove dyspeptic to the Treasury, wrote to them, "Though it is likely, I cannot of course guarantee that one season's work will complete the salvage of the gold, but allowing for all contingencies I should expect to recover upwards of one million pounds worth on the above expenditure."

Damant's measured but upbeat reports of the work gave the impression to the Treasury that they would soon be awash in gold. To the staid civil officers who managed His Majesty's money, the *Laurentic* was an enterprise that drew them to undersea adventure. Not that the Admiralty ever told them much of the operations, and even then only a few officials were really in the know about details concerning what was happening off Lough Swilly. Still, even the rumor of the *Laurentic* and its gold had the potential of making their jobs a little more exciting, a little more romantic. As in 1919, special preparations were made to have the gold delivered straight to Liverpool with the intent that no bullion should touch the Irish shore.

The *Racer* and *CD 1* were commissioned on April 24, 1920. On May 12, the *Racer* arrived in Buncrana and two days later headed to the mouth of Lough Swilly. Moorings were taken up from their sunken location in Ballymastocker Bay and laid efficiently. Damant sent off a report to Bruen, writing, "Progress up to the present is very satisfactory and compares favourably with that of former years."

But the weather quickly deteriorated, with big rollers coming in from the Atlantic, so the first divers, Damant included, did not descend to survey the wreck until May 25. Then, as Damant stood among the ruins of the *Laurentic* peering through his faceplate, his heart sank. Instead of the narrow pit of the working position, bound on either side by the high structures of the former passenger accommodations, everything was smashed flat. The *Laurentic* had become an even more confusing mishmash of corroding steel, wood, and hardened muck. In fact, the working position, which had been clearly delineated by masts and other structures, was lost. The landmarks had shifted relative to each other by as much as thirty feet.

Damant reported, "The shell of the ship has crumpled down flat in most places and boilers have broken out and lie scattered at some distance on the sea floor." He could not tell where to dig. But he optimistically expected to find the old working position in a couple of days of diving and wrote, "I consider the progress quite satisfactory."

The excavation work of 1919 had undermined the stability of those higher areas. Finally, storm and tide during the winter of 1919 to 1920 had torn them down, sliding fresh deck plates and bulkheads over the excavation. Such a collapse would have been catastrophic if the divers were on the bottom. It was probably a lucky thing, but that did not diminish the aggravation of having to remove tons and tons of deck plates anew. There was also no guarantee that Damant would choose to dig at the correct spot. Since the gold had gradually disappeared toward the end of 1919, there was a nagging suspicion that the bulk of the bullion had slipped out of the *Laurentic* through the hole that was created by the mines that sunk it. Not since the initial accordion-like collapse of the wreck in 1917 was morale this low.

In early June, Damant thought he may have found the approximate spot of the gold. He and the divers began the arduous process of exploding and hauling out deck plates. Damant estimated that about three hundred tons of plating and bulkheads needed to be removed just to begin, and a month was lost to the thankless, dangerous work. Diver Ernest Crouch wrote, "We used to shackle on a wire on these plates and remaining on the wreck gave the signal by telephone to pull up seeing they were clear; also taking special precautions to see your air pipe was clear. On many an occasion the diver's air pipe got foul, and he was pulled up with the hoist from which he had to be cleared. Then the plates were hauled inboard and placed upon the deck." When the day's work was done, the *Racer* slipped the mooring buoys and, once clear of the wreck, threw all the plates into the sea. Crouch noted that scrap steel then was selling at four pounds a ton and they were pulling up about forty tons of steel a day.

It was hard work, and although the divers got extra pay for diving, the job itself presented unique difficulties. "It was not a pretty sight when you first got on the wreck," wrote Crouch. "You never knew for certain where you were going to land. When one first started it took you one whole season, eight months, to be able to explain to the boss [Damant] exactly where you were and then one had to think very careful as he knew everything." The wreck was difficult to navigate, but there were landmarks such as the fallen mast on the seafloor and a big derrick that had been near the working position, which stuck up from the wreck by about thirty feet. A diver going down to the *Laurentic* soon learned to note the direction of the tide before going to the bottom. This served as a compass so that a diver could get his bearings just by feeling the direction of the current. Damant had a big board upon which he mounted a plan of the *Laurentic* that had markings for where the divers were operating. Small sheets of copper were laid on it to represent deck plating. The plan was used not only to help prepare operations, but also to instruct new divers. But nothing trumps experience, and after a time, the repetitive work granted preternatural knowledge to the divers. "We could always tell when rough weather was coming along," Crouch wrote, "as we always got a big underground swell and it was very hard to remain on the bottom as you used to get chucked about."

At the beginning of July, the divers cleared a layer of deck plates to reveal a field of smaller debris that needed to be removed painstakingly by hand. This debris was different than what the divers had encountered in 1917 or 1919. In the 1920 collapse, the contents of the upper decks had cascaded into the working position. These included all the trappings one might expect to find on a former luxury liner. Aside from broken-up wood, iron, and cement, there were disintegrating saloon chairs, paneling, porcelain baths, planking, and tiles—there was no sign of any gold. Matters were made worse since, with the general flattening of the wreck, gravel and sand that had been blocked from entering the *Laurentic* began to pass through. It was not in great amounts, but it was steady enough that there was a growing concern that the wreck would silt over. This sediment hardened like concrete in the debris, reinforced by cot frames and spring mattresses that lay about in all directions.

So the divers worked and worked, removing the debris by the bucket. Then on July 7, 1920, their efforts were rewarded when a diver discovered two ingots, embedded three feet inside the rubble. Damant's relief was immediate and intense. Although it was only two ingots, it was evidence that Damant had selected the correct position. But there was little more gold to be found, and by July 23 they had recovered only a total of five ingots.

Based on all the latest intelligence, Damant and Miller agreed that the gold had become divided into two hoards. The first was either exhausted or nearly so. The larger portion was probably some little distance deeper to port under yet more layers of deck plates. It was an educated guess, a hunch perhaps, but it was clear that where they were digging was devoid of treasure. Damant ordered excavation to commence in a new area with the hope that the gold was there.

After several weeks of excavation, the divers found all sorts of items, from naval guns to parquet floor tiling, but there was no sign of any gold. Damant, however, was convinced that some place under all the rubbish was the treasure.

To speed things along, Damant turned to technology—specifically, the pump he had brought aboard the *Racer*. It was the "Invincible," a fifty-horsepower dredging pump that ran at 950 rpm using centrifugal action to suck up sand and debris. Manufactured by J. & H. Gwynne of the Hammersmith Ironworks of London, the Invincible's pumping engines were advertised as being "unequalled for Efficiency, Durability, and Strength." It was fully submersible and capable of being fitted with six-inch hoses, which would be just the right size to start removing all the smaller debris, sand, and mud. The Treasury spent £632 for it, but in light of the potential millions that could be wrested from the sea, it was seen as a sound investment.

The pump was also bulky, weighed about two tons, and had never been used at a depth of 125 feet, which was about where the divers were working at this time, at level with the seafloor. To deploy the Invincible, the *Racer* lowered the pump to the working position where a diver guided it. This, in and of itself, was not an easy job since the working position was narrow and filled with such twisted metal that it was hard to find a place to secure the machine. It took hours just to place it appropriately and, considering the fickle weather of Lough Swilly, made the pump's use a risky proposition. Still, they tried. Damant reported, "So far as I know nothing similar to this pumping of solids has previously been attempted at such a depth and naturally many difficulties arise at first. For instance, we find it harder to prevent the pump choking itself and clearing it, when this occurs, is a stiff job under water."

The pump, when operational, was highly efficient. With it, the divers sucked out as much debris in an hour as they could do by hand in a day, discharging the sediment in the direction of the tide so that it would not darken the water. In this way, the divers first reached the outer skin of the ship. Although there was still no sign of gold, there was still much debris to sift through. But in late August the pump broke down, its electrical parts malfunctioning. Damant did not have the equipment necessary for repairs so he set to modify a twelve-inch pump they had on the *Racer* by reducing its pipe to six inches in the hopes that it would prove capable of sucking up debris straight to the surface. But the depth was too great to allow it to work effectively. The only reliable means to remove the debris was for the divers to remove it manually in buckets. Since with every strong tide or current the sea would wash in sand and other sediment, it became clear to Damant that the only way to get to the gold was not a matter of cleverness but hard labor. Essentially, they needed to dig faster than the sea could fill the pit.

Damant needed to have his divers work in the most efficient way possible. He decided to limit each man's "dip" to thirty minutes. In those thirty minutes, a diver exerted himself to the utmost and filled the hoppers with sand and debris. Since it was a straightforward job, there was rarely a need to extend their time on the bottom. When the thirty minutes were up, the diver was decompressed to the surface in only thirty-three minutes, following the decompression tables. Meanwhile, a fresh diver would be on the bottom working for thirty minutes. In this way, there would always be a diver at work.

Damant wrote, "Had we kept each diver 1½ hours on the bottom he would have to spend a further 1½ hours decompressing, during which time his services would have been lost to us on deck, where probably also when he did appear after 3 hours under water he would not have been much use till he had had another hour's rest.... By limiting the liability for decompression to half an hour I felt justified, as the sea got up, in hanging on till the last moment, and in snatching a dive here and there in intermissions."

While this system of automation worked for most men, Damant found that certain individuals proved more susceptible to the bends then others. In these cases, decompression times were raised 20 percent above Haldane's tables. As a further safeguard, the *Racer* also kept aboard cylinders of compressed oxygen that divers would breathe through a mask for ten minutes after surfacing. Damant

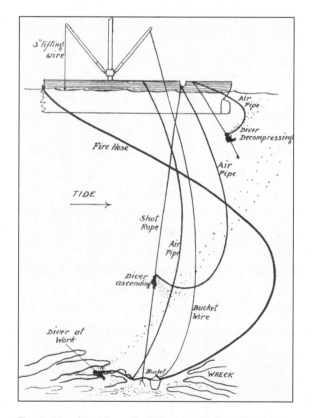

This diagram shows the order of operations and lay of the lines for the divers on the *Laurentic* salvage. Journal of Hygiene *25, no. I (1926):* *47, courtesy of Cambridge University Press*

viewed the oxygen as a final precaution and never did see any cases of the bends after the oxygen was breathed. But Damant admitted that "in the absence of strictly comparable controls this proves nothing, and I was too busy to attempt systematic tests of the value of the method. Still we all came to believe in it; and men who thought they might be going to have bends were free to go to the cylinder and help themselves without fuss or bother to anyone else."*

Damant counted a total of thirty-one cases of the bends over the entire course of the work, typically men with pain in the joints and limbs, not including those men that suddenly acquired patches of discoloration, generally in the abdomen. In most cases, decompression illness occurred within an hour of surfacing, and only once was it delayed by two hours. The worst was one case of temporary blindness and another case of temporary paralysis—both were cured in the recompression chamber.

As the divers racked up dive after dive, the men could sense the onset of the bends before they even surfaced. In cases where a joint or limb was affected, the diver would try to stop the attack by moving the affected area in violent exercise. This would usually work. If not, then he reported the attack, and the diver would be passed into the recompression chamber. This was a notable change from 1917 when, out of ego and pride, divers would not report symptoms until it was almost too late. Divers now marched themselves straight into the chamber and, knowing the decompression tables, would manage it all themselves.

But without any gold forthcoming, Damant drove the men hard. One diver, Augustus Dent, had a bad attack of the bends. It felt like his arm was being torn off. He was carried off to the "diver's oven" and kept inside for six hours to decompress. After he got out, Damant handed him a glass of gin. Dent took it, gulped it down, and said, "Thank you, sir."

---

* The method of breathing pure oxygen is indeed effective, and in later decades it became standard procedure to administer pure oxygen to divers who might have missed a decompression stage. Pure oxygen is also commonly used for normal decompression at shallower depths and has different decompression tables that allow for quicker surfacing times.

"Don't thank me," said Damant. "It was a medical necessity, not a gratuity."

Dent would later recall, "He was a cold fish, was Damant."*

On one occasion, Damant worked on the wreck for an hour. After surfacing, he began to see double. He knew what it was, and that he needed to get into the recompression chamber. However, Dusty Miller had contracted the bends earlier in the day and was almost done with his own decompression, being down to five pounds per square inch.

Miller, seeing Damant's state, blew open the chamber and allowed his commander to enter even though Miller still had forty minutes left to decompress. Damant slipped into the chamber and found that the double vision disappeared after he raised the pressure to ten pounds. Damant fully decompressed, and there were no further problems.

However, Miller's bends came back more aggressively than before. He reentered the chamber, and Damant directly supervised his assistant's decompression. First, the pressure needed to be raised to twenty psi to relieve the symptoms. Following the tables, Damant brought the pressure down to four pounds, but Miller's bends returned. For six and a half hours Damant tried by trial and error to cure Miller. Damant now wished, even though there was no room on the *Racer*, that he had one of the larger models of recompression chambers aboard. The damp tightness of the diver's oven was demoralizing to Miller. By 1:30 AM with a long day of work ahead, all reason was lost. Both men decided to try a hot meal and bed as a cure. Miller continued to suffer all that night and most of the next day before the symptoms finally subsided.

By the end of August, Damant and his men had recovered two more bars of gold. After searching the area where these were found, first under some deck plates and then by digging holes in debris by blasting it with jets of water, they could locate no more. These two ingots were the last

---

* Dent was not only a diver but also a survivor of the *Laurentic*. Dent recalled that Damant had asked for him in 1917 since Dent knew where the gold was within the ship. But Dent could not join the *Volunteer* since a doctor would not pass him as fit for deepwater diving and diagnosed him with a heart suffering from shock. It was only after the war that he joined the *Laurentic* salvage. By that time, his personal knowledge of the ship was useless since the wreck had fully collapsed.

of the season, giving a total of seven bars of gold estimated to be worth
£11,770. To make matters more awkward, the 1920 salvage operations
had cost £23,001, far more than the £12,750 Damant had originally estimated. Instead of the *Racer* bringing to Liverpool a hold full of bullion,
an officer and two seamen used public transportation to deliver the
seven ingots to the Bank of England. If there was any bright point to
the salvage season, it was that there was no whiff of a plot by the IRA to
attack the *Racer*—maybe they knew how unsuccessful Damant had been.

After all of Damant's hopeful assessments, the Treasury wanted an
explanation. If the salvage force continued to recover the remaining
2,347 ingots at the same rate, it would take them over 335 years to
raise the remaining gold. Damant took "great pains," as he put it, and
produced a report for the Treasury department on September 11, 1920,
in which he admitted that the results were "very unsatisfactory." Damant
then proceeded to describe the difficulties of the work and how it was
more than likely that the mass of gold was hiding under some deck
plate. "On one occasion in 1917," Damant wrote, "conditions being
similar, by hoisting out a single small plate a nest of 214 ingots was
exposed and brought to the surface within an hour. The obvious course
is to clear out all the debris in the working position right down to the
skin of the ship and so make sure of finding the gold."

As to the possibility of the gold having slipped out a hole in the
ship immediately after it was mined or torpedoed, Damant dismissed
the chance as remote. He asserted that the Treasury needed to consider four facts about the gold. He wrote:

a) It is certain that it is still there.
b) It can be exposed and salved by removing the overlaying wreckage and debris.
c) The removal of the wreckage is practicable and is what we have
been doing but, on account of the depth of the water, it is a slow process. If silting was taking place seriously the operation might become
impossible but as things are at present we gain on the accumulation.
d) The value of the gold is enormous compared with the cost of
continuing the work. We have had two successful and one unsuccessful season.

Damant urged that the government should continue the work. Admiral Bruen wrote in support, "The recovery of the gold is likely to be a slow process, but that it is in or about the wreck seems pretty certain. This season has been exceptionally bad from a salvage or divers point of view, the weather and the prevailing direction of the wind have combined in delaying the work, otherwise better results would have been probably obtained."*

In the end the decision to proceed rested not with the Admiralty but with the Treasury. On the morning of September 16, 1920, Damant visited London and met with Baddeley, who in his role as Admiralty liaison escorted him to the Treasury. There they met with Sir Warren Fisher, the permanent secretary to the Treasury, and Basil Blackett, the comptroller of the Treasury. Damant and Baddeley explained the situation, how the gold was certainly there, and how they were stymied by weather and the chaotic mess that the *Laurentic* had become. The essential message: the salvage was difficult but not impossible, and if allowed to keep working, they would find the gold. Their arguments, and especially Damant's conviction, won Fisher and Blackett over, and they advised Sir Joseph Austen Chamberlain, the chancellor of the Exchequer, to support the work.**

Thus, Damant was allowed to continue his quest. What he had figured to be an operation that would last only a couple of weeks had turned into an endless odyssey in which his motivation, at first driven by patriotic reasons, had now become a matter of honor and pride. In some respects, the *Laurentic* was at that time his raison d'être. But to the Treasury the *Laurentic* was, no matter how romantic the notion of sunken treasure, a matter of business. If the outlay of expense was more than the return, there was no point of continuing. Damant and Baddeley were told that if results were not satisfactory in 1921, then they would abandon operations and the whole business would most likely be turned over to a private salvage company.

---

* Bruen also had his own reasons for maintaining Damant's unit. Since the elimination of the salvage section, only Damant's team was available as a Royal Navy unit to conduct any salvage in the event of an emergency.
** Chamberlain was the half brother of the more famous Neville Chamberlain.

27

"A Pity to Give Up"

DAMANT SPENT THE WINTER OF 1920 to 1921 investigating the maggots of the feather-horn plumed gnat. Specifically, Damant was curious as to how the crystalline larvae of the *Corethra plumicornis* managed to hover perfectly motionless in water. Damant noticed it was similar to the neutral buoyancy a diver maintained when his air was perfectly balanced. As Damant exposed the gnats to different kinds of gases such as hydrogen, oxygen, and nitrogen, he found that the insects, while momentarily disturbed, were able to correct their positions quickly. It was fascinating work, and he hoped that his findings might be published in one of the preeminent scientific journals. He had already managed to get one note published in the *Physical Society Proceedings* concerning the research titled "Secretion of Gas by the Larva of a Gnat."

But despite Damant's longing to study entomology, he knew he had another purpose: he needed to find the *Laurentic*'s gold. Damant was convinced that the ingots lay in a massive heap somewhere in or around the working position. However, he also believed he was wasting time digging into random places. He contacted Professor Ernest Edward Brooks of Leicester City Technical School, who had worked at the Admiralty Research Station in Harwich during the war. Damant's question to Brooks: *Is there a method to detect gold buried in iron wreckage underwater?*

Brooks was intrigued, and, after consulting with Dr. Charles Vickery Drysdale of the Admiralty Research Station, proposed two possible methods. The first was essentially using a metal detector that could indicate the proximity of gold without contact, and the other thrusting a probe into the debris that could detect gold on contact. Practically speaking no one had ever tried such a thing, so experiments would need to be conducted in a tank. Brooks estimated the cost for the equipment and research would run £15 or less. The Admiralty saw it as a bargain.

It is just as well that the price was low since the experiments were a failure. It was simply too difficult to devise a method to discriminate gold from iron. Brooks proposed another option using a complex apparatus composed of two beams of metal fitted with electrodes that ran a current that penetrated the metal. By turning the beams slightly, it would give a signal to differentiate between iron and gold. Brooks advised, however, "In the first place it cannot be expected that this method or any other will be able to detect gold buried under thick iron plating. In the second place, no one can say without actual trial how much the normal working of the apparatus may be upset by the proximity of enormous masses of iron wreckage, and by the short-circuiting effect of the seawater overhead.... it is quite likely that the diver's copper helmet will have to be reckoned with." The matter was dropped by Damant, although Brooks continued to work on his new device.

Other bad news came regarding the broken Invincible dredging pump. While it had been brought to the Portsmouth Dockyard for repairs in October 1920, by the next spring it was still not fixed, and repairs did not seem likely to occur any time soon due to general labor troubles in the country.

So Damant returned to Lough Swilly and began diving on April 25, 1921, without innovative equipment but lots of hope. Fortunately, there was minimal change to the wreck, and it showed little sign of silting.

Success came early for Damant as the divers found the first gold of the season on May 3, hauling up three ingots. Divers discovered another three bars two days later. But progress was slower than usual since the operations were hampered by gales and swells. They did not uncover another ingot until June 2.

Meanwhile, Damant's plans had become undermined because of his relationship with the commanding officer of the *Racer*, Lieutenant Y. C. N. MacMillan. Diver Ernest Crouch wrote that in MacMillan's opinion he had seniority over Damant since he was an active service officer, whereas Damant was retired. This would not have made a difference to the divers. Crouch wrote, "There was not an officer or man living who could take charge of the salvage operations of *Laurentic* more capable than Commander Damant and all the divers knew it and respected him for it. He was a very stern master, but we all had great faith in him. What he said or done was right."

The relationship between the two became so frayed that in late June 1921 Damant visited Whitehall to complain to Admiral Bruen. He requested that MacMillan be replaced. The request was granted, and a new master of the *Racer* named McCutchan took charge. Forgoing the Admiralty rule for requiring naval personnel, McCutchan was a Royal Fleet Auxiliary (RFA) officer who clearly was subordinate to Damant. The two men got on well, and when they could not work on the wreck sometimes took hikes about Lough Swilly together.

It was at about this time that the divers once more reached the outer skin of the ship. They could clearly see the *Laurentic*'s propeller shaft tunnels next to a field of debris, mud, and sand that they needed to dig through. The tunnels allowed Damant to mark their position with greater accuracy since the forty-foot-long, twelve-foot-wide tunnels were easily discernible. He moved excavation to another suspected spot, farther aft toward a square structure that was once the ship's hospital. This separate compartment was strangely upright, and Damant figured that it had been separated from the ship and had shifted about twenty feet. By his reckoning it was approximately where the gold had slipped to. The divers went to work, slowly removing the hospital and clearing plates.

At this depth, the divers saw strange fauna. Ernest Crouch spotted frogfish, a type of anglerfish that uses an appendage dotted with phosphorescence to attract prey. A diver stuck one with a knife and sent it up in a bucket. Damant was delighted and impressed the men of the *Racer* as he gave them a lecture about this strange creature.

Most of the deck plates had been removed to reveal a small, loose field of debris. As before, the divers removed it by hand. By July 8, 1921, the men had managed to clear a fairly large area, leaving only mud and sand. To help, Damant ordered an improved double-chain standard Priestman sand grab. The device, scheduled to arrive in August, was essentially a gigantic claw to lift cartloads of debris all at once.

In July the divers found more gold. This was not the great hoard that Damant longed for but rather pairs of ingots or, if they were lucky, bars in triplicate. By July 15, after several days of work, the divers exhumed another ten bars from the wreck. These ten came at a price since to get at them the divers had to dig under one of the *Laurentic*'s ten-inch guns. This subsequently crashed into the working position. Fortunately, there were no injuries, but it did delay work for a couple of days as the heavy weapon could not be directly winched to the surface but had to be towed off-site by the *Racer*. It was during this process on July 17 that the divers discovered a clue as to the gold's whereabouts. The divers found box fragments—the crates that had been used to stow the gold. Another six bars were pulled up on July 31.

Wreckage recovered from the *Laurentic* was heavy, twisted, and sharp, posing dangers for the divers.
Journal of Hygiene 25, no. 1 (1926), courtesy of Cambridge University Press

That month had other positive auguries. On July 9, 1921, a truce to the Irish War of Independence was signed that was to go into effect on July 11. While violence still continued, there seemed to be for the moment a reprieve to the political situation in Ireland. The country had become partitioned into Protestant-dominated Northern Ireland and the rest as Southern Ireland. The *Laurentic*, off Donegal, was just inside the boundary of Southern Ireland in an area known as the Borderlands. But there was uncertainty about what was to happen as Southern Ireland would either become a "free state" under the British Empire or attain complete independence. While the matter was being debated, Damant grew concerned as to how the prospect of a completely independent Ireland would affect his work on the *Laurentic*. Eventually, he wrote to the Admiralty, "Under future legislation (unless the point is foreseen) it might be possible for the Government of this part of Ireland either a) to claim the wreck or b) to be in a position to regulate salvage operations within these waters."

In the meantime, the *Laurentic* was still Damant's and he could rightfully expect that the threat of Irish rebels attacking the *Racer* would be at least lessened. Then more good news came from Admiral Bruen. Damant was promoted to commander in recognition of his war services with an effective date of November 11, 1918.

During a long spell of bad weather in early August 1921, the *Racer* headed ashore to Londonderry to install the new Priestman sand grab. The grab was able to dig faster than a diver, and they were even able to lower it while the *Racer* was rolling on its moorings. The drawback was that the grab needed to have a diver on the bottom to move it into the narrow working position. The diver waited on the wreck while the grab was lowered to within a foot or two of the debris. Then the diver attached a wire to the claw and shackled the line to the wreck so that the grab could take a bite of sand. The grab could not be used in all areas because of the awkwardness of the position and random pieces of steel that dotted the wreckage. Under ideal conditions, the grab worked well, but for the *Laurentic*, removing the debris by hand was still the most reliable method.

Meanwhile at Whitehall there was debate as to whether operations should continue into 1922. While Damant had recovered more gold than he did in 1920, the total for 1921 would be 43 bars; there were still 2,304 ingots remaining in the wreck. Even as operations ended in early September, Damant was asked to make a report to the Treasury.

Damant sensed he was close to the main gold hoard. In a long report to the Treasury Damant noted that although they pulled up relatively few bars, it was still more than the year prior, and they were now operating at a profit. He wrote,

> As far as my information goes there must be a mass of 3,000 ingots hidden in this rubbish we are searching and sifting. The fact that we have got 39 this season* shows that we are working about the right spot. Apparently these ingots, which we have been finding in groups of two or three, are outliers from the main mass of gold. At any time a diver may dig down to a cluster of, not two or three, but two or three hundred of them and once located the task of salving the gold is a very simple matter. In the present state of things, with the operations running at a good profit and the reasonable expectation of sooner or later finding the main mass of bullion, I have no hesitation in advising that the operation should continue.

Damant admitted his own failures in providing too rosy an outlook. "I had hoped and expected to find the bulk of the gold before now but after the experience of the last two years it must be recognised that success may be long postponed. In the meantime, it seems clear that the proper policy is to work on doggedly as long as may be necessary and, since the expenses are the same whether much or little gold be salved, to economise as far as possible without hindering the work." To emphasize the difficulty of the salvage, Damant attached a photograph of a simulated debris field on the deck of the *Racer*.

The Treasury deliberated with the Admiralty. Baddeley and Bruen were Damant's staunchest supporters with the latter noting that when diving had not been hampered by the weather, they had found gold. Baddeley asked Admiral Henry F. Oliver, the second sea lord, if the divers could be used again in 1922 if operations were continued. Oliver assented and added, "I think it would be a pity to give up

---

* The report was written before the full 43 bars were found.

A debris field was mocked up on the deck of the
Racer to demonstrate the difficulty of the work.
Courtesy of the National Archives, London, ADM 116 1741

when there is a good chance of coming on thicker patches of ingots."
Baddeley then submitted a report to Blackett at the Treasury, noting,
"Our advice would be to continue the work next year; but as we are
in fact only your agents in the matter, we shall be glad to have your
concurrence." In the meantime, Damant's divers had exhausted the
area where they had found all the ingots that summer. He chose to
start digging in a new place, about twenty feet to aft and starboard of
the old spot.

On August 27, Blackett gave his assent to continue the work. The
salient point was that operations were now working at a profit. The
cost of operations in 1921 was £23,000 and the value of the recovered
bullion was £66,018. Also, Blackett shared Damant's optimism, or
was at least convinced by him that success was at hand. To further
reduce costs, Damant offered and Blackett accepted a proposal to
remove the drifter *CD 1* from the salvage. Baddeley broached the
subject of gratuities the men had been offered in prior years, but

this time pressed for one-half of one percent, rather than the one-eighth percent that had been given in 1917 and 1919. There was some resistance by the Treasury, with one official writing "these people are all Naval ratings, who have to do any such job as this which may be assigned to them" and that the divers and attendants were entitled to extra pay anyway. Baddeley objected and wrote, "I think there is no doubt that encouragement and incentive may make all the difference in the prosecution of this very ticklish job.... Hitherto your financial people have been most willing that this encouragement should be given. I do not think this is a matter that can be dealt with on hard and fast service lines. The success of the enterprise depends entirely on Commander Damant and his men, and a refusal will plainly be very disappointing to that officer." Despite the doubts that the distribution would be so low as to not truly offer incentive, bonuses were granted at one-half of one percent for the 1920 and 1921 seasons. This amounted to a little under six pounds per diver.

Damant returned to the Isle of Wight that September relieved. However, this turned to sorrow as his mother, Mary, fell ill and died on October 30, 1921. He had stood by his strong-willed mother as she lost her husband and two sons. Damant wrote, "The last years of poor, proud, tender hearted Mother were made very, very sad. She was humiliated." He added later in his memoirs, "Each generation has its sorrows and should not also be harrowed with those of former generations."

● ● ●

There was good news, bad news, and exciting news for Commander Damant during the winter of 1922. The good news was that the Irish War of Independence had officially come to an end. The Anglo-Irish Treaty, passed by the Irish parliament on January 7, 1922, established the Irish Free State in which Ireland would share the same status as other British Commonwealth nations such as Canada, South Africa, and Australia. Northern Ireland opted out of this arrangement within a month and remained a part of the United Kingdom with limited home rule. Ireland was to have two separate governments. There was no question that the *Laurentic* would remain under the control of Whitehall.

The bad news was that for many Irish nationalists, the Anglo-Irish Treaty hardly went far enough. Particularly galling to antitreaty forces was the requirement that all members of the Irish parliament take an oath of allegiance to the British monarch. The more ardent nationalists believed that dominion status would never deliver a wholly independent Ireland. A civil war was about to commence.

The exciting news was from Damant's family. Nell was pregnant with a second child. However, the baby was due during the summer, so he would not be present for the birth. Guy and Nell worked out a code since they did not want the radio operator aboard the *Racer* to know about the baby's birth before him. When the baby arrived, Nell's sister would send a telegram indicating that a houseguest had arrived at Thursford. If the guest was "Tommy," it was a boy, "Jane" if a girl.

Damant prepared for the 1922 salvage. He had personnel problems since no provision was made by the Admiralty to man the *Racer* with a naval crew. In past seasons the extra crew had come from men assigned to newly built ships. But the postwar era saw opinion shift toward naval disarmament. From November 1921 to February 1922, Britain and eight other nations gathered in Washington, DC, to discuss the prospects of disarmament. The resulting Washington Naval Treaty limited the construction of capital ships and the tonnage of other war vessels. Concluded on February 6, 1922, the treaty was deeply unpopular at the Admiralty, but the public generally felt that naval spending was excessive as it was. This time, instead of last-minute shuffling of naval personnel, the Admiralty agreed at the suggestion of Damant to man the *Racer* with a crew made up of RFA members. These merchant marine personnel would be paid by the Treasury. The divers, however, remained Royal Navy men.

When the *Racer* was commissioned on March 15, 1922, it was divided between a mercantile crew and a Royal Navy diving party. The RFA crew operated under union rules. One such rule entitled engineering officers to cabins. This had the unintended consequence of placing Damant's right hand, Miller, into a shared space that was seven feet long by just over five feet wide. Damant objected and was able to negotiate a separate cabin for him. Such difficulties, however, did not seem to detract from the overall morale upon the *Racer*.

Ernest Crouch described the merchant crew as "a very good crowd of chaps." What is more, Frederick Little, a master rigger that they had lost after the navy took over the crew in 1920, had returned—Damant had complete confidence in his abilities.

The *Racer* arrived at Buncrana on March 30, 1922. The next day, the ship headed to the seaside village of Portsalon where it set up shop and began the work of retrieving moorings and laying them over the wreck site. The sense of anticipation was agonizing. The *Laurentic* had thrown plenty of twists and turns at Commander Damant since he arrived at Lough Swilly in 1917. Tempered by experience, Damant could only hope for the best but expect the worst even as Miller went over the side as the first diver to survey the wreck on April 4.

Miller landed forty to sixty feet away from the working position. He made his way down through the wreckage, checking conditions. He then peered into the thirty-foot hole that showed the excavation area. Miller noticed that everything seemed clear. Neither silt nor rubble had washed into the area. In fact, it seemed even clearer than when they had left the wreck at the end of the previous summer. But he went no farther. Because of the colder water temperatures, his time was limited on the bottom, and he was brought up after twenty-five minutes.

Next up was Ernest Crouch. He was to enter the working position. His descent was somewhat turbulent, since the tide was coming in. However, he made his way to the working area and secured a shot rope. He looked around through the thick glass of his faceplate.

Crouch telephoned to the surface for a bucket. The heavy weighted porous hopper was dropped over the side and lowered to the diver. Excitement followed when Crouch called up the telephone, "One in the bucket!" A gold bar had been found.

The wicked weather of Lough Swilly had for once worked in Damant's favor and swept away the debris that covered the ingots. Before Crouch's time was up he discovered ten more bars, just lying there exposed.

Nineteen bars of gold were recovered that day, leading one of the divers to comment to Commander Damant, "They gave themselves up like lambs."

28

"Like Lambs"

THE *RACER* SPENT EASTER DAY, April 16, 1922, riding out a gale. While the crew ate tinned corned beef, Commander Damant mulled over the situation. He had already raised twenty-seven ingots, and all signs showed that there were more to come—much more. With so many mercantile crew aboard, and the general knowledge that the *Racer* was salvaging gold, word would surely spread that they were hauling aboard a fortune. Delight, euphoria, and relief mixed freely with foreboding, fear, and suspicion.

Damant's alarm could only have grown after the *Racer* anchored at their base of Portsalon for mail.[*] Postal officials informed him that the mail car bound for Portsalon had been robbed by Irish dissidents and that they had looted £250. It was clear from the state of the envelopes that the mail bound for the *Racer* had been tampered with. In addition, telegraph wires nine miles outside Portsalon had been cut by the partisans.

Damant did not have codes or ciphers aboard the *Racer* to send sensitive wireless messages. Instead, he sent an innocuous report, which conveyed that aside from divers surveying the *Laurentic* "it

---

[*] Damant avoided going to Buncrana since at that time it was suffering raids by Irish Republican forces. Indeed, until July 30, 1922, it was under the control of Republican forces.

would take several weeks for new men to become familiar with the dimly visible landmarks in the wreckage and efficient in the peculiar methods of working."

Simultaneously, Damant typed a special report to be hand-delivered to the Admiralty. He was finding gold, and he was sure to find more. He proposed that arrangements be made to take the gold to Campbeltown, a remote village on the west coast of Scotland. There was a branch of the Bank of Scotland there that Damant thought would be suitable.

When word of Damant's success reached Whitehall, there was elation but also dismay. It seemed that the discovery of the gold was ill timed considering the political situation in Ireland. When Sir Vincent Baddeley read Damant's suggestion to land the gold at Campbeltown, he immediately sent a wireless message to the *Racer* not to sail. The bank at Campbeltown had no facility to deal with large amounts of gold bullion, and the closest rail connection was eighty miles away. Baddeley declared Campbeltown to be "about as an inconvenient place as could be found in the United Kingdom." The Admiralty issued orders to the destroyer *Wolfhound* to go to Lough Swilly and transfer the treasure to them. Meanwhile, the *Racer*, alone, sat off Portsalon and continued to salvage gold.

On the evening of May 1, 1922, at 11:00 PM, all hands were suddenly roused from their slumber. The night watch had heard shots and screaming ashore. Rifles were brought up as well as the Lewis guns. Leather hoses were connected to the ship's boilers, to spray any attacker with hot water. An extra watch was put on, and all that night, eyes scanned the waves, looking for the slightest sign of any boat that might come with a boarding party. But none came.

The *Wolfhound* arrived at Lough Swilly without incident and eleven boxes of gold valued at approximately £66,000 were transferred to it. The destroyer took the gold to the Scottish town of Stranraer where officials from the Bank of England met the ship and had the treasure sent by train to London. But before the *Wolfhound* departed Lough Swilly, it passed along special instructions from the Admiralty. Damant was to have the gold positioned in such a way on deck that if Irish partisans attacked, the gold could be easily tipped into the sea and recovered later.

News was coming from the shore that the situation was growing worse. On May 4 a detachment of IRA soldiers had raided a branch of the Bank of Belfast in Buncrana, robbing it of £800. Soldiers of the Free State arrived leading to a fierce ten-minute firefight. Several were wounded, including two IRA members as well as bystanders; a nineteen-year-old girl had been shot through the lung and a nine-year-old girl in the abdomen. The IRA soldiers had raided Barton's Hotel in Portsalon as well and seized one of the hotel's automobiles. The Irish Civil War between those who wanted complete independence and those who supported the Free State would begin in earnest on June 28, 1922.

Damant's feelings toward the Irish were not unusual for an upper-class Englishman. He referred to Irish Catholics generally as "natives," and he had little respect whatsoever for Irish Republicans, whom he called "brutes." His view seemed to harden over time owing to the various encounters he experienced with them during his years in Ireland, chiefly the near-piratical attack in 1919 and what he viewed as the disrespect shown to the *Laurentic* by locals auctioning the wreck's flotsam in 1917.

But despite the fact that the gold salvaged by the *Racer* would have been a juicy target by dissident groups in Ireland, Damant's own status was different. He wrote, "These brutes would have been delighted to steal our gold but did not bear us any special personal malice as we were not part of 'the forces occupying the country on behalf of a foreign power.'"

Damant, however, could dissemble. Since he worked in a country going through a period of upheaval, he realized that he had to work within their system. Sometimes Damant found it necessary to go by automobile to Londonderry on ship's business. Locals connected him with a specific garage. The owner of the garage was, according to Damant, a "leading rebel" and he needed to give three days' lead time after the man was hired to clear a path through the more disrupted regions where roadblocks and local brigades often appeared. Damant recalled, "This worked well, though on one occasion four sinister looking rogues came into sight, lined up across our road with their hands in their right hand coat pockets where, no doubt, they carried pistols. We pulled up and the driver got down and parlayed, after which they retired behind the hedges on either side and let us pass."

Damant and the men of the *Racer* were far more comfortable mixing among the minority of Protestant Anglo-Irish in places such as Portsalon. There they had made good friends such as a man named Thompson, a young parson who lived in the huge decaying rectory of All Saints Church. Thompson had an Irish boy who assisted him, but the two lived in semisqualor. "They used to box each other and sit up in the drawing room at night with 12 [gauge] bore guns to shoot the rats as they came out to forage," wrote Damant. "Miller and I used to go out there on off days and put the gloves on with him."

Meanwhile, Damant kept up the ruse that nothing unusual was occurring concerning the *Laurentic.* Only in his special hand-delivered reports to the Admiralty was any mention of gold made. Instead, Damant played up how the work was similar to the disappointing 1920 and 1921 seasons. "Conditions on board in this abominable weather are not very comfortable for officers or men, every one is looking forward to a relief from the enforced idleness." When gold was ready to be transferred, Damant passed word surreptitiously to the Admiralty, which then dispatched a destroyer to pick up the cargo. Damant only confirmed the transfer of gold by writing that the *Racer* had *communicated* with the destroyer.

As for the divers, Damant was severe. No diver on the bottom was allowed to leave the gold area at any time without permission. Damant, and Miller for that matter, were really the only two men aboard who could fully account for all actions going on in the working position.

The initial successes of Damant's men steadily petered out. The first gold bars were easy enough to find, but after this initial lot was brought up they became harder to locate, although on most dives they found some bars. Like bread crumbs, the gold brought them deeper and deeper into the debris.

Damant's divers slowly cleared an area of about 440 square feet on the wreck. They were working at, if not slightly below, the level of the seafloor. Sand and stone washed back into the wreck repeatedly. At points, it seemed like they had dug clean through the *Laurentic* and were working the virgin seafloor. This puzzled Damant greatly since they were still pulling up bars of gold. Was it possible that the gold had slipped through the ship completely?

Upon examination, Damant found that the divers were not working on the true seafloor. The outer skin of the *Laurentic* had crumpled and formed corrugated depressions that had filled with sand, stone, and rivet heads—all cemented together by iron rust. The violence of grinding metal and bulkheads had warped the ingots. Many were doubled up into U-shapes. Some were squeezed like putty. Some had rivets and pebbles driven into them. But, deformed as the bars were, they were here—or at least a good amount of them were—at the utmost extremity of the wreck. They were not easily removed, however. Because of the awkwardness of the position of the bays and the overhanging structures about it, the sand grab was useless. If there was any innovation to detect gold amid all this sand, it would have been most welcome.

On June 3, 1922, Professor Ernest Edward Brooks joined the *Racer* to test out his new experimental equipment to detect gold. Ernest Crouch described his device as "a very sensitive galvanometer connected to an electric cable. On the end of this cable was a steel probe [to] which the other end of the electric cable was connected. The steel probe was encased in wood with the point protruding." If the probe touched gold the dial on the galvanometer would move to the right, but if it touched other metal it would move to the left. After carrying out some successful experiments on a bar of gold in a washtub on the upper deck, Brooks donned a diving suit and went over the side of the *Racer* and another diver followed to look out for him. Brooks, an elderly man, soon found his courage leave him and asked to be hauled to the surface. Divers were taught how to use the equipment instead. The divers managed to find seven bars of gold that day, but Brooks's equipment did not do the job. Crouch suspected that the sea pressure made the device malfunction. Damant himself went down with the detector and another diver. The diver dug out a bar of gold and held it for Damant who scraped it with the probe, but the dial went in the wrong direction. He then tried it on one of the wreck's steel girders. It went the wrong way. They then tried it on all sorts of metals with erroneous results. The device never proved useful, although Professor Brooks kept working at the problem. Meanwhile, the divers continued to search and dig for gold.

• • •

On June 10, 1922, Petty Officer William Light suited up for his turn on the bottom. His job was to remove as much sand and stone as could be removed in thirty minutes and, if he was lucky, bring up an ingot or two.

Light slid down the shot rope, carrying sacks. He landed on the *Laurentic* and plodded to the designated spot. It was like a dune of hard sand, cemented with the rust of the wreckage and pressed down hard by water pressure. Atop the dune was a deck plate. The dredging grab was of no use here. The space was too awkward and the folds were at such angles so that there was no way to position it without it bumping onto the unyielding overhanging plates.

Light took his lifeline and air pipe and tied it with a separate piece of rope to a secure part of the wreck. This was meant to be a safety precaution, to avoid his lines from drifting and fouling in the wreckage but more importantly, to prevent him from being lifted bodily by the heavy swells. He paid out about forty feet of air pipe and lifeline, both conjoined at three-foot intervals with stops in order to prevent the separate lines from fouling in different parts of the wreck. Then he turned to the sediment. He needed to remove it. But scratching at the sand wore out Light's fingernails—several of the divers had already worn their fingernails to a quarter inch. The pain when they dried out after decompressing was sharp enough to keep them up at night.

There was an ample supply of diving gloves aboard, not heavy gauntlet-like ones, but far more flexible leather gloves. But the divers had found that the surest way to find gold in the dark bays was by touch. At the beginning of his time on the *Laurentic* salvage, diver Light could not tell the difference between steel, brass, copper, or gold. But now, after two months' work, his fingers were so sensitized to the feel of gold as a physical substance that he could pick out a bar easily.

In order to remove the sand, Light needed a special fire hose that had been tied to the top of the bay. Taking it, Light pressed the hose against the cemented sand and shingle. He turned on the water, bringing the pressure up to seventy psi. The jet of water loosened the sand, and Light forced in the head of the hose like a crowbar. Pebbles, stones, pieces of rivets, and other metal debris flew through the water, stinging the diver's hands as he worked.

After a few moments he telephoned to the *Racer* to turn off the water so that the cloud of darkness caused by the flying debris could clear away. Light began to scoop. The ship's blacksmith had fabricated a shovel-like opening at the top of his sack that forced it open so that the diver could clear sand and grit more efficiently into sacks.

It was a rather straightforward, mundane task. In order to keep up the morale and motivate the divers, Damant weighed the amount

Divers used these customized hand spades to dig out and collect the silt and sand that had washed into the wreck.
Journal of Hygiene *25, no. 1 (1926), courtesy of Cambridge University Press*

of sand each diver brought up. This was duly tallied so each diver could see who was slacking off and who was doing his fair share. In the spirit of competition, the divers started to devise new ways to bring up more sand. That is how the sack with the scoop came about. Commander Damant was delighted at the initiative but some of the divers gave up after seeing how unbeatable Albert Balson, the strongest of the divers, was in sending up sand. Of course, the biggest prize was to find gold. When working at the bays, this meant removing much of the grit in order to get to the ingots, which were typically found at the very bottom.

The overhanging plate above forced Light to bend down and work headfirst and downward. To do this, he needed to turn down his air intake to the minimum, at times shutting it off completely. The air in the dress, meanwhile, pooled upward into Light's leggings. As this filled up, Light necessarily had to back out and once able to get upright allowed the air to rise into his helmet and escape through

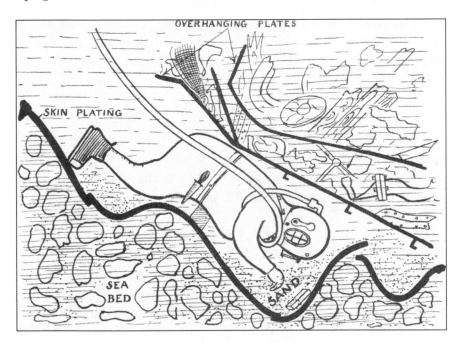

Gold had slipped between deck plates and the outer skin of the wreck. In order to get to them, divers like William Light had to burrow in headfirst, a highly dangerous position. Journal of Hygiene *25, no. 1 (1926): 40, courtesy of Cambridge University Press*

the outlet. He then went back at it again. Damant compared this method to a terrier digging at a rabbit hole.

Light only had about fifteen minutes left, so he loosened, scooped, filled his sack, and went back at it again. It was common for the divers to fill the sacks with over two hundred pounds of sand and rock before having it winched to the surface. But then Light's fingertips touched something soft and metallic. He had found an ingot.

He reached, flicking it with his fingertips. The sediment and sand fell back in, swiftly hardening about his hands in a viselike grip. He worked at the bar more, trying to loosen it from the gravel's hold.

Just then, he felt his legs go upward. He had waited too long. The air, pooled in the leggings in his diving dress, had floated up to the overhanging plate. He could not crawl backward.

Light called up to the *Racer*. The air needed to be turned off.

This was done, but Light had no means to get rid of the excess air in the suit. The only outlet for it was in his helmet, which now was the lowest point on his body. Then a heavy groundswell of water pulled him up despite his desperate struggle to hang on. He irresistibly shot up and out of the bay, feetfirst.

He flew through the water before being jerked to a stop by the line he tied to the wreck. He floated upside down about forty feet above the wreck. He could neither be seen from the surface nor from the *Laurentic*. Light could do nothing. His suit was blown up. There was no fulcrum for him to capsize himself so as to get the air out of his suit.

There was something else. He telephoned to the *Racer*. "I am filling up with water." Light was not sure from where. "Only a little," he added.

Upside down was the absolute worst position a diver could be since any water that got into his suit would naturally pool inside the helmet. It only took a quart or more of water to cover a man's nose and mouth, drowning him.

Meanwhile, Edwin Blachford was beginning his descent to the *Laurentic*. He was telephoned by Commander Damant who ordered

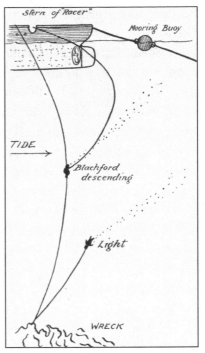

This drawing illustrates the plight of diver Light. Journal of Hygiene *25, no. 1 (1926): 41, courtesy of Cambridge University Press*

him to swing over to Light's air pipe. Blachford grabbed the line, and slid down until he landed on the wreck.

Blachford could not see Light anywhere. In fact, he could see little of anything since the disturbance of the blow-up had caused sediment to cloud the greenish water. Eventually, Blachford came to understand that Light was not there but above him, out of sight. He found his way to the place where Light had secured his lines to the *Laurentic*.

Damant ordered Blachford to cut the rope holding Light's line. The idea was this would free Light and allow Blachford to slowly ease him to the surface, hoping that Light would be able to upright himself. Blachford, using his diver's knife, cut the lanyard while holding tightly to Light's line.

But the strain on Blachford's hands by Light's line was far too powerful for him to hold. What Blachford did not notice, or thought little of, was that Light's lines were between his legs. With a snap it capsized Blachford who quickly fouled into Light's line and flew upward. Now both divers soared upward, diving dresses blown up.

As they rose, the air in their suits, under lessening sea pressure, expanded even more.

Damant knew he had made a fatal error in judgment. He should have had Blachford climb up Light's air pipe from below so that by using all his strength Blachford might capsize Light right side up and so allow him to release the excess air. Now two of his divers were flying upward, liable to crash into the *Racer*'s hull.

But Lough Swilly had a current running to the stern of the *Racer*. It was this push of the sea that made both men burst to the surface and clear of the *Racer*. Ernest Crouch witnessed the overinflated Light shoot six feet out of the water. The diver's leather belt snapped off and then the strings holding his leaden boots fell away. This loss of weight and the luck of clearing the ship allowed him to bob at the surface. This was true of Blachford, too, although he remained in his diving dress.

Light was brought aboard immediately. Having no other injuries he was sent to the diver's oven, the recompression chamber. Blachford, however, was sent to the bottom to stage decompress.

Work continued since conditions were good. Four more bars of gold were recovered that day.

● ● ●

The person aboard the *Racer* who was most intrigued by the Light-Blachford episode was Professor Brooks. But instead of being fearful of diving as he was at first, he pressed to be allowed to try a dive. Much against Commander Damant's better judgment, Brooks was allowed to don a diving dress and take a dip.

But Damant would not allow Brooks to go deep, restricting him to the harbor. The other divers, who had grown fond of the professor, dressed him and sent him down thirty feet. It was a minimal dive, and shallower than the depth where he would be prone to decompression sickness, but Ernest Crouch gave him credit considering it "a very brave thing for a man of his age to do." Every few feet, Brooks checked in on the telephone, telling the men how he was feeling. The professor even took a dinner plate–shaped object containing four quartz prisms. He wanted to see how the seawater would affect the polarization of light at depth.

The experience was wholly unique for Brooks. During his dive, he came across a large flatfish and thinking of diver stories that said such a fish could be caught by sneaking up behind it and then sticking it with a diving knife, he decided to try. He could not do it, but his remarks through the telephone amused the divers. When Brooks's twenty minutes were up, it took some coaxing to get him off the bottom.

Brooks left the *Laurentic* shortly after his dive. He published a brief article in the journal *Nature* about the experience, but he never contributed anything materially toward salvaging the *Laurentic*'s gold except raising the men's morale.

• • •

As all this gold came up, Damant stayed in close contact with British destroyers through wireless telegraph who often came into Lough Swilly to transfer the ingots, first the *Wolfhound* and later the *Warwick*. The destroyers tried to stay by the *Racer* when they could for protection, but the *Racer* was often alone. Damant heard rumors that rebels were active in the upper part of Lough Swilly and had commandeered a motorboat. Rarely did the *Racer* come into Portsalon even for water, which Damant ordered be distilled from seawater. To supplement their meals, the crew retrieved fish that had been stunned by explosive charges used on the *Laurentic*.

When the *Racer* did come ashore (usually at Portsalon) it was to receive news such as the winner of the latest prizefight, or to witness trucks filled with Irish Free State soldiers arriving and practicing drills on the local golf course. Those were fun evenings for the crew, who drank with the soldiers at venues like Barton's Hotel. Still, there was a palpable sense of danger in the air. The only truly safe port was Londonderry, which being in Northern Ireland was fully controlled by the British government. There, the *Racer* would go from time to time for coal, boiler cleaning, or repairs. The crew was sometimes invited to balls at the local army barracks.

With so many days of rough weather in Lough Swilly, it was often impractical to do the salvage work. But the men of the *Racer* took on odd jobs about the waters. Divers scraped the accumulated mussels from the *Racer*'s bottom. They used the ship's big derrick to fish up someone's motor launch that had sunk in ten fathoms of water.

On one occasion, an oil tanker's anchor chain broke. The *Racer* anchored near the spot, waited for the slack water, then sent a diver down. Finding an anchor, the diver shackled a line onto it. The diver came up, and the wire was connected to the *Racer*'s winch. They hove up a very muddy anchor. Hands gathered around to observe.

"That looks a very small anchor for a 7,000 ton tanker."

A pause.

"It's our own anchor! Overboard with it immediately!"

Laughter.

There was more to the work than simply shifting sand and stone, retrieving gold, and taking precautions against piracy. Damant had been ordered by the Admiralty to write a chapter on salvage and lessons learned during the war for a navy manual, which kept him busy during his idle hours. He still had an insatiable appetite for scientific discovery and the strongest of desires to be a recognized physiologist. When the crew caught a large sunfish, Damant dissected off the head and parts of the body. He left the rest for the crew to eat, but had the dissected portions put in a barrel and salted down for a museum. This may have been a follow-up to a note that he had published in *Nature* in 1920 concerning the buoyancy of sunfish. Damant also took to exploring the little hidden recesses of the shore—a risky proposition considering the ongoing civil war.

One evening, Damant chose to go rowing and found a beach inaccessible from the land. Immediately behind it, clawed from the cliffs, was a great cave with a lofty stone roof. Damant beached his dinghy and looked about. He heard a soft rustling interspaced with ticking noises. Looking about carefully he found that the source of the noise came from countless fleas that hopped about the rocks in the cave.* Damant could not figure why the insects were in such

---

* Damant would later comment, "People to whom I have told this story have looked

a place. His paper on the *Corethra plumicornis* was almost complete, and perhaps he figured that this might be a new object of study. He tried to catch one for a better examination, but failed. He then remembered reading somewhere that if he took a candle and stood it in a saucer of oil, it would attract the fleas, which would hop into the oil and be trapped as they tried to get to the light. Promptly, Damant rowed back to the *Racer*, procured the necessary materials, and set the trap. He returned again to the ship, confident that he would soon have excellent specimens of a wholly unique species of flea to win him zoological fame.

Full dark settled upon Lough Swilly, and the *Racer* stood offshore. That night, the ship had an escorting destroyer to keep it company. In the middle of the night, the destroyer suddenly switched on its bright searchlight. There was some sort of commotion as a boat was dropped off the side. Damant was called onto deck and hailed the boat as it passed. He could see that the officer and crew aboard were all armed.

The boat promptly came alongside the *Racer*. The officer explained to Damant that they had seen a light flickering in a cave ashore. It was surely Irish rebels.

Damant's explanation was received, as he put it, "in pained silence."

The next day, Damant returned to the cave to find that while many flies had been caught in the oil, there were only two fleas. These were later identified by the Science Museum in London as belonging to a species that were commonly found in pigeon nests. Damant later returned to the cave and noticed that the upper parts of the cave ledges were streaked with pigeon droppings. He could hear the birds cooing in the gloom.

Besides rowing about the shore, Damant also roamed the hills of Lough Swilly with McCutchan. One of his favorite walks was a three- to four-mile hike along the sandy shore called Stocker Strand. Some-

---

incredulous and said 'Surely no one could hear a flea jump?' No, perhaps not, but I could hear thousands jumping! One can't hear a single tiny bubble burst but a fizzy drink, freshly poured out makes quite a noise."

times, he and his companion would visit a Miss Hart, a middle-aged Anglo-Irish woman who lived a lonely life in a charming estate called Carrablagh near the cliffs by the sea. She had lost two of her nephews to drowning in the waters of the lough. Now she invited officers of the *Racer* to come for tea or picnics along the ocean strand. On July 5, 1922, there was a heavy swell in Lough Swilly, not a good day for diving, but a good day for a hike. As the pair came over the crest of one hill, they encountered four magpies just in front of them. McCutchan then recited the beginning of an old nursery rhyme that augured fortune by the number of magpies one saw. *One for sorrow, two for joy, three for a girl, four for a boy.*

Damant did not think much of it except that while he knew what *one* and *two* stood for, this was the first time he heard the meanings of *three* and *four.*

The next day, he received a telegram, dated the day prior. It was from his sister-in-law. *Tommy's arrived 6.15 a.m. All is well.* It was the code that meant Nell had given birth to a boy. Damant was pleased, but unsure. Writing home, he inquired if "Tommy's" was singular or plural. Maybe Nell had twins. He found out that there was only one baby and his son, Harry Guybon Damant, would ever afterward be called Tommy.

• • •

By the end of July 1922, the gold was becoming scarce once again. Renewing the search by removing fresh wreckage, Damant noticed that certain bulkheads that they hauled up were streaked with gold. Following the clues, by August 13 the divers had discovered the ingots again. But this time, instead of pulling up the gold as singles or pairs, they found the concentrated mass that Damant had been pining for. To Damant's surprise, the gold was not so much in the center of the working area as he had expected, but in the outlying area. It was still difficult work, since the gold was embedded in the grit and sand. After an interruption owing to weather conditions during the last half of August, work commenced again. Each day, more and more bars were pulled up. Thirty-two ingots were pulled up on September 3, and between September 4 and 10, 115 bars were recovered. Seventy-seven bars were recovered on September 23 alone and another fifty-four the day after. Even as the autumn weather set in, gold kept coming up, which made all hands loath to leave the job. Between October 2 and October 8, 295 bars were recovered, and the area showed no signs of exhaustion.

There was so much gold that the *Racer* did not have boxes for it. Instead, the salvors relied on every scrap of wood they could scavenge from the escorting destroyer *Tilbury*. By the time the *Racer* had to give up the work on October 13 because of weather and the air compressor breaking down, the divers had hauled from the wreckage 895 bars of gold for the 1922 season. While there were still 1,409 bars of gold left of the original 3,211, Damant knew he had found the mother lode.

29

"His Sturdy Optimism"

THERE WAS NO QUESTION THAT work would resume on the *Laurentic* in 1923. The Admiralty increased the diving party to twelve, and plans were made to have a permanent destroyer-escort for the *Racer*. On April 7 the *Racer* arrived at Portsalon and quickly began preparatory work. The *Laurentic* had suffered some silting over the winter, and plating had slid into the working position—but it was no where as disruptive as the disastrous winter of 1919 to 1920. By late April Damant and his divers reached the gold again.

The divers used the same methods to extract the gold as they did in prior seasons—blasting and hand-scooping the sand and debris. Their efforts paid off. Between April 24 and 29, divers hauled 124 ingots out of a seabed of rounded boulders and sand. Destroyers such as the *Sarpedon* and the *Raider* tag-teamed the transfer and delivery of gold to Chatham, from where it was transported by lorry to the Bank of England with two royal marines standing guard.

Meanwhile, the threat of the Irish Civil War soon dissipated as the Irish Free State, backed by the finances and arms of the United Kingdom, defeated Republican forces and brought an end to the civil war on May 24, 1923. By the late spring it seemed that there was nothing to interfere with Damant's plans to raise the bulk of the *Laurentic*'s gold. However, rumors of new problems began to surface, but instead of the possibility of German U-boats or Irish partisans who might threaten to attack the salvage from without, this time the trouble was from within.

In the prior year, the *Laurentic*'s gold had become well known to the general public. It was rumored that a dealer from the East End of London had heard of the gold and invited two divers from the *Racer* for drinks and bribed them to steal gold for him. Yet how was a diver to do such a thing? There were officials from the Treasury present aboard the *Racer*, and all bars were carefully tallied. The plot, as outlined, had divers tying cords onto ingots they discovered under the sea and attaching buoys to them. After the *Racer* finished its work for the day, confederates on a fishing boat would pull out the buoys and haul up the ingots. It was reported that some bars had already gone missing.

Despite police efforts to locate the supposed stolen bars, they were never found. In fact, there is no documentary evidence that any bars had been stolen or lost once they were found. Damant, however, heard the rumors and in 1922 called the entire company on deck and warned them they would lose their gratuities if there was any tampering with the gold. Nothing came of it until June 1923 when somebody reported to Damant that diver Ernest Crouch had been seen with the London dealer.

On June 20, 1923, Damant dismissed the diver from the salvage without telling him the reasons why. Crouch returned to his duties as a diver and instructor at HMS *Excellent*, and Damant, lacking any evidence, did not pursue the matter further. Crouch, who was a highly successful diver on the *Laurentic* salvage, wrote some years later his own account of the operations. In it, he never mentioned anything concerning his dismissal but did take time to compare the amount of money the divers were awarded as bounty compared to what a commercial salvage diver would earn, insinuating inherent unfairness.

For example, for the highly successful 1922 salvage season, the Admiralty instituted a one-eighth percent bonus to be split among the men. Even though the divers each received a share of whatever bounty the Treasury placed on the recovery, it made no difference to the divers from a monetary standpoint if they brought up more or less gold since bonuses were distributed equally by rating. A seaman rigger received a bounty of almost fourteen pounds sterling for that season. Crouch, as a diver, earned almost forty-nine pounds in addition to his regular pay and diving bonuses. Commander Damant was given just over £221. But a commercial diver would have potentially made much more since he may have been entitled to a larger percentage of the salvaged material. The divers all would have been painfully aware of the moneymaking potential working in the private sector and the temptation of the *Laurentic*'s gold. All the same, Crouch praised Damant's leadership, and there is no documentary proof that there was any plot to steal any of the treasure. In the absence of other evidence, and since there was no hearing or trial, it must be assumed that Crouch was innocent in the matter.

Likewise, the divers could not, even if they wanted to, steal gold. Diver Augustus Dent recalled, "Damant was a very strict man on the divers that were working in the gold area. Only Damant and his officers knew just what was going on down there." Divers were limited to only work in that specific area and could not leave it without permission. Dent said of the very last bar of gold he found, "It was not in the gold area, and I had to ask Damant's permission to collect it. I would also say it was not possible to hide a bar of gold anywhere without Damant and his officers knowing that something was wrong down on the site. Bars of gold were heavy and divers could not simply hurl it off the area.... Some people would say a diver could have left a marker buoy to mark the spot, but that would be quite impossible. Damant was no fool." This rings true. Divers going down were heavily monitored, and even if one wanted to tie a line and buoy to an ingot, these accessories were not permitted equipment. The notion of stolen gold from the *Laurentic* is a rumor that would last for decades to come.

As the summer wore on, the divers made sport of the work and competed to haul up the most gold. Damant noted, "Human nature being what it is, there was a tendency for some men to spend their whole half-hour in poking about for odd bars and getting the derrick wires down to turn over likely plates, leaving the dull sand-shifting to the next fellow. It was odd to find oneself cursing X for bringing up untold gold and blessing Y for producing a sack of dirty sand and stones." The winner of the competition sent up £45,000 worth of gold on a single dive. For his labors, he was awarded a tin of cigarettes. Able Seaman Michael "Mickie" Maddison was the overall gold champion who, it was reported, recovered 200 ingots in the course of the diving season. His nearest rival was Petty Officer William Light, who hauled up 170. Maddison credited his victory to one day when he managed to haul up 43 bars in two separate dives.

So successful were Damant and the divers that by July 18, 1923, there were only 328 bars of gold left on the wreck. Thrilled at the great success, Sir Vincent Baddeley wrote to the First Lord of the Admiralty, "The greatest possible credit is due to Commander Damant for his skill and judgment in dealing with the whole matter. It was his sturdy optimism alone that induced the Admiralty and the Treasury to continue the operations after such a long period of disappointment."

As a celebration of sorts, when the *Racer* voyaged to Northern Ireland for its scheduled boiler cleaning, Damant headed home. For the long periods he was away, Nell had at times grown suspicious that

A group shot of Damant's salvage team circa 1923. Miller is seated second from left; Damant is seated third from left. *Courtesy of Mary Harrison*

her husband may be having an affair. To dissuade her of any such notion, Guy often talked about the affairs of the *other* men. This may have produced the opposite effect of what Guy intended.

When Guy arrived home he picked up Nell and Baboo—Tommy was still too young—and dashed back with them to Ireland. He brought them to Portsalon, where those friends he had made were concentrated. Picnics and children's parties along the coast were the order of the day. Guy stayed ashore when he could with Nell at Barton's Hotel, and they were often visited by Parson Thompson of All Saints Church who joined them for nights of dancing and idling.

The clock was ticking to a close. Damant advised the Admiralty that it would be feasible to continue operations until the bars grew very scarce. At that point, the Admiralty and the Treasury could determine the risk versus reward of the salvage operations.

The gold indeed grew sparser into and throughout August. Damant knew approximately where the gold was—under great flaps of the ship's skin that had been torn and folded back upon themselves. Damant identified that this area may have been the location where the *Laurentic* was hit by the mines. The thickness of the bottom plating and the way it was folded made it highly difficult to dismember through explosive charges. What is more, the area was completely exposed to the seafloor, and silting was frequent.

Meanwhile, rumor and news of the *Laurentic*'s gold were spreading. A source claiming to be an officer and diver aboard the *Racer* named Lieutenant G. Williams contacted the press for exclusive interviews. He told them that he was the first diver on the wreck in 1917 and saw the bodies of those killed in the ship, which included men, women, and children. (There were no women and children aboard the *Laurentic*.) He claimed that while working on the wreck he was dragged for seven miles underwater while the salvage ship was chased by a German U-boat. He asserted that the divers faced deadly dangers from all forms of sea life. Sharks were not so bad since they tended to fear a diver's bubbles, but the fiercest was the octopus, which "goes for anything it sees moving. The danger is that if a large one is encountered it may throw out one of its feelers, with a long row of suckers, round you, and immediately encircle you with its other tentacles and bind your arms helplessly by your side before you can slash at them with your knife." He also claimed that they found gold using Professor Brooks's condemned metal detector.

Almost entirely fabricated, the source was not G. Williams but the *Racer*'s former wireless telegraphy operator, a civilian listed on the books as "T. S. Williams." Not much is known about Williams, neither his background nor his full name. However, his false reports were quickly exposed by Commander Damant who had to send an explanatory letter to his superiors at the Admiralty. Williams had been sacked from the *Racer* for faking messages, was never on the *Volunteer* in 1917, and had never dived a day in his life.

Neither the Admiralty nor Damant did much to discount Williams's story except to give a more factual account of what was happening. But even then there was hesitation. At no point did Damant ever let a reporter aboard the *Racer*, and so more false legends of the *Laurentic* grew.

As September came, conditions grew worse as sand and silt continued to fill the wreck. However by October, when salvage operations closed, Damant and his men had recovered a staggering 1,255 bars of gold. One-eighth percent of this treasure, at a little over £2,463, was divided up among the men. Of the original 3,211 bars, there were now 154 left.

Damant was satisfied with the work that had taken six salvage seasons over the course of seven years. But now that he was so close, and because he was confident as to where the remaining gold was, he recommended to the Treasury and Admiralty to go on for one more season to try and raise the rest of the gold.

Commander Damant had the full confidence of the government, and he received orders to go one last time to Lough Swilly. He boarded the *Racer* in Portsmouth, and the ship steamed to the Old Castle Point buoy, where a local fisherman he had hired met him at the ship with all of Damant's heavy baggage. After transferring it, the *Racer* passed through the Solent, coming in view of Thursford, where his family waved farewell from the windows. The *Racer* went on its old tack—through the Needles, past Portland, Land's End, the

Maidens, Rathlin Island, Malin Head, and finally Lough Swilly. He arrived on April 4, 1924.

It seemed that fortune still favored Damant, since there was little silting on the wreck. His divers were bringing up bars in April. But soon the bars became elusive. Damant reported to the Admiralty on May 11, 1924, that the gold had passed through the skin of the ship through tears and portholes before the collapse of the wreck was complete. "Since that time settling and creeping of the skin plating over the bottom has taken place so that most of the bars are out of reach from the holes through which they dropped and lie sandwiched between the stony bottom and unbroken parts of the ship's side."

To get at the gold, the divers dug holes through the openings until a space was created where they could fit blasting charges. Setting this off enlarged the crack where a diver could get himself downward and clear out the loosened sediment to see if any gold was present. Stones and boulders were raised. Several charges were needed to remove each piece of the thick port plating.

Success! A diver looks at a bounty of gold from the *Laurentic*.
Courtesy of the National Archives, London, ADM 116 1741

By mid-June there were thirty-nine bars of gold left on the wreck. The Director of Naval Equipment calculated that even if the team recovered one bar of gold a week, it would more than pay for operations since an ingot was worth roughly £1,500 while the cost of operations ran about £600 per week.

Damant carried on, and his divers digging under the wreck raised seven more bars by June 22. Through July the hunt continued and by the twentieth, after pulling up two more ingots, the tally of outstanding gold was twenty-six bars. But, bad weather kicked up and operations ceased. On August 3, Damant sent off a message to the Admiralty stating that diving could continue until October, but it would only be profitable if they recover at least three bars of gold. "It is not certain that this proportion or indeed any of the gold will be salved," wrote Damant. "The Treasury stands, at best, to gain some £35,000. At worst to lose some £3,600 plus something more, depending on the inherent risk to personnel of such work.... In my opinion the prospects certainly justify a policy of going on till the beginning of October with the object of getting as many bars as possible before finally closing down, but I do not wish to press this view which may be unconsciously coloured or thought to be influenced by the reluctance which everyone feels at terminating his own employment as well as that of others."

The Admiralty instructed Damant to carry on. But unsettled weather had washed fresh silt into the wreck that had to be removed. The divers got back to work, and on August 11 they were rewarded with a single bar.

After this, the weather further deteriorated, and the divers could not get down to the wreck until August 29. Large quantities of fresh sand and rock had washed into the wreck. Damant wrote, "It is now so late in the season that one cannot count on being able to restore the position and I consider the chance of being able to recover more gold to be a good deal less than it was a fortnight ago."

Through September, Damant and the divers strove on, but new gales washed even more sand into the wreck. It was too late in the season for them to remove it all. As divers searched the surrounding areas for any lost bars that might have been blown away from the wreck by explosions, it became clear that the bar found on August 11 was to be the last. On September 16, 1924, after seven salvage seasons in eight years in which the divers dove on the *Laurentic* about five thousand times, the Admiralty called off operations.

With the final 129 bars pulled up in 1924, Damant and his men had raised 3,186 bars of the original 3,211 that sank with the *Laurentic* in 1917. Commander Damant, while not quite getting one hundred percent of the gold, was quite satisfied with obtaining over ninety-nine percent of it. Furthermore, total cost of operations for the seven years was £128,000, or 2.5 percent of the £5 million of the raised treasure. The government was thrilled. Sir Vincent Baddeley wrote, "Commander Damant has by steady perseverance and resource proved that his original view was correct, and that the recovery of gold from the wreck of the *Laurentic* was possible, although this was not the view of other salvage experts." Sir Otto Niemeyer, comptroller of finance at the Treasury, sent his appreciation to Damant "how much the Treasury, quite apart from their natural glee at the recovery of their pelf, appreciate his fine professional feat. I don't think anyone else has equaled this particular catch!"

Niemeyer's statement was true. As of the writing of this book, the recovery of the *Laurentic*'s gold is the largest recovery in weight of a sunken gold hoard. It is even more remarkable that there were no serious injuries and no deaths, considering the limits of diving technology then as well as the work taking place in highly hazardous conditions.

Damant submitted his final report on September 21, 1924:

> This satisfactory result is due above all things to the loyal and do-gged work of Naval divers, inspired by no selfish motive of reward but by the simple idea of doing their utmost for the job and the credit of the Service. Among these men there have been neither offences, complaints, or punishments.... It is with profound gra-titude to those who have helped me to foresee and guard against danger that I record the fact that there has been no loss of life or serious accident in the whole course of the work.

Damant called special attention to Miller. He wrote, "Besides being my assistant throughout and having charge of all the plant has done more diving and himself found more gold than any other diver on the work.* His technical advice in connection with cutting up the wreck and his resource in emergencies have been of the greatest value."

Year	Number of Ingots Salvaged	Value of the Gold	Cost of Operations
1917	542	£836,358	£5,000 (estimated)
1918	No operations		
1919	315	£484,209	£12,018
1920	7	£11,770	£23,001
1921	43	£66,018	£23,000 (estimated)
1922	895	£1,390,603	£21,116
1923	1,255	£1,970,638	£24,534
1924	129	£199,469	£20,000 (estimated)
Totals	**3,186**	**£4,959,065**	**£128,669**

Total amount of gold bars that went down on wreck: 3,211. Original calculated value: £4,996,317

For the final season, the Treasury originally wanted to give Damant and his men the usual bonus of one-eighth of one percent. This, however, was disputed by Sir Vincent who noted that the final work in 1924 was quite difficult and that because the numbers of the bars were so few, the bonus should match that given for the 1920 and 1921 seasons, one-half of one percent. But the Treasury balked and only after strong argument by Sir Vincent did they compromise at one-quarter of one percent. Damant closed operations and prepared the *Racer* for the voyage back to England. Yet before he left, he wanted to give a gift to the people he and his men had interacted with for so many years.

In June 1924 diver Augustus Dent had located one of the *Laurentic*'s massive bells. This inspired Commander Damant with the notion

---

* This was over the course of the entire salvage, as opposed to winners of gold competitions for individual salvage seasons.

of presenting it to All Saints Church in Portsalon. Damant wrote, "Our good friends ashore were the remnant of the Protestant, anglophile gentry, isolated in a rather hostile Catholic countryside and their little tin church meant something to them." So after the Admiralty agreed to the plan, Damant had the bell raised and taken ashore in September 1924. The *Laurentic*'s bell was a good deal heavier than the bell already in place at the church so an architect had to be called in to ensure that the wooden frame of the belfry would hold.

The *Racer*'s blacksmith and shipwright bolstered the structure, and several of Commander Damant's crew hoisted the bell into place. The church members were pleased with the gift and invited the entire ship's company to attend a service. There the blushing men of the *Racer* heard about themselves in a sermon although, according to Damant, "the bell was supposed to commemorate the shipwreck and loss of life." One of the men who attended the service and helped to hoist the bell into place was Augustus Dent, who would later remark, "I can still hear its sharp, clear chimes after seven long years of silence as it echoed around the hills."

30

Rewards

Sᴵʀ Vɪɴᴄᴇɴᴛ Bᴀᴅᴅᴇʟᴇʏ ʀᴇᴄᴏᴍᴍᴇɴᴅᴇᴅ ᴀᴄᴄᴇʟᴇʀᴀᴛᴇᴅ promotions and honors for the men of the *Racer*. Eleven of the divers and crew of the salvage team were awarded medals of the civil division of the Order of the British Empire and several were given accelerated promotions, including Miller who was promoted a year ahead of schedule to Commissioned Shipwright.

Damant received his first major recognition even while he was still engaged in the last year of the *Laurentic* salvage. On June 3, 1924, Damant received a telegram from an old friend: "Congratulations. You wear it round your neck!!" Puzzled, Damant did not know what this meant until the next day when the destroyer *Sparrowhawk*, escorting the *Racer*, signaled that Damant was to be made a commander of the Order of the British Empire (CBE). Damant was pleased since this was a step-up from the OBE that he had received in 1919.

Damant journeyed to London where he met Nell and stayed at the Piccadilly Hotel in Westminster.* The hotel, while opulent, was nothing compared to the investiture ceremony Damant attended at Buckingham Palace. He waited with other award recipients in the picture galleries where Damant enjoyed looking at portraits of

---

* The location of this hotel was on Piccadilly Street and is now occupied by the Le Méridien Hotel.

notables of the British Empire past and present, some of whom he was acquainted with. Then finally he was called into line and went forward to see King George V. Damant recalled, "When the time came to joining the queue and have the thing pinned on by the King, I was impressed by the devotion to duty, not only of His Majesty, but of the Royal semicircle formed, standing, behind his chair. It included the aged Duke of Connaught in Jack boots grasping his Field Marshal Baton." A blue cross with florets signifying the new CBE that would be appended after his name was hung around his neck. It was a great day.

At this time London was holding the British Empire Exhibition in a newly constructed stadium later known as Wembley. Among the various exhibits, the Admiralty had asked Damant to have some models of the work on the *Laurentic* constructed. These were mocked up and sunk into a tank of obscuring green water. Damant went with Nell to see the exhibit and received congratulations from people who had heard that "the giant *Racer* was attracting millions." This, however, referred not to the salvage ship but a dangerous roller coaster of the same moniker.[*]

In touring the exhibition, they also came upon a performance of the Zancigs, a troupe of stage magicians and mentalists who were quite popular in Britain and the United States. Nell went up to one of the mentalists on the platform. She came down thirty seconds later. When Guy asked her what the performer said, she replied, "Your name is Eleanor, you will have three children, and never want for a penny." Nell was amazed that the mentalist knew her full name, but she only had two children.

The most interesting part of the exhibition to Damant, and the part of the exhibit he spent many words describing in detail, were the performing fleas. He wrote, "The coach had traces made of stiffish hairs along which five or six fleas were glued by their backs with the legs free. As long as the fleas had been glued on with their heads pointing up in the right direction and their legs continued to jump

---

[*] The Giant Racer was a roller coaster at Coney Island, New York, that operated from 1911 to 1926. In 1911 two women were killed, and three men were severely hurt in 1925 when testing the ride. The roller coaster was removed in 1926 to make room for the famous Cyclone.

and agitate the coach would go forward, and so it did at a good rate. The showman fed the fleas his own blood (or pretended to) when they tired. Other teams of fleas were working treadmills and other devices."

After the work on the *Laurentic* ended, Damant reverted back to the navy's retired list. He was to return permanently to Nell at Thursford and continue with his scientific investigations. As a retired commander, he might have expected to be promoted on the navy's retired list to captain in several years, thus increasing his pension.

He was starting to settle into his new post-*Laurentic* life when he started receiving letters. But these were addressed to *Captain* Damant. He received enough of them that he was compelled to write to the Admiralty on December 5, 1924, to "enquire, seriously and with proper respect" if it was true. The notice was published in the *London Gazette* the same day that Damant had sent the letter. The Admiralty officially notified him on December 8 that his promotion was effective November 7.

⚫ ⚫ ⚫

Some emerged who desired a share in the *Laurentic*'s gold and glory. Boatswain Geoffrey Unsworth, the man who in 1917 helped in the rescue efforts and had located the *Laurentic* by sweeping, pressed for a claim in the gold bonuses that had been granted to the salvage team. This was denied. Then there was Ernest Crouch, the diver who was summarily dismissed by Damant, who learned that his fellow divers had received OBEs and accelerations in seniority. He wanted the same. Crouch was unaware of Damant's suspicions about him plotting to tamper with the gold. The Admiralty was unaware of this as well since Damant never took the case forward. As a result, the Admiralty contacted Damant for his opinion. Damant wrote back and explained his suspicions, adding, "I cannot conscientiously recommend a man whom I still strongly suspect, but I may be in error and, recognising this, cannot demur if their Lordships sees fit to reward him." The Admiralty dismissed Crouch's claim and did not inform him as to the reasons.

Then there was a book published by Faber and Gwyer in 1926 titled *Diving for Treasure and Other Adventures Beneath the Sea* by a Lieutenant Commander G. Williams. In it were the improbable claims of underwater adventure that freely mixed fiction and fact that the dismissed wireless operator, T. S. Williams, had publicized in the newspapers in 1923—only expanded to include more adventures and run-ins with Irish partisans. The newspaper, the *Daily Sketch*, was suspicious and contacted Damant. Furious, Damant wrote an exposé of Williams that they published as a feature article. Faber and Gwyer contacted Damant, apologized, and withdrew the book from circulation. Damant wrote that he kept a copy of the book, which contained a prominent photograph of him (captioned as C. C. Damant), scowling. "Even that was a bit libelous," wrote Damant.

Guy and Nell had a third child in 1929, a daughter named Mary, which fulfilled the prediction made by the Zancigs. Guy, like his mother before him, read Dickens to his children and as they grew older and went to school corresponded with them in Latin. For pleasure, he raced his yacht and took bicycling trips, often with his old friend Arthur Edwin Boycott.

Damant made money from his naval pension, but he also did lucrative consulting work on the use of compressed air in construction, such as the tunnels built for the Dartford Crossing over the Thames, or refinements for staged decompression theory. One of the firms he worked especially closely with was the diving equipment manufacturer Siebe Gorman. He was great friends with its director, Sir Robert Henry Davis. Damant observed advances in diving technology, such as German-designed armored diving suits and was consulted on the seemingly impossible salvage of the liner *Egypt*'s cargo of gold bullion, which had gone down in a collision at seventy fathoms in the Bay of Biscay in 1922. Damant thought this last effort was impossible, but the Italian salvage firm Sorima proved him wrong.

Damant also returned to the biological research that he loved so much. His study on the buoyancy of the larvae of the *Corethra plumicornis* was published in the *Journal of Physiology* shortly after he finished *Laurentic* operations in 1924. "Few but professional physiologists ever appear among its contributors," wrote Damant. He went on to publish more papers, researching topics such as the gas in fish's swimming bladders and in seaweed, as well as the physiology of whales when diving. He lectured on working in and with compressed air and worked toward developing effective apparatus for people to use to escape from a sunken submarine as well as experimenting with helium-oxygen mixtures that could allow divers to go deeper. After the outbreak of the Second World War, Damant returned to the Royal Navy. He helped form a new salvage section, but the operation was later turned over to Admiral Alan Dewar—evidently Captain Damant was not a great administrator. Damant went on to direct salvage in the Mediterranean. During the war, Dusty Miller, then a retired lieutenant commander, entered the service and once more served as Damant's assistant.

As Damant aged, he remained sharp and cogent, continuing his consulting work. He witnessed with fascination the development of "frogmen" using scuba gear and commented on how they could be used in commercial salvage. In 1945, at the urging of his children, Damant started penning his memoirs, which took a decade to complete.

While in the final stages of his work on the *Laurentic*, Damant had allowed himself to be interviewed by reporters, and on one occasion was on a broadcast of a radio program. For many years would-be writers approached Captain Damant and asked him to tell the tale of the *Laurentic*. But Damant, averse to any sort of limelight, rarely granted interviews.

One of the few permitted interviews was with the American writer James Dugan, who had collaborated with and written about the celebrated French undersea explorer Jacques Cousteau. In the 1950s Dugan corresponded with Damant, who finally agreed to meet at the United Service Club. Damant sat Dugan under a portrait of Rear Admiral Sir George Cockburn—the admiral who had burned Washington, DC, during the War of 1812. This subtle gesture was not lost on Dugan.

"I do not like publicity," Damant said to Dugan. When he pressed for more information, Damant simply redirected him. "It wasn't like this in the old Navy," he said. "No publicity, no nicknames. We hadn't a journalist in sight the seven years on the *Laurentic*."

Damant said to Dugan, "Look here, there's no use in writing about what we did. It's over and done with. Why don't you write about these new chaps, the frogmen, all lashed up with teevee sets?"

He never gave many details to Dugan, or any others for that matter. But he did read Dugan's *Man Under the Sea*. While Captain Damant disliked its "journalistic" writing style, he later admitted how exciting it was to read.

Even as he grew older, Damant retained his dry, self-effacing humor. His relative, Derek Damant, who later became a bishop, was ordained a priest in 1958 at the University of South Africa. As a gift, Guy sent him the ship's Bible taken from the wreck of the German liner *Eider,* which had gone down off the Isle of Wight in 1892.* Guy inscribed on the Bible that it was a gift from the "ille urinator," from the Latin *urinare,* "to dive into water."

Captain Guybon Chesney Castell Damant, CBE, passed away quietly in his home of Thursford on the Isle of Wight on June 29, 1963, from colon cancer at age eighty-one. He was cremated and his ashes scattered in Northwood Cemetery on the Isle of Wight. His voluminous papers, correspondence, and manuscripts were handed into the care of his son Tom. As the years passed, various writers hearing the tale of his father's adventures on the *Laurentic* and inside the U-boats approached him for access to these files. But these projects fell to the wayside even until Tom's death in 2011. These papers then fell into the hands of Damant's youngest child, Mary, and were stowed away. Some papers, including many of his scientific ephemera, were donated to the Royal Society in London.

Damant became an outstanding figure in the history of diving. His research and experiences set the stage for deep-sea diving in ways that are still being used today. His covert work on the U-boats during the First World War is hardly remembered—although it materially contributed to the Allied victory. But it is the *Laurentic* for which Damant is known best. He acknowledged this, writing that it was the "highest point of my career." But all those who follow tales of lost

---

* The Bible fell into the family's hands from Harry Damant's work as an agent of Lloyd's.

treasure know that Captain Damant did not quite complete the job. There were twenty-five bars of gold left on the bottom of Lough Swilly after the *Racer* left in 1924.

Captain Damant commented in 1925, "There is always a possibility of heavy gales washing away sand so as to expose some of the 25 ingots believed to remain in the wreck of the *Laurentic* and therefore a chance, however slender, of recovering more gold, but I should not advise any one to risk money in speculating on it."

31

Speculating in Gold

As EARLY AS 1925, VARIOUS COMPANIES approached the British government with the idea of risking money to speculate on the *Laurentic*'s gold. The Admiralty had the idea of auctioning the salvage rights to the wreck, but delayed any contract since it was not clear if there were any confidential materials inside the ship that were still of value. Upon reflection, the Admiralty reconsidered when it was approached in 1926 by a ship-breaking company. Sir Vincent Baddeley agreed with Captain Damant on the dubiousness of making the *Laurentic* a profitable venture. "My own belief is that, even if any further salvage operations *did* succeed in recovering some of the gold, the cost would exceed the value of anything that would be recovered." Still, the Admiralty offered a no-cure, no-pay contract at a fifty-fifty split between the British government and the company. This deal fell through probably after some prudent calculations were made by the ship breaker.

On May 19, 1931, the British government signed over salvage rights to the Malet Salvage Syndicate. The company, formed by Commander Herbert Rivers Malet of the Royal Navy Volunteer Reserve, a former salvage officer during the war, and directed by Frank Christie, had negotiated a contract whereby they were allowed to retain 75 percent of the value of any bullion and the British Treasury would receive the remainder.

Malet was a small company and without financial backing could not hope to achieve the same complexity and thoroughness of Damant's salvage operations. They used two ships in the course of the work, first the *Estoy* and later the *Attendant*. Commander Malet did not have a recompression chamber at his disposal and had only two divers, former Royal Navy men named John Tyler and Dan Godfrey.

To do the job, the salvors first lowered an observation chamber—an enclosed steel submersible device with thick glass portholes that allowed a man from the inside to see the state of the wreck. Based on observations, Malet was better able to direct the divers as to where to excavate. The divers, using only crowbars, searched not in the area of Damant's working position but rather along the outlying areas. They found two ingots in the 1931 salvage season and two more the next year. This was not quite enough to pay for operations, but the Malet Salvage Syndicate kept at the job, thinking that if they could make one strike and recover the remaining bars it would pay for all.

But payment for the bars they had recovered was not without controversy. On September 16, 1931, Britain went off the gold standard in response to outflows of bullion and capital from the Treasury. As a result, the market value of gold increased dramatically even though the statutory value of gold (the value declared by the government) remained at the lower rate. The Treasury paid for the bullion at the lower, governmental rate, much to the consternation of the Malet Salvage Syndicate. It took almost a year of negotiations before the Treasury agreed in January 1933 to pay the lower rate for the first two bars since they were recovered before Britain abandoned the gold standard, and later ingots at the market rate.

Malet recovered a total of five bars between 1931 and 1934.[*] It never was a profitable venture for Malet, and in November 1934 Christie asked for a £2,000 loan from the Treasury with the *Attendant*

---

[*] Malet even found the *Laurentic*'s safe, but this was lost when the chain hauling it to the surface snapped. There was some confusion when in 1934, after finding the fifth bar, it was erroneously reported in some newspapers that the salvage team had recovered all the remaining gold.

as collateral so that they could continue the work. The Treasury, however, would not or could not authorize the loan. After 1934 the Malet Salvage Syndicate ceased work on the wreck, although it renewed its salvage rights yearly until 1940 when the company went bankrupt. Frank Christie attempted to get an extension in his own name, but this never came to pass.

Throughout the Second World War and for several years after, the *Laurentic* and its twenty gold ingots lay undisturbed. While individuals would sometimes inquire about the wreck, the next serious effort to find the remaining treasure was performed by Risdon Beazley, a major salvage company. They negotiated a five-year contract that would give them 90 percent of the value of the first five bars found, 85 percent of the value of the next five, and 80 percent for the remainder. This agreement was signed in 1952 with special permission from the Republic of Ireland, which by that time had become completely independent of the United Kingdom. Risdon Beazley began its efforts shortly thereafter.

After working on the wreck for a year with their vessel *Topmast*, the company managed to recover £2,868 worth of scrap metal, including some bronze propeller blades, but they could not locate any gold. Risdon Beazley pressed to purchase the hull, not the cargo, for a token sum of £200 so that it could enforce the law of trespass on the wreck. However, the British government refused, with one Treasury official writing, "The wreck of the vessel itself (as distinct from the cargo) has generally been regarded as valueless from a salvage standpoint.... The firm's ownership of the wreck would entitle them to be consulted as to the terms and conditions under which any future salvage operations might be undertaken in regard to the cargo (i.e. the gold). It sounds too much like the sale of a 'birthright for a mess of pottage.'" Risdon Beazley soon gave up salvage operations not only because of the refusal of the government to sell the hull but also perhaps because representatives of the company had read Damant's own pessimistic reports of recovering more gold and had spoken with diver Godfrey from the Malet salvage. Godfrey believed that there was no more gold to be found on the *Laurentic*—or at least it would be impossible to find.

Naturally, there had been rumors over the years as to the possibility that the remaining twenty bars of gold had been spirited from the wreck or somehow stolen after they were raised. One rumor told of a sailor who brought a gold bar to an antique shop in Londonderry. Allegedly, the owner cut up the bar into smaller pieces using a hacksaw and sent it out. A week later, two detectives came to investigate but found nothing. Another story spoke of a freight yard in Londonderry. The yard had a large gate that was held open by a blackened metal block. As a horse and cart were passing into the yard one day, the wheel of the cart caught the block and scratched it. Workmen noticed a shine to the block with a letter *L* etched on its side.

Both of these rumors are unsubstantiated, belonging to the realm of urban legends and the wishful thinking of conspiracy mongers. What's more, the bars of gold from the *Laurentic* were engraved from where they originated, either the bank or country of origin, not the first letter of the ship that they were on. The working position was well monitored when salvage was underway, and the gold was too hard to get at as to make theft feasible. According to records, all the gold bars recovered were received in good order by the Treasury. Could there have been stolen bars? Yes, there is always a possibility. Is it probable? No.

Even while Risdon Beazley considered the *Laurentic*, others hearing of the fabled twenty ingots sent inquiries to the government, including a Mr. Frank Maguire of Glasgow who in 1955, after writing that he was preparing for salvage work on the ship, inquired of three pieces of data concerning the *Laurentic*:

1) Her exact position
2) The whereabouts of the bullion room
3) Amount of gold bars salvaged by the *Racer*

The letter did not inspire confidence on the part of the British government. Risdon Beazley held the rights to the wreck and didn't do any further salvage until their contract expired in 1957.

• • •

The lure of sunken treasure is compelling to young men. Such was the case for the Cossum brothers. Ray and Eric Cossum grew up in Folkestone, Kent, in a family of ten siblings. The English Channel was their backdrop and the context for many stories of shipwrecks they heard as youths. The brothers were first introduced to Lough Swilly when they would go on holiday with their family to Buncrana. It was on one of these vacations that while looking out at the waters Eric remarked to his brother that there was a sunken treasure ship there and its name was *Laurentic.* Ray said, "The name had drawn us like a magnet."

Riches to be wrested from the sea through adventure was a fascinating prospect and could bring the brothers wealth, fame, and ultimately a sense of purpose. Ray Cossum was entranced by the waters of the sea lough. He shared the physicality of his father, a sergeant major in the army who was an able boxer. In 1964, the thirty-two-year-old Ray, wearing his swimming trunks and a pair of Lone Ranger goggles, swam the five miles from Rathmullan to Buncrana. He emerged from the water to applause as people gathered by the sea to witness the feat. He was hooked on long-distance swimming ever since and swam the English Channel on August 1, 1970, at a time of thirteen hours and forty-one minutes, claiming to be the first Irishman to swim it. One of his sons, Desmond, also became passionate about endurance swimming, and they trained an Irish junior team that broke the world record for a Channel swim in 1978. At the time of this writing, Ray is a vice president of the Channel Swimming Association.

Ray served in the Royal Navy for eight years, five of which were in the submarine service as an escape instructor. While he was in the navy, he was based in Londonderry and there met and married Bridget "Bridie" Loughrey in 1951. Derry became his home, but he was often abroad serving as a diver on deep-sea salvage jobs worldwide and working on rigs in the North Sea and also on drill ships in the Sunda Strait and other locations in Asia. All the same, Ray Cossum always felt tied to the English Channel. He wrote, "I have worked as a diver on the bottom of the English Channel, I have swum the English Channel, I am Vice President of the Channel Swimming Association, I have passed through the Channel in submarines, I have been through the Channel Tunnel, I have flown over the Channel, and passed over the Channel on ships." But as strong as Ray Cossum's ties are to the English Channel, it was at Lough Swilly where he gained the most notice.

As Ray and Eric grew older, their dreams returned to the Lake of Shadows and its ship of gold. In 1967 they decided to try to discover the wreck for themselves. Although the brothers knew the approximate area of the wreck, they could not identify the precise location. In the summer of 1967 the pair found themselves in a small trawler, *Girl Christine*, heading out of Lough Swilly. Portsalon passed by on the west as they headed toward Fanad Head. The high oceanic waters began to raise the trawler as they used sonar to scan the ocean bed. Suddenly, the needle on the device climbed. The brothers shrieked with delight and bade the captain to stop.

The duo and their friend Tom Gallagher, an exporter and shipping agent, boarded a rubber raft and had the ship take them in tow. The Cossums had rigged a proton magnetometer metal detector to the raft, and they anxiously watched it as they passed over the area. The detector flickered—there was a huge magnetic gradient.

The Cossums and Gallagher suited up in scuba gear to see what was on the bottom. Ray remembered, "Our hearts were pounding, and I could feel the half-fear gnawing at the pit of my stomach as

Ray Cossum (standing) and Eric Cossum prepare for a dive down to the *Laurentic* circa mid-1960s.
© *Ray and Des Cossum (Cossum Diving Syndicate)*

we slipped over the side. But the second I hit the water I was alright. Together, we headed into the gloom. As we descended, dull, strange shapes began to loom into view. It was her—the *Laurentic*.... We all unashamedly hugged each other moaning like banshees into our mouthpieces with excitement, and Tom and I did swimming rolls of victory." As a souvenir, Ray and Eric lifted a porthole from the wreck.

The *Laurentic* did not disappoint the Cossums. It was a huge tangle of ruined steel mixed with megalithic machinery. But *knowing* the scale of the *Laurentic* and *experiencing* it are two different things. Ray compared it to a huge "football field of scrap," adding, "Even today it is quite amazing how, when working in a certain area, you will suddenly stumble on a piece of machinery of enormous proportions you had never seen before. There is always a thrill of the unexpected on the great wreck."

Now that the Cossums knew where the ship lay, they wanted to verify that the gold was still in it. In a thorough research effort using Admiralty records and newspapers and conducting interviews with one of Damant's divers as well as crew of the Malet salvage attempt, the Cossums became more knowledgeable about the *Laurentic* than anybody since Guy Damant and Dusty Miller. They were convinced that the gold was still there—they just needed to get the right to recover it. They spoke to representatives from Risdon Beazley, who informed the Cossums that the company owned the wreck.

But the brothers were dubious. So, in March 1969, Eric applied to the Ministry of Defence to get the salvage rights. The result of his negotiations was found in a telegram that Ray received on March 22: "WE OWN LAURENTIC." The terms they worked out with the British government were a ninety-ten split of the value of the gold, with 90 percent going to the brothers. The brothers formed Cossum Syndicate Ltd, with Ray and Eric as the principals. The brothers were later joined by Ray's son Desmond who shared much of his father's passion for the lost liner.

The first dives that Ray and Eric made on the *Laurentic* were done from a twelve-foot C craft inflatable with a twelve-horsepower outboard engine. They did not have a compass, GPS, or radio. Most of their equipment, suits, and harness were designed by Eric. He even crafted their first air compressor using spare aircraft parts. The compressor always fretted the brothers. The machine was designed to produce two thousand pounds per square inch of compressed air. However, Ray said it sounded like "crushing stones" and was always breaking down. But they were young and the allure of the gold was too strong for them to be overmindful of safety.

Soon enough, the Cossums learned of the wicked weather off Lough Swilly. On one occasion the sea suddenly turned on them forcing Ray's diving companion to shout, "Go back! For God's sake Ray, go back!" They returned to Portsalon with dark waves chasing them all the way.

These early years of salvage were filled with some successes. They found brass and copper from the portholes of the *Laurentic*, which helped finance further dives. The brothers continually dived on the wreck into the early 1970s with Ray's son Desmond becoming an eager partner in the work, as well as his other son, Grahame, joining them at times.

In dive after dive they found artifacts. They brought up coins scattered about the old gold area, but there was never a sign of gold. Finally, in 1979 the Cossums decided they needed professional assistance. They contacted a group of businessmen and struck a deal in exchange for help in locating the gold, the company would receive the value of any scrap they raised.

The salvage firm that they hired used an ancient vessel, the *Allerton*, a World War I–vintage tank carrier. The Cossums nicknamed the ship the *Black Pig* after a ship in a popular comic strip titled *Captain Pugwash*. There was no crane or recompression chamber, and it looked like a hulk.

The crew was equally motley. The principal diver, Victor "Vic" Cowan Dickie, was tall, strong, and temperamental. On one occasion, he came up from a dive demanding some different equipment so that he could raise more scrap. The Cossums noted that Vic was not adhering to the decompression tables. While Vic explained that he worked on his own diving tables, his son raised the volume on a boom box. Vic grabbed the box and smashed it to pieces on the deck of the *Black Pig*. He promptly dived again, crashing about the wreck, pulling up scrap and then coming back up—seemingly immune to decompression illness.

Vic was excellent at finding the brass and copper that the Cossums had overlooked in a decade of diving. In fact, it was Vic who helped them locate another bell of the *Laurentic*, which had hung in the bridge. The bell was missing its clapper, which was not unusual since clappers were typically removed until needed in watches. The bell had many indentations on it, as if it were struck repeatedly hard by a hammer—perhaps damaged in the *Laurentic*'s final hour. This find was a surprise to Ray Cossum, who knew of the bell that hung in the church at Portsalon: "We had dived many times on the wreck as had many other divers and no one had seen the bell. It was easy now to understand how we had missed the gold. I was even more convinced the gold was still there."

The evening that Vic had raised the *Laurentic*'s bell, he collapsed on deck. After the captain examined him, they knew he had the bends. The *Black Pig*'s radio was not working. Slowly, they moved the 250-pound man into an inflatable motorized boat and then sped back to the Portsalon pier. From there, they telephoned for help. But the Irish Rescue Air Service was involved with a sea rescue. They got them in touch with the British service and two and a half hours later a Royal Marines helicopter hovered overhead.

Ray Cossum (right) with his son, Desmond, holding the *Laurentic*'s bell.
© *Ray and Des Cossum (Cossum Diving Syndicate)*

This was during the time of the Troubles in Northern Ireland, and the helicopter would not land. The pilot shouted, "We do not leave the chopper! You bring the injured man to us!" A crowd had gathered, and several others helped bring Vic to them. They flew off to Northern Ireland where he was placed in a recompression chamber. The doctor commented that his blood "had a head on it like a pint of Guinness." Vic recovered, but between that, and the company directors' decision to dock the pay of Vic's son for visiting his father in the hospital, the brothers ended the agreement. The company took the scrap, and the Cossums kept the bell.

After studying the artifact for a short while and basking in their good fortune to have found it, the Cossums sold the bell to Paul Rowlands, a businessman from Euro Salvage. Rowlands's father then loaned the bell to a company that then went into liquidation. The bell disappeared. After Ray found out what happened he regretted selling the bell, and now his personal quest encompasses not only the *Laurentic*'s gold but also locating the lost bell.

After the mixed results with the *Black Pig*, the Cossums then partnered with other more professional salvage firms. They first worked a deal out with the Holyhead Towing Company in 1984. The firm excavated in Damant's working position hoping that several bars were overlooked. They operated off the tug *Afon Goch*, and used a seventy-five-foot pontoon equipped with a two-man recompression chamber. The weather was generally bad, but the salvage company excavated a forty-by-sixty-foot pit of shingle and sand in thirty days of work. While they recovered one of the *Laurentic*'s guns, they too could not locate any gold.

The next company was Consortium Recovery Limited in 1992, to which the Cossums deeded their rights to the wreck. The Cossums were kept as consultants and had a right to a portion of the value of the gold. This company, using the *Holga Dane*, excavated out and away from Damant's original position. An extensive search was made, and then the salvors performed a sweep of the old working position. But although Consortium Recovery took home many portholes and even a large amount of old munitions from the *Laurentic*'s magazine, there was no gold. The company intended to return, but it soon dissolved and the rights were returned to the Cossums.

With no gold being found, the Cossums became discouraged. Eric, who was sixty-four at the time (and Ray sixty), said, "It's time to give up. Because of our ages it is too much for us. We know the gold is there but it will have to take a different approach and not use a big salvage boat like Consortium Recovery's because it would cost a great deal of money. We believe it should be done with a boat just big enough to do the work. There is no easy way to recover the gold or the Cossum Syndicate Limited would have found it. But we are not big enough to do so, and I believe it's time to give up."

The Cossums became convinced that the twenty gold bars lay in a concentrated area. Consortium Recovery, before leaving the work, advised that it was possible that a couple of boxes of gold slid down a corridor or shaft as the ship broke up. But the means of getting at the gold are clearly difficult. Ray contends that the best way to make a sustainable attempt would be through a smaller operation using a more compact vessel that would pay for itself through the proceeds of scrap from the wreck.

As the years pass, there are occasional reports of gold being found from the *Laurentic*. In 1992, a radio station in Donegal reported that a gold bar had been recovered by a twelve-man diving team. It even got reported on CNN in the United States. But the claim turned out to originate from two brothers in Belfast who were pleasure diving on the *Laurentic*. They went to a local pub with a fake bar made of brass and filled with lead. As news of the claim spread, Ray Cossum was investigated by customs and excise officials. Even after this matter was cleared up, other false news reports followed.

Eric Cossum passed away in 2016 before he could be interviewed for this book, but Ray, even at eighty-four, still exudes an eager, boyish energy when speaking of the *Laurentic*. When I asked him directly where he thought the gold was, he quickly replied as if he had heard the question a thousand times, "If I told you, everybody would be diving on the wreck." After some pressing, Ray speculated that the gold probably lies somewhere under one of the *Laurentic*'s other guns toward the edge of Damant's working position, citing how Damant had found a certain quantity of gold under a similar gun that led him on the right track in July 1921. But even after removing the gun, the likelihood is that the gold, being so dense, would have sunk even deeper into the wreck.

To legally dive on the *Laurentic* a diver needs the permission of the Cossums. But many people have chosen to ignore this, including a museum curator who was stealing artifacts from the wreck. At the petitioning of Ray, the government strengthened the laws protecting such wrecks, but it is admittedly hard to enforce. When divers ask the Cossums for permission, they generally get a positive response, such as when a group of amateur divers from Downings, led by Kevin McShane, approached Ray about recovering a seven-meter gun from the *Laurentic*'s bow. Ray assented. The divers, over the course of three years, used lifting chains and a customized flotation bag to raise the gun and finally recover it in 2007. They presented it to the town of Downings. Ray was pleased to see it restored and set by the harbor.

While a gun is nice, the gold would be stellar. But the probability is that the cost of actually getting to the gold would be the same if not more than its value. Ray commented, "At my age, I don't think I'll ever see the gold." But Ray doesn't seem depressed or saddened about this—the *Laurentic*'s gold to him was in many ways not the actual bullion but the act of being part of an ongoing adventure. In a newspaper interview, Ray commented, "I've been lucky to have experienced everything I've done but also lucky to have met the many people who have made it all possible. We all rely on our brothers, sisters, wives, and friends and should never take them for granted. With the benefit of hindsight this is more clear than ever, and I'd like to thank everyone for helping me along the way."

Today, the *Laurentic* is viewed in the diving community as an excellent wreck to dive on. Underwater photographer Steve Jones dived with eight others for pleasure to the *Laurentic*. He noted, "The extensive salvage combined with nearly a hundred years of sea action have left the wreck well broken up and quite flat, with deck and hull plates lying over each other like a collapsed pack of cards, but it is still easy to appreciate the scale of this 168-meter-long liner. The bow has broken off and lies on its side, and further down the port side a large deck gun acts as a good navigation marker, pointing you to rows of scotch boilers and the triple expansion engine blocks. This wreck teems with fish life and the sheltered position means it's a good choice if the winds prevent venturing further afield on the other outstanding wrecks in the waters off Malin Head."

Diving on the *Laurentic* grew more complicated in 2017 when, on the hundredth anniversary of its sinking, the wreck officially became protected by Irish law under the terms of the National Monuments Act that require a license to dive on the wreck since the ship will become a designated historic site. However, this will not interfere with the rights of the Cossums who have been assured of their ownership by the Irish government. In fact, the new legislation may prove more helpful in preventing illegal treasure hunting on the wreck. Ray Cossum met with the government and came to terms that he would retain his rights and be allowed to carry on as before. He even signed a copy of his book, *We Own Laurentic*, for them.

The *Laurentic* has been honored in other ways. The Ulster Canada Initiative launched the *Laurentic* Conference in 2009, to honor the dead of the *Laurentic* and foster ties between Northwest Ireland and Canada. The conference, whose motto is Remembrance, Reconciliation, and Prosperity, has speakers who discuss matters of international trade, energy, and other transatlantic issues. The organization annually honors the *Laurentic*'s dead by laying a wreath at the St. Mura's graveyard at Fahan and then at the St. Mary's Church cemetery where many of the victims had been buried.

As some go the graveyard at Fahan to see the memorial cross erected to the men of the *Laurentic*, some may wander into the nearby church, where there hangs a painting of the ship with its single funnel whipping black smoke in its speed. Below it is W. R. Latham's poem "The Loss of the *Laurentic*" that, notwithstanding its historic inaccuracies, sets the *Laurentic* in its epic context.

In nineteen seventeen the proud Laurentic
Was bound from Ireland to the U.S.A.
When Germans sank her out in the Atlantic
Off Donegal one bitter Winter day.

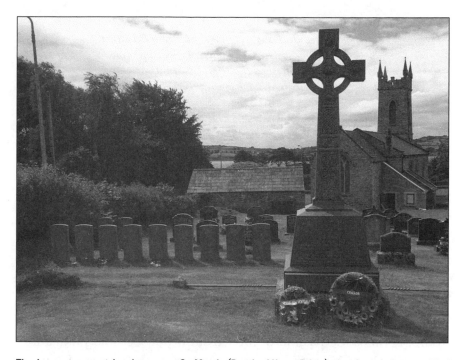

The *Laurentic* memorial and graves at St. Mura's (Parish of Upper Fahan) church yard. *Courtesy of Nigel Henderson, History Hub Ulster*

None saw the swift torpedo that destroyed her
None saw the submarine that launched the blow
They only felt the shattering explosion
That stopped the engines throbbing heart below.

The wounded vessel quivered, paused, and listed
Plunged to her death beneath the hungry waves
And in that fearful wilderness of water
300 gallant soldiers found their graves.

A precious ship and precious lives were lost there
And lost the precious cargo in her hold
Five million pounds of gleaming glittering ingots
Three thousand and two hundred bars of gold.

The finest divers in the British Navy
Skilled men of courage and tenacity
At home in that strange world of swirling water
Were sent to wrest that treasure from the sea.

They dared the hazards of the winds and tides then
Of shifting sand, strong current, floating mine,
Of cutting edges that could mean disaster
Of falling wreckage fouling pipe and line.

For seven years they battled to recover
The wealth that lay there wasting in the deep
Until at last they freed those prisoned riches
The jealous sea had fought so hard to keep.

Man by his skill can build an Ocean Liner.
Man by his skill can send her to her doom,
Man by his skill can bring back the buried treasure,
But not the dead from their untimely tomb.

We might expect the story of the *Laurentic* to continue. One day when the tides are right and the sands shift or the last deck plates are uncovered a diver may see a warped ingot emerge from its tomb. Perhaps the passion of the Cossums will see final validation—but anybody seeking this treasure needs the persistence of Captain Damant, or more. For twenty fathoms under the sea, off Lough Swilly, some two miles from Fanad Head, lies the *Laurentic* with its twenty bars of gold.

ACKNOWLEDGMENTS

As with all my books, my greatest support and assistance has been from my wife, Michelle, who has now been through three books with me and has looked over the earliest drafts of each work with care and *loving* criticism.

There are many organizations and individuals who assisted in the creation of this book. The following are some of those who provided especial help and to whom I direct my thanks.

To Dr. John Bevan, Chairman of the Historical Diving Society (UK), thank you so much for your technical comments and assistance in helping me get straight the differences between the American and British styles of diving. Also, thank you for providing for this book valuable documents and photographs that helped to humanize the *Laurentic* epic.

To Ruth Bloom, thank you for your able research assistance and helping me to get in touch with some of the key players in this story. This book would not have been possible without your help.

To Donald P. Brennan, thank you for reading another of my manuscripts and providing discerning feedback to help strengthen the narrative.

To Ray and Des Cossum, what is there to say but thank you? You have been personally involved with the *Laurentic* for decades, and I appreciate your willingness to open up to me with your experiences and support.

To Hannah Cunliffe, thank you so much for your research assistance. The documents you found for me were one of a kind.

To Charles Darwent, I owe you an especial thanks. Your eager willingness to assist me and connect me with your family not only increased the length of this manuscript by twenty thousand words, but also allowed it to attain a level of character depth that it did not have before.

To Mary Damant Harrison, I hope you find this book a fitting tribute to your father, a truly remarkable man.

To Jon Hazelbaker, member of the board of the History of Diving Museum (FL), for commentary and answering the odd technical questions concerning deck whips and air pipes: I truly appreciate your passion for the subject.

To Dr. Innes McCartney, thank you for your work, both academic and practical, in confirming the truths of the sunken U-boats of World War I. Thank you also for commenting on my manuscript.

To Ronan McConnell and the Derry City and Strabane District Council for assistance in obtaining important primary documents.

To Tomas Termote, thank you for the technical assistance and photographs of U-boats. Your contribution made for a more accurate narrative.

To DCC (SS/SW) David L. Johnston, USNR, and Ric Hedman TN (SS) USN, American submarine history experts and managers of Pigboats.com. Thanks again for providing your feedback to build a better book.

To Michael Poirier of the *Titanic International Society*, thank you so much for going beyond the call of duty. You and your colleagues' dedication to the history of liners is impressive. Thank you for coordinating the odd photograph or the random fact.

To Alice Walsh, archives collections officer of the National Museum of the Royal Navy, thank you very much for your reference assistance in helping me find some of the correct sources.

To the Friends of East Cowes and the East Cowes Heritage Centre, particularly to Ken Wheeler and Ken Perkins, thank you for providing useful genealogical information for this work.

To the professional archivists at the British National Archives, thank you for preserving the key documents that made the heart of this narrative possible.

NOTES

Abbreviations

AFT: G. C. C. Damant, "A Father's Tale" (unpublished manuscript, August 18, 1954). Microsoft Word file transcribed from the original.

Notes: G. C. C. Damant, "Notes on the 'Laurentic' Salvage Operations and the Prevention of Compressed Air Illness," *Journal of Hygiene* 25, no. 1 (1926): 26–49.

1. The *Titanic* in Miniature

The majority of information informing the narrative of the sinking of the *Laurentic* and rescue efforts undertaken after its sinking is taken from ADM 116/1553 "Loss of the H.M.S. *Laurentic*," which contains depositions, testimony, and official logs taken from the court of inquiry over the matter.

Information concerning the interior description of the *Laurentic* and its engineering plant is taken from "Three Notable Launches," *The Engineer*, September 18, 1908; "Triple-Screw Steamer Laurentic," *The Engineer*, April 23, 1909.

For Captain Reginald Norton's Service Record, see ADM 196/43/370 "Norton, Reginald Arthur," National Archives, Kew, London.

For a general overview of the Live Bait Squadron, see Alan Coles, *Three Before Breakfast* (White Plains, NY: Kenneth Mason, 1979).

"I have the honour to submit": Archibald Hurd and H. C. Bywater, *From Heligoland to Keeling Island: One Hundred Days of Naval War* (London: Hodder and Stoughton, 1914), 156.

2. The Damants of Cowes

Most of the narrative concerning Damant's biography is derived from AFT.

Details concerning the marriage of Harry Damant and Mary Wilson from the *Manchester Courier and Lancashire General Advertiser*, October 4, 1879.

Details concerning the political officer Guybon Damant's death from correspondence with Charles Darwent; *Hampshire Advertiser*, October 22, 1879; October 25, 1879; and November 5, 1879

Details concerning the death and grave of George Sancroft Damant from correspondence with Charles Darwent and Mary Harrison. Note that the gravestone is no longer at the West Cowes Cemetery. After the bombings during the Second World War the gravestone was removed and kept at their home of Thursford.

"on the cheap": AFT.

For a physical description of G. C. C. Damant, I relied on photographs and a description provided by Damant's daughter, Mary Harrison.

Information on the Grange school is scanty in all sources except for advertisements in newspapers, thus I relied on Damant's recollections in AFT. It is notable that while Damant's memoirs name the headmaster as Watson, advertisements found in the *Isle of Wight County Press* name the headmaster as Wilson. Since there was no apparent source that could corroborate either account, I kept the Watson reference.

Information on Naval Cadetship requirements and curriculum from M. L. Pechell, *Professions for Boys and How to Enter Them* (London: Beeton, 1899), 3–7; W. Laird Clowes, *All About the Royal Navy* (London: Cassell, 1891), 157–163.

"Careless and Dirty": AFT.

playing goalie on the Grange's football team: *Isle of Wight County Press*, November 16, 1895.

For results of Damant's cadetship exams, see *Birmingham Daily Post*, December 25, 1895.

3. The U-Boat War

For movements of the *Laurentic*, see ADM 116/1553.

For goings-on at the Admiralty during the First World War and the U-boat campaign, the best source is Arthur J. Marder's multivolume *From the Dreadnought to Scapa Flow: The Royal Navy in the Fisher Era*, rev. ed. (1966; repr., Annapolis, MD: Naval Institute Press, 2013). Also see C. I. Hamilton, *The Making of the Modern Admiralty: British Naval Policy-Making, 1805–1927* (Cambridge: Cambridge University Press, 2011), for more detailed information concerning politics at the Admiralty.

"an unwarranted invasion of the sovereignty": "Removal of Enemy Subjects from American Vessels," *The American Journal of International Law* 10, no. 4 (1916): 427–432, doi:10.2307/2212622.

"The course of events hitherto": Admiral Reinhard Scheer, *Germany's High Sea Fleet in the World War* (London: Cassell, 1920), 245.

"There is no possibility of bringing the war": Scheer, *Germany's High Sea Fleet*, 247.

"England will be forced to sue for peace": *Official German Documents*, 2:1214–1216, quoted from Michael H. Hunt, *Crises in U.S. Foreign Policy* (New Haven: Yale University Press, 1996), 44.

4. "I Have No Good Word to Say for It"

For general information on the *Britannia,* see Commander E. P. Statham, *The Story of the "Britannia": The Training Ship for Naval Cadets; with Some Account of Previous Methods of Naval Education, and of the New Scheme of 1903* (London: Cassell, 1904).

"I have no good word to say for it": AFT.

For Damant's official record, see ADM 196/46/148, "Damant, Guybon Chesney Castell," National Archives, Kew, London.

"There my boy, what do you think": AFT.

"Administration has always been my bugbear": AFT.

"knew nothing whatever about it": AFT.

"Come on, Andrew!": AFT.

"This saves one": AFT.

"What the mesoblast of the Death's Head Moth": H. G. Wells, *The Complete Short Stories of H.G. Wells,* ed. J. R. Hammond (London: Phoenix, 1998), 85.

"What could this be?": AFT.

"Though not feeling particularly ill, I grew feeble": AFT.

"to have court martialled": AFT.

"Private subscriptions awarded": AFT.

"One morning at sea with the fleet": AFT.

"mass of mud": AFT.

For a general history of HMS *Excellent,* see Commander R. Travers Young, *The House That Jack Built: The Story of the H.M.S. Excellent* (Gale and Polden, 1955); R. D. Oliver, *H.M.S. "Excellent": 1830–1930* (Portsmouth: Charpentier Ltd., 1930).

5. The Lake of Shadows

For movements of the *Laurentic,* see ADM 116/1553.

For personal information concerning Frank Finnis, see AFT.

Regarding activities of officers going ashore to Buncrana, see Jack Scoltock and Ray Cossum, *We Own Laurentic: The Story of "the Gold Ship"* (Coleraine, UK: Impact, 2000).

6. Through the Looking Glass

"singularly attractive personality": **Times of London,** January 27, 1939.

"It was an unpopular item": AFT.

"Suppose a diver at work on a stage": Robert H. Davis, *A Diving Manual and Handbook of Submarine Appliances* (London: Siebe, Gorman, 1924), 14.

For information concerning the diving dress during this period, see John Bevan, *The Infernal Diver: The Lives of John and Charles Deane, Their Invention of the Diving Helmet, and Its First Application to Salvage, Treasure Hunting, Civil Engineering and Military Uses* (London: Submex, 1996); Davis, *Diving Manual.*

"Send for the doctor": *Report of a Committee Appointed by the Lords Commissioners of the Admiralty to Consider and Report upon the Conditions of Deep-Water Diving; Together with Index, Appendices, and Illustrations* (London: Eyre and Spottiswoode, 1907).

"his skin was cyanosed": Archibald McKinlay, "Case of Death from Syncope Caused by Caisson Disease," in Great Britain Parliament, House of Commons, *Papers by Command*, vol. 42 (Arkose, 1901), 102.

"on incising the scalp": McKinlay, "Case of Death," 102.

"The heart was normal in size": McKinlay, "Case of Death," 103.

For information on caisson disease, see Leonard Hill, *Caisson Sickness and the Physiology of Work in Compressed Air* (London: Arnold, 1912); James Dugan, *Man Under the Sea* (New York: Harper, 1956); Davis, *Diving Manual.*

"I felt like Alice through the looking glass": AFT.

"I found going under water": Dugan, 64–65.

"Officers did not dive": AFT.

7. Spark

For movements of the *Laurentic* and information concerning Bower, see ADM 116/1553.

For information concerning the Crippen case, see Scoltock and Cossum, *We Own Laurentic*; Erik Larson, *Thunderstruck* (New York: Broadway Books, 2007).

8. Suffer

"professors from Oxford": AFT.

For an excellent biography of J. S. Haldane, see Martin Goodman, *Suffer and Survive: The Extreme Life of J.S. Haldane* (London: Simon and Schuster, 2007).

"Experiments are still needed": AFT.

For Haldane's experiments concerning ventilation and diving pumps, see *Report of a Committee*; Goodman, *Suffer and Survive.*

Damant's impressions of Haldane and his participation in the experiments can be found in *Report of a Committee*; Goodman, *Suffer and Survive*; A. E. Boycott, G. C. C. Damant, and J. S. Haldane, "The Prevention of Compressed-Air Illness," *Journal of Hygiene* 8 (1908): 342–443, doi: http://dx.doi.org/10.1017/S0022172400003399; AFT.

"Have you got it?": AFT.

"I suddenly woke up": AFT.

"like heaven on earth": AFT.

air experiments on goats can be found in Boycott, Damant, and Haldane, "Prevention of Compressed-Air Illness."

"Goats, while they are not perhaps such delicate": Boycott, Damant, and Haldane, "The Prevention of Compressed-Air Illness," 379.

"During the breeding season": Boycott, Damant, and Haldane, "The Prevention of Compressed-Air Illness," 383.

"Harris the Sausage King": AFT.

"It is needlessly slow": Boycott, Damant, and Haldane, "The Prevention of Compressed-Air Illness," 425.

"did not want publicity-seeking": Goodman, *Suffer and Survive*, 193.

9. SOS

For activities of the *U-80*, see Scoltock and Cossum, *We Own Laurentic*.

"Abandon ship!": ADM 116/1553, written deposition and testimony of Reginald Norton.

"Have you sent for help?": ADM 116/1553, testimony of Reginald Norton and Arthur Bower.

"Have you received my S.O.S.?": ADM 116/1553, testimony of Arthur Bower.

10. Loch Striven

The fullest account of the diving trials off Loch Striven may be found in *Report of a Committee*. See also Goodman, *Suffer and Survive*; AFT.

The sequence for dressing a diver was taken from R. H. Davis, *Diving Scientifically and Practically Considered: Being a Diving Manual and Handbook of Submarine Appliances* (London: Siebe, Gorman, 1915); Davis, *Diving Manual*. Damant was a contributor to these manuals.

"I dipped first in 36 fathoms": Damant's diving log taken from a copy kept by the Friends of East Cowes.

"It was quite possible that they would wind up": AFT.

"is the greatest depth ever definitely recorded": *Report of a Committee*, 10; Boycott, Damant, and Haldane, "The Prevention of Compressed-Air Illness"

11. Abandon Ship!

For the movements of the *Laurentic* and evacuation, see ADM 116/1553.

"Leave them where they are and go to your boat": ADM 116/1553, testimony of Reginald Norton.

"I am going to lower you away now": ADM 116/1553, testimony of Hugh Rogers.

12. The Inspector

For an overview of *Torpedo Boat 99, see* Thomas W. Corbin, *The Romance of Submarine Engineering: Containing Interesting Descriptions in Nontechnical Language of the Construction of Submarine Boats ... and Many Other Feats of Engineering Beneath the Surface of the Water,* (Philadelphia: J. B. Lippincott, 1913).

Damant's personal life while working at Lister is fully described in AFT.

"young and so fresh": AFT.

"Here's a chance for you Damant": AFT.

Damant's first published piece: G. C. C. Damant, "The Normal Temperature of the Goat" in "Proceedings of the Physiological Society, December 1, 1907," *Journal of Physiology* 35, supplement, December 1, (1907).

"will be of some value in supplying": Damant, "The Normal Temperature of the Goat"

"The job was more troublesome": AFT.

For Damant and Boycott's other papers, see A. E. Boycott and G. C. C. Damant, "A Note on the Quantities of Marsh-Gas, Hydrogen and Carbon Dioxide Produced in the Alimentary Canal of Goats," *Journal of Physiology* 36, nos. 4–5 (1907): 283–287, doi:10.1113/jphysiol.1907.sp001233; and "Some Lesions of the Spinal Cord Produced by Experimental Caisson Disease," *Journal of Pathology and Bacteriology* 12, no. 3 (1908): 507–515, doi:10.1002/path.1700120305.

The narrative of the *Torpedo Boat 99* incident and Damant's subsequent troubles is drawn from Corbin, *Romance of Submarine Engineering;* B. J. Hyde and S. Leverett, "A Fight for Life Under Water," *Wide World Magazine* (May 1908) 153–156; *Western Times,* July 17, 1907; *Los Angeles Herald,* August 4, 1907; *Nottingham Evening Post,* July 16, 1907; *Star,* Issue 9036, September 17, 1907; *Evening Telegraph and Post,* July 16, 1907; *Gloucester Citizen,* July 16, 1907; *Aberdeen Daily Journal,* July 17, 1907; *Gloucestershire Echo,* July 17, 1907; *Lancashire Daily Post,* July 17, 1907; *Manchester Courier,* July 17, 1907; *Bath Chronicle,* July 17, 1907; *Portsmouth Evening News,* July 18, 1907.

"Oh, it's not so strong as that": *Western Times,* July 17, 1907.

"I am all right": *Western Times,* July 17, 1907.

"All right, I will come down and help you": *Western Times,* July 17, 1907.

"It was heartrending to find": Hyde and Leverett, "Fight for Life," 155.

"All the time I struggled": Hyde and Leverett, "Fight for Life," 156.

"could hardly have been safely kept": Boycott, Damant, and Haldane, "Prevention of Compressed-Air Illness," 369.

"the mesenteric fat, which was very abundant": Boycott, Damant, and Haldane, "Prevention of Compressed-Air Illness," 369.

"This is the only known case of prolonged exposure": Boycott, Damant, and Haldane, "The Prevention of Compressed-Air Illness," 369.

"The practical conclusions are clear": A. E. Boycott and G. C. C. Damant, "Experiments on the Influence of Fatness on Susceptibility to Caisson Disease," *Journal of Hygiene* 8, no. 4 (1908): 455, www.jstor.org/stable/4619377.

For Damant's further troubles with *Torpedo Boat 99*, see *Cheltenham Chronicle and Gloucestershire Graphic*, July 20, 1907; *Yorkshire Evening Post*, July 20, 1907; *Cornishman*, July 25, 1907; *Gloucestershire Echo*, July 20, 1907; *Western Gazette*, July 25, 1907.

Damant's appointment as Inspector of Diving and his subsequent promotions are noted in his official record in ADM 196/46/148; also, see *Lincolnshire Echo*, October 25, 1907.

"I took a turn at getting some secret": AFT.

"He became much better at once": G. C. C. Damant and E. R. Lockwood-Thomas, "A Case of Compressed-Air Illness Cured by Recompression," *BMJ* 2, no. 2543 (1909): 881, doi:10.1136/bmj.2.2543.881.

"acquired great skill as a diver and is a well-read physiologist": ADM 196/46/148.

13. The Cold Sea

For information regarding the lifeboats of the *Laurentic*, see ADM 116/1553.

"Observe rocket": ADM 116/1553, testimony of Frank Finnis.

"The evidence shows": ADM 116/1553, "Finding of Court Martial on Loss of H.M.S. *Laurentic*"

14. The Fortunes of House Damant

"It's the view, not the house": AFT.

Details concerning the death of Harry Damant, see *Nottingham Evening Post*, August 15, 1910; AFT.

Details concerning the will of Harry Damant, see Will of Harry Castell Damant grant of probate dated October 17, 1910.

"prettiest girl in Cowes": Correspondence with Mary Harrison.

"We lost our unity": AFT.

"a generalised irritable weakness of the entire nervous system, characterised": Thomas Dixon Savill, *Clinical Lectures on Neurasthenia* (London: Henry J. Glaisher, 1908), 25; also, see Ivo Geikie Cobb, *A Manual of Neurasthenia (Nervous Exhaustion)*, (New York: William Wood, 1920).

For John Alister Damant's Service Record, see ADM 196/144/629 "Damant, John
Alister," National Archives, Kew, London.

"suicide during temporary insanity": *Daily Mail*, November 19, 1910; see also: *Nottingham
Evening News*, November 17, 1910.

G. C. C. Damant's life after his retirement and before conducting the *Laurentic*
salvage is chiefly derived from AFT.

"to teach boys to think and act": *Isle of Wight County Press*, June 4, 1913.

"frivolous tendencies": Correspondence with Mary Harrison.

"No one had the least idea of what a war would be like": AFT.

"My pay was good": AFT.

"Great black anti-aircraft shell bursts crashed all round us": AFT.

"Wounded were lying in stretchers": AFT.

"easy ones for me": AFT.

15. The Council of the Sea Lords

For a description of the Admiralty and Whitehall, see Colin Brown, *Whitehall: The
Street That Shaped a Nation* (London: Simon and Schuster, 2009).

"most ugly edifice": Brown, *Whitehall*, 203.

"The normal day's work": Sir Charles Walker, *Thirty-Six Years at the Admiralty* (London:
Lincoln Williams, 1933), 112.

"the mob from the north": Hamilton, *Making of the Modern Admiralty*, 247.

For specific information concerning the amount of gold on the *Laurentic*, I relied
on figures provided from Treasury documents, see T 160/505/4 "Gold bars
salved from the *Laurentic*," National Archives, Kew, London.

For information concerning the credit of the Allies and war financing, see Hew
Strachan, *Financing the First World War* (Oxford: Oxford University Press, 2004);
Martin Horn, *Britain, France, and the Financing of the First World War* (Montreal:
McGill-Queen's University Press, 2002).

For the intended transportation and use of the *Laurentic*'s gold, see M7/157 "Gold
and Silver," Bank of England Archive, www.bankofengland.co.uk.

For the information given to Damant about the *Laurentic* at the Admiralty, see AFT.

"I walked on air": Dugan, *Man Under the Sea*, 66.

16. Twenty Fathoms Deep

For Damant's visit to the graveyard, see AFT.

"guns, mountings, rangefinders and other articles of value": ADM 116/1740, S.V. 062,
minute sheet no. 1, January 31, 1917.

For an excellent history of the Royal Navy's Salvage Section, see Tony Booth, *Admiralty Salvage in Peace and War, 1906–2006* (Barnsley, UK: Pen and Sword, 2007).

"genial old boy": AFT.

For information concerning Frederick Young, see Booth, *Admiralty Salvage*; Desmond
    Young, *Ship Ashore: Adventures in Salvage* (London: J. Cape, 1932).

"exposed to the full run of North Atlantic weather": Notes, 26.

For the selection of the *Volunteer*, see AFT; ADM 116/1740.

"I had had just enough experience of diving": AFT.

"bug trap": AFT.

For the movements and refitting of the *Volunteer*, see ADM 116/1740.

"quiet, decent man": AFT.

"splendid seaman and rigger": AFT.

The selection of divers may be found in ADM 116/1740. Damant only specifi-
    cally names three in the records. There were probably others who were later
    involved with Damant on his U-boat operations, notably Balson and Frater.

It should be noted that I found no primary source documents that actually refer to
    Miller as "Dusty." The nickname thus may be a later appellation in secondary
    sources attempting to provide color to the narrative. In any event, for this story
    I have chosen to retain the nickname because of its ubiquity and popularity
    and because there is no direct evidence contradicting its veracity.

"strong personality": ADM 196/157/756, "Miller, Ernest Charles," National Archives,
    Kew, London.

For Damant's assessment of Miller, see AFT.

The number of men aboard the *Volunteer*: ADM 116/1740.

The outfitting of the *Volunteer*: ADM 116/1740; Notes.

"air chamber"; *"diver's oven"*: Logbook kept by Dan Goodwin in HM Salvage Ship
    RACER, 1922, MSS/76/065.1—LAURENTIC, National Maritime Museum,
    Greenwich, London.

For Clement Greatorex's orders, see ADM 116/1740.

Information regarding Geoffrey Unsworth is found in A. Hyatt Verrill, *They Found
    Gold: The Story of Successful Treasure Hunts* (1936; repr., Glorieta, NM: Rio
    Grande, 1972), 217–218.

For details concerning Damant's preparations in Buncrana, see ADM 116/1740.

For the first dives to the *Laurentic*, see ADM 116/1740; "The Recollections of
    Ernest Crouch Regarding the 'Laurentic' Salvage" (unpublished, undated
    manuscript), Historical Diving Society; Notes.

"Given a spell of fine weather": ADM 116/1740, letter dated March 6, 1917.

17. The Path to the Strong Room

The first days of the *Laurentic* operation, including ship movements and weather,
    are fully covered in the primary documents found in ADM 116/1740. A good,
    general narrative of the work is also contained in Notes.

"along the high starboard rail": Notes, 27.

"In blasting rocks or wrecks": "The Month: Science and Arts," *Chambers's Journal of Popular Literature, Science and Arts*, vol. 47 (1870): 847.

"Flour in sacks which had been under a head": Notes, 29.

"I've got to the strong room, sir": Dugan, *Man Under the Sea*, 67.

A description of the actual gold bars, and what was branded on them may be found in "Recollections of Ernest Crouch"; AFT.

Miller's encounter with caisson disease is discussed in Notes.

18. The Storm

ADM 116/1740 and Damant's Notes form the core source material for this chapter with the exception of the work on the U-boat. That description is taken chiefly from Robert M. Grant's *U-Boat Hunters: Code Breakers, Divers and the Defeat of the U-Boats, 1914–1918* (Annapolis, MD: Naval Institute Press, 2003).

The gale and problems with the salvage are found in ADM 116/1740; Notes; AFT.

"How much for all that lies on the beach": AFT.

"three enormous boilers with strips of wood": AFT.

The diversion to Sunderland is recorded in Grant, *U-Boat Hunters*.

"Hullo Schirm, you here too?": Clive Dunn and Gillian Dunn, *Sunderland in the Great War* (Barnsley, UK: Pen and Sword, 2014), 64.

"It is considered that with satisfactory weather": ADM 116/1740, correspondence dated April 5, 1917.

Damant had written about the collapse of the wreck in his Notes, published in 1926. In the article, he claimed that after the divers returned to the wreck they could get no farther than a few feet into the entry port. However, his reports at the time derived from primary sources in ADM 116/1740 indicate clearly that they initially could get as far as the strong room, but after that point the corridors were crushed. It is likely that the *Laurentic* was still settling and they were losing headroom until they realized that they had to blast open the tunnel.

"I hope that salvage has not been discontinued": ADM 116/1740, letter dated April 24, 1917.

"There was a mistaken idea at the Admiralty": AFT.

"Into this ten foot space"; *"The process is extremely slow"*: ADM 116/1740, report dated May 4, 1917.

"The gold's not here, sir!": Dugan, *Man Under the Sea*, 68.

19. "Give Me More Air"

For ongoing operations in dismantling the *Laurentic* through the use of explosives, see ADM 116/1740; Notes.

For the dead fish and Damant's fascination with them, see Notes; also, see "Recollections of Ernest Crouch"; Goodwin logbook.

"I and other divers": Notes, 32.

For Miller's interactions with the dogfish, see "A War Secret," *Saturday Evening Post*, October 23, 1926.

Mention of the diver's getting the bends is best described in Notes.

"One may understand the situation": Notes, 30.

The incident with diver Edwin Blachford is fully described in Notes.

Details concerning the procedure to remove the deck plates by putting explosives underneath them in ADM 116/1740, report dated June 1, 1917; Notes.

"Lower my pipe"; *"Take in the slack of the firing circuit"*; *"Give me all the air you can, sir"*; *"That's right, give me more yet"*; *"Give me more air"*: Notes, 31.

"It may be objected that undue risks": Notes, 31.

How the salvage operation found the gold again is described in ADM 116/1740, report dated May 23, 1917; Notes, 32.

Miller's second case of caisson disease is described in Notes.

How the gold was sent to the Bank of Ireland in ADM 116/1740.

For Greatorex's telegram, see ADM 116/1740.

The variety of bars is described in "Recollections of Ernest Crouch," 7.

"One in the bucket!": See "Recollections of Ernest Crouch"; Goodwin logbook.

A description of minesweeping procedures is found in *Mine Sweeping Manual: United States Navy* (Washington: G.P.O., 1917); H. Taprell Dorling, *Swept Channels; Being an Account of the Work of the Minesweepers in the Great War* (London: Hodder and Stoughton, 1935).

For injuries to the divers done by exploded mines, see ADM 116/1740, report dated June 12, 1917; Notes.

"For days afterwards the tide": AFT.

"The Germans knew nothing about the Laurentic": AFT.

For information concerning the operations in June 1917, see ADM 116/1740.

"There is reason to believe that other large quantities": ADM 116/1740, report dated June 25, 1917.

"By his energy": ADM 116/1740, correspondence dated July 4, 1917.

"These operations require the greatest perseverance": ADM 116/1740, "Award to Officers and Men on Salvage Operations on *Laurentic*," dated July 14, 1917, SV0454.

"The stuff is small": ADM 116/1740, report dated July 13, 1917.

"confident that by patiently": ADM 116/1740, report dated July 13, 1917.

The later operations in 1917 are documented in ADM 116/1740.

For the birth of Eleanor Brook, see AFT.

For the suspension of work and gratuities, see ADM 116/1740.

20. Schooling in Salvage

For Damant's meeting with Young, see AFT.

For the reassignment to the *Vernon*, see ADM 116/1740, reference sheet dated October 2, 1917.

For statistics concerning war losses of British ships to the U-boats, see Marder, *From the Dreadnought*, vol. 4, 102; Patrick Beesly, *Room 40: British Naval Intelligence 1914–18* (London: Hamilton, 1982), 252; Arthur Salter, *Allied Shipping Control, an Experiment in International Administration* (Oxford: Clarendon, 1921), 388, https://archive.org/.

"The British had suffered serious": Marder, *From the Dreadnought*, vol. 4, 52.

"the gravest peril": John Rushworth Jellicoe, *The Crisis of the Naval War* (London: Cassell, 1920), vii.

For information on U-boats, see Gino Deceuninck et al., "World War I Underwater Cultural Heritage in the Belgian Part of the North Sea: A Preliminary Overview," in *Underwater Cultural Heritage from World War I*, 65–77.

For antisubmarine efforts, see Marder, *From the Dreadnought*.

For technical details of antisubmarine equipment and munitions, see Norman Friedman, *Naval Weapons of World War One: Guns, Torpedoes, Mines and ASW Weapons of All Nations: An Illustrated Directory* (Barnsley, UK: Seaforth Publishing, 2011).

The debate over convoys is thoroughly covered in Marder, *From the Dreadnought*; Beesly, *Room 40*.

"The oceans at once": quoted from Marder, *From the Dreadnought*, vol. 5, 89.

"I am getting very concerned": quoted in Marder, *From the Dreadnought*, vol. 5, 106–107.

For information concerning Saltzwedel, see Guðmundur Helgason, "The U-Boat Wars 1939–1945 (Kriegsmarine) and 1914–1918 (Kaiserliche Marine) and Allied Warships of WWII," accessed July 19, 2016, http://uboat.net/.

For technical information concerning the U-boats, see Friedman, *Naval Weapons*; Eberhard Rössler, *The U-boat: The Evolution and Technical History of German Submarines* (Annapolis, MD: Naval Institute Press, 1981).

For the last action of the *UB-81*, see Grant, *U-Boat Hunters*, 62–63.

For Damant's efforts to raise the *UB-81*, see ADM 116/1632; AFT.

For Damant's visit to the Isle of Wight for the holiday, see AFT.

For Damant's work on the Comrie Castle, see AFT.

"That's better": AFT.

"On each of the two lower decks": AFT.

"I don't think that I should have succeeded": AFT.

For the *O.B. Jennings* and *War Knight* collision, see ADM 137/3450 "Collision Between SS 'War Knight' and U.S. 'O.B. Jennings' in Convoy," National Archives, Kew, London; Joe Gores, *Marine Salvage: The Unforgiving Business of No Cure, No Pay* (Garden City, NY: Doubleday, 1971).

"Pitch black, greasy smoke": AFT.

"an excellent piece of salvage work": ADM 116/1638.

21. Codes and Ciphers

For political developments at the Admiralty, see Hamilton, *Making of the Modern Admiralty*; Marder, *From the Dreadnought*.

"fighting face with a monocle set in it": Marder, *From the Dreadnought*, vol. 5, 4–5.

For the history of Room 40, see Beesly, *Room 40*. Also, see W. M. James, *The Eyes of the Navy: A Biographical Study of Admiral Sir Reginald Hall, K.C.M.G., C.B., LL. D., D.C.L.* (London: Methuen, 1955); David Ramsay, *"Blinker" Hall, Spymaster: The Man Who Brought America into World War I* (Stroud, UK: Spellmount, 2008); Innes McCartney, "The 'Tin Openers' Myth and Reality: Intelligence from U-boat Wrecks During WW1," Proceedings of the Twenty-Fourth Annual Historical Diving Conference, 2014.

For the captured German codebooks, see Beesly, *Room 40*; McCartney, "'Tin Openers.'"

For biographical information on Admiral Blinker Hall, see Ramsay, *"Blinker" Hall*; James, *Eyes of the Navy*; Beesly, *Room 40*.

"a perfectly marvelous person but the coldest-hearted"; *"Well, it was not a target of any military"*: Beesly, *Room 40*, 37–38.

For the work of *Room 40* including the Zimmermann telegram, see Beesly, *Room 40*.

"one of the most attractive of men": Marder, *From the Dreadnought*, vol. 7, 70.

For information concerning Keyes, see Booth, *Admiralty Salvage*; Marder, *From the Dreadnought*.

For information on Hall's intelligence efforts, see Beesly, *Room 40*; James, *Eyes of the Navy*.

For the loss of Hall's spy in Germany and his proposal to Damant, see AFT.

"speed and knowledge": ADM 116/1634, memorandum dated March 29, 1918.

"This was an exciting job": AFT.

22. The U-Boat Hunter

For the formation of Damant's special section and his promotion, see ADM 116/1640.

For information on the *Moonfleet*, see McCartney, "'Tin Openers'"; AFT.

For Damant's case before the operation on the *O.B. Jennings*, see ADM 116/1632.

"An alternative to diving in these cases": ADM 116/1632, report dated April 24, 1918.

"mare's nests"; Details concerning Damant's disappointing cases in AFT.

For information on the case of the *UB-33*, see Grant, 66–67; Robert Ho Davis, *Deep Diving and Submarine Operations: A Manual for Deep Sea Divers and Compressed Air Workers* (London: Siebe, Gorman, 1955); "Submarine Episodes," *Seagoer* 5, no.1 (1937): 86–97; AFT; and especially ADM 116/1634.

"I see and conquer": Davis, *Deep Diving*, 351.

Regarding the shooting of the officer: Note that in Damant's account in AFT he writes that Gregor was shot in the back. The primary source material reported by Damant states that he was shot in the stomach and head. In this case, I opted to choose the Admiralty sources because they were written at the time of the incident.

"That's him"; *"Go on and get the signal books"*: AFT.

"long and doubtful"; *"This would open up the boat"*: ADM 116/1634, report on salvage operations dated May 21, 1918.

"No": "Submarine Episodes."

"I shall never forget the expression": "A War Secret," 46.

"They give one a bit of a shock": "A War Secret," 46.

"the greatest energy and determination": ADM 116/1634, report on salvage operations dated May 29, 1918.

"zeal and ability"; *"I consider that much material"*: ADM 116/1634, report on salvage operations dated June 19, 1918.

"VERY URGENT": ADM 116/1634, telegram dated May 31, 1918.

23. Underwater Espionage

The nickname "Tin-openers" was, by my best guess, created by the writer Kendall McDonald in his 2003 short, dramatized, and often inaccurate book *The Tin Openers: The Secret Underwater War Against the U-Boats 1914–18* (Storrington: Historic Military Press, 2003). It seems that McDonald used as his main source the "A War Secret" article from the *Saturday Evening Post* and embellished on some of its own hyperboles.

"Bundling pumps, gear, and some dry clothing": AFT.

For figures on U-boat depredations, see Marder, *From the Dreadnought*.

Details concerning the proposal to open a special diving school at the *Excellent* in ADM 116/1634.

"You will understand that Mr Miller": ADM 116/1634, Telegram dated June 7, 1918.

The episode of the *Lorna*; *"Kamerad!"*; *"Help!"*: Henry John Newbolt, *Submarine and Anti-submarine* (London: Longmans, Green, and Co., 1918), 225.

The work on the *UB-74*: AFT; ADM 116/1634.

The *UC-11*: Grant, *U-Boat Hunters*; ADM 116/1634; Dugan, *Man Under the Sea*.

"A bit of luck, that": Dugan, *Man Under the Sea*, 66.

"The results obtained show that most violent explosions": ADM 116/1634, report dated
    July 2, 1918.

The UC-64: ADM 116/1851 "Salvage Record no. 22," 1918–1919, National Archives,
    Kew, London.

"I don't think prospects of getting papers": ADM 116/1851, report dated June 20, 1918.

"Explosives must be used": ADM 116/1851, report dated June 20, 1918.

"Explored fore part of wreck": ADM 116/1851, telegram dated August 11, 1918; also,
    see Grant, *U-Boat Hunters*, 74.

"With a rifle": AFT.

"Guns, bodies, mysterious electric boxes": AFT.

"One used to wonder": AFT.

"The divers are not paid as Salvage Divers": Notes of John Bevan, Historical Diving
    Society (UK).

"On several days the divers were severely shaken": ADM 116/1740, letter dated March
    27, 1919.

"Don't tell me that it is old wreckage": AFT.

Details on the *UB-109* in ADM 116/1851; AFT.

Details concerning the story about the flat boxes in AFT.

"waiting for a day and hour": AFT.

"The lighters looked very attractive": AFT.

Details on the *UC-70* in ADM 116/1851; AFT; Grant, *U-Boat Hunters*.

For Nell's visit, see AFT.

"a most brutal officer": Grant, *U-Boat Hunters*, 83.

"Read with interest and admiration": ADM 116/1851, report dated October 16, 1918.

"impossible for the Fleet": Marder, *From the Dreadnought*, vol. 5, 173.

On the *UB-116*, see Grant, *U-Boat Hunters*; AFT; ADM 116/1851.

"The idea had taken root in their minds": Marder, *From the Dreadnought*, vol. 5, 173.

"a decent man and we got on without friction": AFT.

"inspired with the idea of striking a last": AFT.

"The Scapa water was very clear": AFT.

"I have been shocked to hear": AFT.

"skewered together in bundles": AFT.

"weights had been secured to them": AFT.

"hounded back to his Manse": AFT.

"Sirens blowing, bells clanging": AFT.

"splicing the main brace": Marder, *From the Dreadnought*, vol. 5, 187.

"all jumps and activity": AFT.

Details concerning promotions and recognition for Blachford and Clear in ADM
    116/1740, letter dated March 24, 1919.

"I had been awarded": AFT.

"There was another string to my bow": AFT.

24. "Every Prospect of Success"

Regarding Royal Navy post war operations, see Norman Polmar and Edward
  Whitman, *Hunters and Killers: Anti-submarine Warfare from 1776 to 1943*, vol. 1
  (Annapolis, MD: Naval Institute Press, 2015), 89–90.

For information regarding the Salvage Section's postwar operations, see Booth,
  Admiralty Salvage.

For information regarding Young's work in Belgium, see Desmond Young, *Ship
  Ashore,* "Admiralty Navy Estimates, 1919–1920," last modified August 29, 2014,
  www.naval-history.net/WW1NavyBritishAdmiraltyEstimates1919.htm.

"The only complaint": Desmond Young, *Ship Ashore,* 155–156.

"At the time of suspending operations": ADM 116/1740, reference sheet dated July
  3, 1918.

"It was rumoured that private salvage firms": AFT.

For Damant's immediate postwar activities, see AFT.

For the selection of a proper ship, see AFT; ADM 116/1740.

"Any steam craft or lighter": ADM 116/1740, telegram dated May 6, 1919.

"She isn't much to look at, and she ain't so very big": H. Howell, Shipwright Diver,
  Journal with photographs, recording salvage operations, mainly related to HMS Racer,
  1917–1920, reference number 2007/47, National Museum of the Royal Navy,
  Portsmouth, UK.

On the reconditioning of the *Racer,* see ADM 116/1740, reference sheet dated
  May 5, 1919.

On the *Moor,* see ADM 116/1740, correspondence dated April 1, 1919.

"other, unproductive work": ADM 116/1740, reference sheet dated May 1, 1919.

Harold Jones: ADM 116/1740, telegram dated May 7, 1919.

"now wasting valuable time": ADM 116/1740, telegram dated May 6, 1919.

"I consider it impracticable to get a preliminary survey": ADM 116/1740, telegram dated
  May 15, 1919.

"A fair amount of plating and debris": ADM 116/1740, telegram dated May 31, 1919.

"The Naval Salvage Advisor at Ostend": ADM 116/1740, report dated June 14, 1919.

"does not in my opinion warrant heavy government expenditure": ADM 116/1740, telegram dated June 19, 1919.

"The case would have to be settled out of court": Booth, *Admiralty Salvage,* 84.

For the proposal by James Dredging, see ADM 116/1740, telegram dated August
  28, 1919.

"so far as it is possible to judge": ADM 116/1740, reference sheet dated June 5, 1919.

For biographical information on Sir Vincent Baddeley, see *Times of London,*
  December 31, 1935; July 28, 1961; July 29, 1961.

"Bank of England may be easily able to make arrangements": ADM 116/1740, correspondence dated June 21, 1919.

"anxious that the fact that this gold": ADM 116/1740, correspondence dated June 21, 1919.

For expenses of the *Racer*, see ADM 116/1740, report dated July 18, 1919.

25. The Return to Lough Swilly

Regarding the new volunteer divers, see "Recollections of Ernest Crouch," 11.

"With a sardonic wit he could talk": AFT.

On Clear's departure and Damant's rank, see ADM 116/1740.

For information concerning this tumultuous period in Irish history, see Richard Killeen, *A Short History of the Irish Revolution* (Dublin: Gill and Macmillan, 2007); Michael Hopkinson, *The Irish War of Independence* (Montreal: McGill-Queen's University Press, 2002).

For information concerning the Soloheadbeg ambush, see Dan Breen, *My Fight for Irish Freedom* (Dublin: Talbot, 1924); *Times of London,* July 8, 1919; *Irish Times,* January 22, 1919; *Irish Times,* January 23, 1919; *Weekly Irish Times,* January 25, 1919.

"the special difficulties connected with transit of explosives": ADM 116/1740, reference sheet dated May 10, 1919.

Regarding movements of the *Racer* and *Corycia* and establishment of mooring gear, see ADM 116/1740.

"There is no doubt as to the position": ADM 116/1740, reference sheet dated July 19, 1919.

"You landed on the wreck": "Recollections of Ernest Crouch," 14.

On typical operations during the 1919 salvage season, see ADM 116/1740, correspondence dated July 12, 1919.

"I find that I can do far more work per day": ADM 116/1740, correspondence dated July 12, 1919.

On Crouch locating the gold, see "Recollections of Ernest Crouch," 14.

For the figures as to how much gold was brought up, see ADM 116/1740.

"How happy I was!!": AFT.

On the accident with the explosives, see AFT; "Recollections of Ernest Crouch"; ADM 116/1740.

"In harbour that night we cleared these out": AFT.

On Damant's search for easier means to recover the gold, see ADM 116/1740; ADM 116/1741 "Laurentic"—Salvage of Bullion, 1921–1924, National Archives, Kew, London.

"a very dark hold": "Recollections of Ernest Crouch," 16.

inquiries from newspapers: ADM 116/1740.

"I expect to get considerably larger quantities of gold": ADM 116/1740, report dated August 27, 1919.

"It is thought that all the gold": *Irish Times*, August 18, 1919.

"While treasure-seekers in Tobermory Bay": *Evening Telegraph and Post*, August 12, 1919.

"I think it would be wise to do as little as possible": ADM 116/1740, correspondence dated August 20, 1919.

Details concerning the visit by Haldane in AFT; "Recollections of Ernest Crouch," 15–16.

"a very strange coincidence": "Recollections of Ernest Crouch," 15.

"There is no difficulty that could not be overcome": ADM 116/1740, report dated September 7, 1919.

Details concerning costs of the diving season in T 160/505/4, statement A, 1919.

"I consider that the rest of the gold recoverable": ADM 116/1740, report dated October 9, 1919.

"very good pay but working": "Recollections of Ernest Crouch," 18.

Details concerning a diver's earnings in "Recollections of Ernest Crouch"; ADM 116/1740.

On the incident with the fishing boats, see AFT.

"I never again saw boats fishing" AFT.

"an unknown quantity of gold in 25 boxes": AFT.

"I consider that a full season's work in 1920": ADM 116/1740, report dated September 1, 1919.

"The general view on board the Admiralty": *Evening Telegraph and Post*, August 27, 1919.

"looked very sweet in a suede jersey and grey skirt": AFT.

26. Invincible

For the transition to the 1920 salvage season, see ADM 116/1740; ADM 116/1741.

The cost of operations: ADM 116/1740, letter dated November 1, 1919.

For the political situation in Ireland, see Killeen, *Short History*; Hopkinson, *Irish War*.

On the debate over whether to continue operations in 1920, see ADM 116/1740.

"Taking into consideration the proximity": ADM 116/1740, Salvage on S.S. "Laurentic" in 1920, Proposals for Next Year's Operations, November 6, 1919.

"During the operations this summer": ADM 116/1740, letter dated November 1, 1919.

"Though it is likely, I cannot of course guarantee": ADM 116/1740, letter dated December 11, 1919.

For operations on the work during the 1920 season, see ADM 116/1741; "Recollections of Ernest Crouch"

"Progress up to the present is very satisfactory": ADM 116/1741, report dated May 14, 1920.

"The shell of the ship has crumpled down"; *"I consider the progress quite satisfactory"*: ADM 116/1741, report dated May 28, 1920.

"We used to shackle on a wire on these plates": "Recollections of Ernest Crouch," 19.

"It was not a pretty sight when you first got on the wreck": "Recollections of Ernest Crouch," 38.

"We could always tell when rough weather was coming along": "Recollections of Ernest Crouch," 21.

For the plans of the *Laurentic* that Damant marked up, see "Recollections of Ernest Crouch."

"unequalled for Efficiency, Durability, and Strength": J&H Gwynne, "'Invincible' Centrifugal Suction Dredgers," advertisement, *The Steamship*, June 1903, 55.

For all the various correspondence regarding the pump, see ADM 116/1741.

"So far as I know nothing similar to this pumping": ADM 116/1741, report dated August 13, 1920.

For Damant's comments regarding decompression sickness during the operations, see Notes.

"had we kept each diver 1½ hours on the bottom": Notes, 31.

"in the absence of strictly comparable controls this proves nothing": Notes, 36.

"Thank you, sir "; *"Don't thank me"*; *"He was a cold fish"*: Scoltock and Cossum, *We Own Laurentic*, 35.

Damant and Miller's bout with decompression sickness is discussed in Notes, 38.

For the wrap-up of the dismal 1920 salvage season, see ADM 116/1740.

"great pains": AFT.

"very unsatisfactory"; *"On one occasion in 1917"*: T 160/505/4, report dated September 11, 1920.

"The recovery of the gold is likely to be a slow process": ADM 116/1740, note dated September 15, 1920.

27. "A Pity to Give Up"

For information concerning Damant's experiments, see AFT. The actual research was published in the *Physical Society Proceedings* and the *Journal of Physiology*, check under Damant in the bibliography for the full citations.

For the inquiry to Professor Brooks, see ADM 116/1740, correspondence dated November 29, 1920.

"In the first place it cannot be expected that this method": ADM 116/1740, letter dated November 29, 1920.

The operations of 1920 and 1921: ADM 116/1741.

For Damant's personal life, see AFT.

"There was not an officer or man living who could take charge": "Recollections of Ernest Crouch," 30.

"Under future legislation": ADM 116/1741, paper dated September 12, 1921.

"As far as my information goes there must be a mass of 3,000 ingots": ADM 116/1741, letter dated August 21, 1921.

"I had hoped and expected to find the bulk of the gold": ADM 116/1741, letter dated August 21, 1921.

"I think it would be a pity to give up": ADM 116/1741, paper dated August 21, 1921.

"Our advice would be to continue the work next year": ADM 116/1741, paper dated August 21, 1921.

For the costs of the 1921 operations, see T 160/505/4, paper dated October 26, 1921.

"these people are all Naval ratings": T 161/151/14 Reward to Crew of 'Racer' in Respect of Salvage of Gold from 'Laurentic,' National Archives, Kew, London, letter dated November 25, 1921.

"I think there is no doubt that encouragement and incentive": T 161/151/14, letter dated November 25, 1921.

"The last years of poor, proud, tender hearted Mother": AFT.

"a very good crowd of chaps": "Recollections of Ernest Crouch," 30.

Operations in 1922: ADM 116/1741; also see "Recollections of Ernest Crouch"; Goodwin logbook.

"One in the bucket!": "Recollections of Ernest Crouch," 30. It should be noted that the Crouch source is the only one that names the specific diver who first found the gold in 1922. I accepted Crouch's claim without other corroboration.

"They gave themselves up like lambs": Notes, 17.

28. "Like Lambs"

On the Easter holiday and the troubles in Ireland, see Goodwin logbook, 4.

"it would take several weeks": ADM 116/1741, report dated April 9, 1922.

For the special reports, see ADM 116/1741.

"about as an inconvenient place as could be found": ADM 116/1741, memorandum dated May 1, 1922.

Details concerning the incident of May 1, 1922, in Goodwin logbook, 5.

On the transfer of gold, see ADM 116/1741.

For the incidents in Buncrana and Portsalon, see Goodwin logbook, 6.; *Aberdeen Daily Journal*, May 5, 1922.

On Damant's feelings toward the Irish, see AFT.

"These brutes would have been delighted": AFT.

"This worked well, though on one occasion four sinister": AFT.

"They used to box each other and sit up": AFT.

"Conditions on board in this abominable weather": ADM 116/1741, report dated May 7, 1922.

On control over the gold area, see Scoltock and Cossum, *We Own Laurentic*, 52–53.

Continued work on the wreck in clearing out the 440-square-foot area is described in Notes.

"a very sensitive galvanometer connected to an electric cable": "Recollections of Ernest Crouch," 30.

For other mention of Professor Brooks, see Goodwin logbook, 11.

The episode with William Light is most thoroughly described in Notes; also, see "Recollections of Ernest Crouch"; Goodwin logbook.

"I am filling up with water": "Recollections of Ernest Crouch," 34.

"Only a little": Notes, 40.

"a very brave thing for a man of his age to do": "Recollections of Ernest Crouch," 36.

E. E. Brooks published his experiments as a note in "Polarisation of Diffused Light under the Sea," *Nature* 110, no. 2751 (1922): 114, doi:10.1038/110114a0.

Operations are documented in ADM 116/1741.

For leisure time for the crew, see Goodwin logbook.

"That looks a very small anchor for a 7,000 ton tanker": AFT.

On the sunfish, see Goodwin logbook, 26; Damant's note in *Nature* 106, 242–243. Damant published a later note on the sunfish's locomotion in *Nature* 116, 543.

On the fleas in the cave, see AFT.

"People to whom I have told this story": AFT.

"in pained silence": AFT.

On Tommy's birth, see AFT.

On later operations in 1922, see Notes; ADM 116/1741.

29. "His Sturdy Optimism"

On salvage operations in 1923 and 1924, see ADM 116/1741.

Details concerning questions and rumors about a conspiracy to steal the gold in Scoltock and Cossum, *We Own Laurentic*. The case of Crouch is found in ADM 1/8706/200, "S.S. Laurentic—Salvage of Gold," National Archives, Kew, London.

Details concerning diver pay in ADM 116/1741.

"Damant was a very strict man": Scoltock and Cossum, *We Own Laurentic*, 53.

"Human nature being what it is, there was a tendency": Notes, 43.

On Maddison's achievement, see Scoltock and Cossum, *We Own Laurentic*. The prize of a tin of cigarettes is found in Notes.

"The greatest possible credit is due to Commander Damant": ADM 116/1741, letter dated July 19, 1923.

On Nell's jealousy, see correspondence with Charles Darwent and Mary Harrison.

On Nell's visit to Portsalon, see AFT.

The case of G. Williams was reported in local newspapers, and his actual presence on the *Racer* is found in ADM 116/1741. Damant discusses him contemptuously in AFT.

"goes for anything it sees moving": *Evening Telegraph and Post*, August 29, 1923.

Counts of gold bars are found in ADM 116/1741.

For Damant's last voyage to Lough Swilly, see AFT.

"Since that time settling and creeping": ADM 116/1741, report dated May 11, 1924.

"It is not certain that this proportion": ADM 116/1741, report dated August 3, 1924.

"It is now so late in the season that one cannot": ADM 116/1741, report dated August 31, 1924.

"Commander Damant has by steady perseverance": ADM 116/1741, undated note [September 1924.]

"how much the Treasury, quite apart from their natural glee": ADM 116/1741, letter dated July 1, 1924.

"This satisfactory result": ADM 1 8706/200, letter dated September 21, 1924.

"Our good friends ashore": AFT.

"the bell was supposed to commemorate": AFT.

"I can still hear its sharp, clear chimes": Scoltock and Cossum, *We Own Laurentic*, 43.

30. Rewards

For information concerning the promotion of members of the salvage team, see ADM 1 8706/200.

For Damant's award of the CBE, see AFT.

"Congratulations. You wear it round your neck!!": AFT.

"When the time came to joining the queue": AFT.

"The giant Racer *was attracting millions"*: AFT.

"Your name is Eleanor": AFT.

"The coach had traces made of stiffish hairs": AFT.

"enquire, seriously and with proper respect": ADM 1 8706/200, letter dated December 5, 1924.

"I cannot conscientiously recommend a man": ADM 1 8706/200, letter dated April 6, 1925.

For Williams's book, see: Williams, *Diving for Treasure and Other Adventures Beneath the Sea* (London: Faber and Gwyer, 1926).

"Even that was a bit libelous": AFT.

On Damant's post-*Laurentic* career, see AFT.

"Few but professional physiologists": AFT.

"I do not like publicity": Dugan, *Man Under the Sea*, 64.

"highest point of my career": AFT.

31. Speculating in Gold

For information on the Malet Salvage Syndicate, see T 160/505/4; Scoltock and Cossum, *We Own Laurentic*; T 231/1214 "SS *Laurentic*" 1952–1956, National Archives, Kew, London.

"My own belief is that": T 160/505/4, letter dated May 17, 1926. Italics replaced original underlined word.

For the Risdon Beazley salvage efforts, see ADM 1 22403 "Recovery of Salvage from S.S. 'Laurentic,'" National Archives, Kew, London. Interestingly, the archives of Risdon Beazley had no record of their time working on the *Laurentic*, although Admiralty records clearly show that they did.

"The wreck of the vessel itself": T 231/1214, letter dated August 14, 1952.

On rumors concerning the whereabouts of the missing gold bars, see Scoltock and Cossum, *We Own Laurentic.*

For the letter from Frank Maguire, see ADM 1 22403, letter dated December 7, 1955.

For biographical information about the Cossums, see Scoltock and Cossum, *We Own Laurentic*; supplementary information provided in an interview with Ray Cossum.

"The name had drawn us like a magnet": Scoltock and Cossum, *We Own Laurentic*, 54.

"I have worked as a diver": Letter to author from Ray Cossum.

"Our hearts were pounding": Scoltock and Cossum, *We Own Laurentic*, 55.

"football field of scrap": Scoltock and Cossum, *We Own Laurentic*, 55–56.

"WE OWN LAURENTIC": Scoltock and Cossum, *We Own Laurentic*, 7.

"crushing stones": Scoltock and Cossum, *We Own Laurentic*, 67.

"Go back!": Scoltock and Cossum, *We Own Laurentic*, 67.

"We had dived many times on the wreck": Scoltock and Cossum, *We Own Laurentic*, 76.

"We do not leave the chopper!": Scoltock and Cossum, *We Own Laurentic*, 75–77.

"It's time to give up": Scoltock and Cossum, *We Own Laurentic*, 89.

"If I told you, everybody would be diving on the wreck": Interview with Ray Cossum.

"I've been lucky to have experienced everything": Undated clipping provided by Ray Cossum.

"The extensive salvage combined": Correspondence with Steve Jones dated July 18, 2016.

BIBLIOGRAPHY

If you are reading this section, you are no doubt interested in the sources used for the construction of this book or have a deeper interest in *Laurentic* lore. While the bibliography that follows is quite extensive, there are several source materials that were the basis for the majority of the narrative.

Of particular importance are the sources collected from the National Archives in London. Among the various materials, there are two very large bound volumes of official documents that contain all the correspondence and reports on the *Laurentic* salvage operations, these being ADM 116/1740 and ADM 116/1741. These volumes formed the baseline of the narrative, and when sources came into conflict in points of minor to major importance these were used to mediate the correct version of events. Also important among these documents was ADM 116/1553 which was the full record of the court of inquiry over the sinking of the *Laurentic*.

A truly valuable work that enabled me to fully flesh out the character of G. C. C. Damant was his unpublished autobiography, "A Father's Tale," which was sent to me as an electronic transcription by a family member. The original is currently lost, and as a result, in the notes section no pagination is possible. In addition, Damant's account in his "Notes on the 'Laurentic' Salvage Operations" published in the *Journal of Hygiene* was also highly useful in providing a broad overview of the salvage, although this paper, written a few years after events, does conflict at times with the Admiralty records. Damant's paper "The Prevention of Compressed-Air Illness," written with Haldane and Boycott, in combination with the official report of the trials off Loch Striven were most enlightening in showing the story of the development of staged decompression.

Some of the most difficult sections to write from a research point of view were the chapters concerning Damant's work inside the U-boats in 1918. Most of the easily available secondary sources were hyperbolic or simply erroneous. The best factual reference work on this topic is Grant's *U-Boat Hunters* and Innes McCartney's various publications. These enabled me to locate the correct primary source material at the National Archives in the "Salvage Record" series. This provided a factual baseline from which information in the secondary sources could be corroborated. This was bolstered by Damant's own accounts in "A Father's Tale," which is the only place in which he extensively described the work outside of its technical difficulties in the official documentation. Using these two types of source materials, it was possible to provide an accurate narrative concerning his team's covert work.

As the work developed, other accounts came to light, particularly the account of Ernest Crouch from the Historical Diving Society. His recollections provide one of the few instances in which we see the detailed experiences of the divers. Also important for corroboration was the logbook of Dan Goodwin who was aboard the *Racer* in 1922.

Events after Damant's salvage operations were mainly taken from various Admiralty records up to the 1960s. Information concerning the last several decades of work on the wreck has been chiefly derived from an independently published account of the work by the wreck owner, Ray Cossum, as well as interviews and correspondence with him for which I am highly grateful.

Archival Documents

National Archives, Kew, London

ADM 1/8706/200 "S.S. Laurentic—Salvage of Gold."
ADM 1 22403 "Recovery of Salvage from S.S. 'Laurentic.'
ADM 53/38756 Logbook for the *Corycia*, September 30, 1918 to December 13, 1919.
ADM 53/57036-57045 Logbook of the *Racer*, April 1919 to September 1920.
ADM 116/1553 "Loss of H.M.S. *Laurentic*."
ADM 116/1632 "Salvage Record no. 20." 1918.
ADM 116/1634 "Salvage Record no. 21." 1918.
ADM 116/1638 "Salvage Record no. 32." 1918.
ADM 116/1640 "Salvage Record no. 35." 1918.
ADM 116/1740 "Laurentic"—Salvage of Bullion, 1917–1920.
ADM 116/1741 "Laurentic"—Salvage of Bullion, 1921–1924.
ADM 116/1851 "Salvage Record no. 22." 1918–1919.
ADM 137/3450 "Collision Between SS 'War Knight' and U.S. 'O.B. Jennings' in Convoy."
ADM 188/328/191844 "Clear, George."
ADM 188/378/215995 "Dent, Augustus Henry."
ADM 188/398/225900 "Light, William."
ADM 188/403/228024 "Blachford, Edwin Henry."
ADM 196/43/370 "Norton, Reginald Arthur."
ADM 196/46/148 "Damant, Guybon Chesney Castell."
ADM 196/52/282 "Damant, John Alister."
ADM 196/144/629 "Damant, John Alister."
ADM 196/157/756 "Miller, Ernest Charles."
ADM 363/188/94 "Balson, Albert."
DO 35/3998 "Attempted salvage by UK authorities, of gold from SS LAURENTIC, sunk off Irish Coast outside their territorial waters, in 1917," 1952.
MFQ 1/1322/5 "Section and plan of the hold of SS *Laurentic*."

T 160/505/4 "Gold bars salved from the *Laurentic.*"
T 161/151/14 "Reward to Crew of 'Racer' in Respect of Salvage of Gold from 'Laurentic.'"
T 231/1214 "SS *Laurentic.*" 1952–1956.

National Museum of the Royal Navy, Portsmouth, UK

Howell, H. *Journal with photographs, recording salvage operations, mainly related to HMS Racer.* 1917–1920. Reference number 2007/47.

Bank of England Archive

M7/157 "Gold and Silver." www.bankofengland.co.uk.

National Maritime Museum, Greenwich, London

Goodwin, Dan. MSS/76/065.1—LAURENTIC, Logbook kept by Dan Goodwin in HM Salvage Ship RACER, 1922.

Derry City and Strabane District Council Tower Museum

Oral History Recordings, Ray Cossum Collection:
Mss.30.1.17-26: Henry Augustus Dent; Paddy Murphy
Mss.30.1.15; Mss.30.1.30: Don Gillespie.

Historical Diving Society, UK

"The Recollections of Ernest Crouch Regarding the "Laurentic" Salvage." Unpublished, undated manuscript, Historical Diving Society.

Other

Damant, G. C. C. "A Father's Tale." Unpublished autobiography of Guybon Chesney Castell Damant written at intervals between 1945 and 1954.

Articles

Boycott, A. E., and G. C. C. Damant. "Experiments on the Influence of Fatness on Susceptibility to Caisson Disease." *Journal of Hygiene* 8, no. 4 (1908): 445–456. www.jstor.org/stable/4619377.
———. "A Note on the Quantities of Marsh-Gas, Hydrogen and Carbon Dioxide Produced in the Alimentary Canal of Goats." *Journal of Physiology* 36, nos. 4–5 (1907): 283–287. doi:10.1113/jphysiol.1907.sp001233.

———. "Some Lesions of the Spinal Cord Produced by Experimental Caisson Disease." *Journal of Pathology and Bacteriology* 12, no. 3 (1908): 507–515. doi:10.1002/path.1700120305.

Boycott, A. E., G. C. C. Damant, and J. S. Haldane. "The Prevention of Compressed-Air Illness." *Journal of Hygiene* 8, (1908): 342–443. doi: http://dx.doi.org/10.1017/S0022172400003399

Damant, G. C. C. "The Adjustment of the Buoyancy of the Larva of Corethra Plumicornis." *Journal of Physiology* 59, nos. 4–5 (1924): 345–356. doi:10.1113/jphysiol.1924.sp002190.

———. "A Diver's Notes on Submarine Phenomena." *Nature* 106, no. 2660 (1920): 242–243. doi:10.1038/106242b0.

———. "Locomotion of the Sunfish." *Nature* 116, no. 2919 (1925): 543. doi:10.1038/116543b0.

———. "The Normal Temperature of the Goat." In "Proceedings of the Physiological Society, December 1, 1907," *Journal of Physiology* 35, supplement (December 1, 1907).

———. "Notes on the 'Laurentic' Salvage Operations and the Prevention of Compressed Air Illness." *Journal of Hygiene* 25, no. 1 (1926): 26–49. www.jstor.org/stable/3859567.

———. "Secretion of Gas by the Larva of a Gnat." *Physical Society Proceedings*, March 12, 1921.

Damant, G. C. C. and E. R. Lockwood-Thomas. "A Case of Compressed-Air Illness Cured by Recompression." *BMJ* 2, no. 2543 (1909): 881–882. doi:10.1136/bmj.2.2543.881.

"England & Wales, National Probate Calendar (Index of Wills and Administrations), 1858–1966." England and Wales, National Probate Calendar (Index of Wills and Administrations), 1858–1966. http://search.ancestry.co.uk/search/db.aspx?dbid=1904.

Haldane, J. S., J. G. Priestley, "The Regulation of the Lung-Ventilation." *Journal of Physiology*, 1905. doi: 10.1113/jphysiol.1905.sp001081.

Hyde, B. J., and S. Leverett. "A Fight for Life Under Water." *Wide World Magazine* (May 1908): 153–156.

McCartney, Innes. "The 'Tin Openers' Myth and Reality: Intelligence from U-boat Wrecks During WW1." Proceedings of the Twenty-Fourth Annual Historical Diving Conference, 2014, 19–40.

McKinlay, Archibald. "Case of Death from Syncope Caused by Caisson Disease." In Great Britain Parliament, House of Commons, *Papers by Command*, 102–104. Vol. 42. Arkose, 1901.

"Submarine Episodes," *Seagoer* 5, no. 1 (1937): 86–97.

"A War Secret," *Saturday Evening Post*, October 23, 1926.

Books

Beesly, Patrick. *Room 40: British Naval Intelligence 1914–18*. London: Hamilton, 1982.

Booth, Tony. *Admiralty Salvage in Peace and War, 1906–2006*. Barnsley, UK: Pen and Sword Maritime, 2007.

Brown, Colin. *Whitehall: The Street That Shaped a Nation*. London: Simon and Schuster, 2009.

Corbin, Thomas W. *The Romance of Submarine Engineering: Containing Interesting Descriptions in Nontechnical Language of the Construction of Submarine Boats ... and Many Other Feats of Engineering Beneath the Surface of the Water*. Philadelphia: J.B. Lippincott, 1913.

Davis, Robert H. *Deep Diving and Submarine Operations: A Manual for Deep Sea Divers and Compressed Air Workers*. London: Siebe, Gorman, 1955.

———. *Diving Scientifically and Practically Considered: Being a Diving Manual and Handbook of Submarine Appliances*. London: Siebe, Gorman, 1915.

———. *A Diving Manual and Handbook of Submarine Appliances*. London: Siebe, Gorman, 1924.

Dugan, James. *Man Under the Sea*. New York: Harper, 1956.

Ecott, Tim. *Neutral Buoyancy: Adventures in a Liquid World*. New York: Atlantic Monthly Press, 2001.

Fitch, Tad, and Michael Poirier. *Into the Danger Zone: Sea Crossings of the First World War*. History Press, 2015.

Friedman, Norman. *Naval Weapons of World War One: Guns, Torpedoes, Mines and ASW Weapons of All Nations: An Illustrated Directory*. Barnsley, UK: Seaforth Publishing, 2011.

Goodman, Martin. *Suffer and Survive: The Extreme Life of J.S. Haldane*. London: Simon and Schuster, 2007.

Grant, Robert M. *U-Boat Hunters: Code Breakers, Divers and the Defeat of the U-boats, 1914–1918*. Annapolis, MD: Naval Institute Press, 2003.

Hamilton, C.I. *The Making of the Modern Admiralty: British Naval Policy-Making, 1805–1927*. Cambridge: Cambridge University Press, 2011.

Hopkinson, Michael. *The Irish War of Independence*. Montreal: McGill-Queen's University Press, 2002.

James, W. M. *The Eyes of the Navy: A Biographical Study of Admiral Sir Reginald Hall, K.C.M.G., C.B., LL. D., D.C.L.* London: Methuen, 1955.

Killeen, Richard. *A Short History of the Irish Revolution*. Dublin: Gill and Macmillan, 2007.

Lang, Michael A., and Alf. O. Brubakk, eds. *The Future of Diving: 100 Years of Haldane and Beyond*. Washington, D.C.: Smithsonian Institution Scholarly Press, 2009. www.si.edu/dive/library_haldane.htm.

Marder, Arthur J. *From the Dreadnought to Scapa Flow: The Royal Navy in the Fisher Era*. 5 vols. Oxford: Oxford University Press, 1966; repr. Annapolis, MD: Naval Institute Press, 2013.

McCartney, Innes. "The Historical Archaeology of World War I U-boats and the Compilation of Admiralty History." In *Underwater Cultural Heritage from World War I: Proceedings of the Scientific Conference on the Occasion of the Centenary of World War I, Bruges, Belgium, 26 and 27 June 2014*. Paris: United Nations Educational, Scientific and Cultural Organization, 2014, 11–18. www.unesco.org /culture/underwater/world-warI.pdf

———. *The Maritime Archaeology of a Modern Conflict: Comparing the Archaeology of German Submarine Wrecks to the Historical Text*. New York: Routledge, 2014.

————. *Lost Patrols: Submarine Wrecks of the English Channel.* Penzance: Periscope, 2003.

Ramsay, David. *"Blinker" Hall, Spymaster: The Man Who Brought America into World War I.* Stroud, UK: Spellmount, 2008.

Report of a Committee Appointed by the Lords Commissioners of the Admiralty to Consider and Report upon the Conditions of Deep-water Diving; Together with Index, Appendices, and Illustrations. London: Eyre and Spottiswoode, 1907.

Scheer, Admiral Reinhard. *Germany's High Sea Fleet in the World War.* London: Cassell, 1920.

Scoltock, Jack, and Ray Cossum. *We Own Laurentic: The Story of "the Gold Ship."* Coleraine: Impact, 2000.

Young, Commander R. Travers. *The House That Jack Built: The Story of the H.M.S. Excellent.* Gale and Polden, 1955.

Young, Desmond. *Ship Ashore: Adventures in Salvage.* London: J. Cape, 1932.

Interviews and Correspondence

Dr. John Bevan
Ray Cossum
Derek Damant
Charles Darwent
Mary Harrison
Steve Jones

INDEX

Familial parenthetical qualifiers indicate family relationship to Guy Damant. Page numbers in italic refer to illustrations.